Conte

Fairy Tales, Myth, and Psychoanalytic Theory
Feminism and Retelling the Tale

VERONICA L. SCHANOES
Queens College, CUNY, USA

LONDON AND NEW YORK

First published 2014 by Ashgate Publishing

Published 2016 by Routledge
2 Park Square, Milton Park, Abingdon, Oxfordshire OX14 4RN
711 Third Avenue, New York, NY 10017, USA

First issued in paperback 2016

Routledge is an imprint of the Taylor & Francis Group, an informa business

British Library Cataloguing in Publication Data
A catalogue record for this book is available from the British Library

The Library of Congress has cataloged the printed edition as follows:
Schanoes, Veronica L.
  Fairy tales, myth, and psychoanalytic theory: feminism and retelling the tale / by Veronica
    L. Schanoes.
    pages cm
  Includes bibliographical references and index.
  ISBN 978-1-4094-5044-3 (hardcover: alk. paper)
  1. Fairy tales—History and criticism. 2. Psychoanalysis and literature. 3. Feminist literary criticism 4. Feminism and literature. 5. Mothers and daughters in literature. I. Title.
  GR550.S29 2014
  398.2'082—dc23

                                                                        2013035938

ISBN 13: 978-1-138-24807-6 (pbk)
ISBN 13: 978-1-4094-5044-3 (hbk)

FAIRY TALES, MYTH, AND
PSYCHOANALYTIC THEORY

Matthew Gurteen

For my mother, April Schanoes,
who read me fairy tales, and taught me feminism
and for Helen Pilinovsky,
best friend, wise colleague, loving companion

Acknowledgments

When I look into the mirror of this book, I see a number of faces looking back at me, and I am grateful to each and every one of them. Those of us who work in the field of fairy tales and fantasy literature are particularly fortunate to have such a wonderfully supportive array of colleagues to welcome us. I wish in particular to thank Farah Mendlesohn, who has mentored me for many years, beginning with her thoughts on the conference paper that grew into this project; her incisive and perceptive commentary and her friendship, as well as her high standards, are the best guide a scholar could wish for. Cristina Bacchilega's comments on an early version of the project that became this book were utterly invaluable, and her kindness is no less impressive. Though not in the field of fairy tales or fantasy literature, two of my colleagues at Queens College offered essential guidance during critical periods of this work's gestation; Carrie Hintz and Talia Schaffer went above and beyond the call of senior colleague-dom in their willingness to help and work with me. Brian Attebery and Donald Haase have also been generous and thoughtful with their time and counsel. Heidi Anne Heiner has provided rich and valuable resources for all fairy-tale scholars and aficionados.

I have been very fortunate in the department that welcomed me to Queens College–CUNY. Numerous colleagues have made professional life warm and satisfying: Balaka Basu, Ryan Black, Glenn Burger, Jeffrey Cassvan, Seo-Young Chu, Nancy Comley, Nicole Cooley, Annmarie Drury, Hugh English, Duncan Faherty, Kevin Ferguson, Miles Grier, Gloria Fisk, Thomas Frosch, Kimiko Hahn, Caroline Hong, Brian Kim, Steven Kruger, Richard McCoy, Wayne Moreland, David Richter, Harold Schecter, Richard Schotter, Roger Sederat, Sian Silyn Roberts, Kim Smith, Jason Tougaw, Amy Tucker, Andrea Walkden, Amy Wan, Joyce Warren, Bette Weidman, Karen Weingarten, John Weir, and Gordon Whatley.

I had the privilege of earning my PhD from the best program I could imagine. My advisors, Vicki Mahaffey, Sheila Murnaghan, and Jean-Paul Rabaté, were as thoughtful, intelligent, rigorous, and understanding as any advisors could be. Emily Steiner, Peter Decherney, Kevin Platt, Karina Sotnik, and Phyllis Rackin provided me with indispensable guidance and instruction; I learned more than I could have imagined at the beginning of graduate school. And I am very grateful to Anne Prescott of Barnard College, who set me on this path in the first place.

One of the great pleasures of working on contemporary literature is getting to know the authors and editors. Every author and editor I have worked with has been no less than gracious, and many of them are true friends. All of them deserve my deepest gratitude: Ellen Datlow, Kathryn Davis, Gregory Frost, Liz Gorinsky, Gavin Grant, Roz Kaveney, Ellen Kushner, Kelly Link, Robin McKinley, Patrick Nielsen Hayden, Alicia Ostriker, Delia Sherman, Catherynne M. Valente, and Terri Windling.

I rejoice in wonderful friends who are both witty and kind. I am particularly thinking of Brett Cox and Jeanne Beckwith, Dale Bailey, Melissa Bobe, David Chope, John Langan, Donna Levinsohn, Erika Lin, Jonas Oxgaard, Valerie Pierce-Grove, Rose Fox, and Genevieve Valentine. My best friend and the sister of my heart, Jenna Felice, did not live to see this project completed. When she died, I thought that I would never again find a friend whom I could love so dearly, and who would love me the same way, who would be a best friend. But Helen Pilinovsky brought me that good fortune, and I am deeply grateful.

My family has been a source of unstinting support: my cousin, Georgia Hodes; my grandfather, Marvin Zuckerman; my aunts and uncles, Paula Gorlitz and Steven Zuckerman, and Barbara and Steve Goldstein; my sisters Vanessa Felice and Genevieve Schanoes have all helped me in ways too numerous to name. My father David Schanoes and Bonnie Johnson have been two of my staunchest supporters. I have dedicated this project to my mother, April Schanoes. Her constant encouragement and faith in me have never wavered. My imagination has been structured by her Andrew Lang fairy-tale books and her Oz books; it is thanks to her that I know the importance of love, fantasy, and feminism. I have always been able to turn to her and to my stepfather, John Semivan, for support, and I have always been able to count on them to listen to me and to understand.

Finally, there are the people who have filled my life with more joy than anybody could ask for: Sofia Rabaté, Sophie and Asher Decherney, Dasha and Poli Sotnik-Platt, Emma and Cora Hodes-Wood, Ursula Grant, and my beloved godson, Oberon Oxgaard. Never has an auntie or friend been luckier, happier, or prouder than I am.

Grateful acknowledgment is made:

to the PSC-CUNY Research Fund for enabling this research.

for the use of excerpts from *Strategies of Fantasy* by Brian Attebery. © 1992, Brian Attebery. Reprinted with permission of Indiana University Press.

for the use of excerpts from *Inspiriting Influences* by Michael Awkward. © 1989 Columbia University Press. Reprinted with permission of the publisher.

for excerpts from *The Anxiety of Influence* by Harold Bloom (1997), by permission of Oxford University Press.

to Yale University Press for permission to reprint excerpts from Olga Broumas's *Beginning with O*, © 1977 by Olga Broumas.

for excerpts from *The Bloody Chamber*, *The Magic Toyshop*, and *Shaking a Leg*, © Angela Carter 1979, 1967, and 1997, respectively. Reproduced by permission of the Estate of Angela Carter c/o Rogers, Coleridge & White Ltd., 20 Powis Mews, London W11 1Jn.

to ICM for permission to reprint excerpts from Angela Carter's *The Sadeian Woman* (1978).

to the publisher for permission to reprint the passages from "The Language of Sisterhood" (*The State of the Language*, University of California Press, 1979) by Angela Carter.

for excerpts from *The Reproduction of Mothering* by Nancy Chodorow (1999). By permission of University of California Press.

for excerpts from "Learning from the Outsider Within: The Sociological Significance of Black Feminist Thought," by Patricia Hill Collins, originally appearing in *Social Problems* (1986). By permission of University of California Press.

for the passages from *The Girl Who Trod on a Loaf* by Kathryn Davis, © 1993 by Kathryn Davis. Used by permission of Alfred A. Knopf, a division of Random House, Inc.

for excerpts from *Collected Papers*, vol. 4, by Sigmund Freud, trans. James Strachey (1959) appearing on pages xx. © 1959 Sigmund Freud. Reprinted by permission of Basic Books, a member of the Perseus Books Group.

to Writers House for permissions to use excerpts from Gregory Frost's "The Root of the Matter," from Ellen Datlow and Terri Windling's *Snow White, Blood Red* (1993).

for the passages from *Smoke and Mirrors* by Neil Gaiman. © 1999 by Neil Gaiman. Reprinted courtesy of HarperCollins Publishers and Writers' House.

for the passages from *Meadowlands* by Louise Glück. © 1997 by Louise Glück. Reprinted courtesy of HarperCollins Publishers.

for passages from *Changing the Story* by Gayle Greene. © 1991, Gayle Greene. Reprinted by permission of Indiana University Press.

for excerpts from *The Keepsake*, © 1997 by Kirsty Gunn. Used by permission of Grove/Atlantic, Inc.

to the publisher and author for permission to reprint passages from *The Postmodern Fantastic in Contemporary British Fiction* (Wissenschaftlicher Verlag Trier, 2004) by Martin Horstkotte.

for the passages reprinted from *Critical and Creative Perspectives on Fairy Tales* by Vanessa Joosen. © 2011, Wayne State University Press, with the permission of Wayne State University Press, Detroit, Michigan, 48201.

for excerpts from *Women's Growth in Connection* edited by Judith V. Jordan (1991). By permission of Guilford Publications.

for excerpts from *Women's Growth in Diversity* edited by Judith V. Jordan (1997). By permission of Guilford Publications.

to Tor Books for permission to reprint excerpts from Tanith Lee's *White as Snow* (2001).

to the author and publisher for permission to reprint the passages from *Stranger Things Happen* (Small Beer Press, 2001) by Kelly Link.

for excerpts from *Death in Childbirth* by Irvine Loudon (1992) by permission of Oxford University Press.

to Writers House and to Robin McKinley for permissions to use excerpts from Robin McKinley's *Deerskin* (1993).

for excerpts from *The Mirror: A History* by Sabine Melchior-Bonnet, trans. Katherine H. Jewett (2002). Used by permission of Taylor & Francis Group, LLC.

for the passages from *Beloved* by Toni Morrison, © 1987 by Toni Morrison. Used by permission of Alfred A. Knopf, a division of Random House, Inc.

for excerpts from Warren F. Motte's "Reflections on Mirrors." *Modern Language Notes* 120.4 (2005): 785–6. © 2005 by Johns Hopkins University Press. Reprinted with permission of Johns Hopkins University Press.

for the passages from "Penelope's Song: The Lyric Odysseys of Linda Pastan and Louise Glück" (*Classical and Modern Literature*, 2002) by Sheila Murnaghan and Deborah H. Roberts, by permission of the publisher.

to Alicia Ostriker for permissions to use excerpts from her *Stealing the Language: The Emergence of Women's Poetry in America* (1987).

to the author and publisher for permissions to use excerpts from *Witches Abroad* by Sir Terry Pratchett (Victor Gollancz Ltd., 1991).

to the following for permission to reprint the excerpts from *Of Woman Born: Motherhood as Experience and Institution* by Adrienne Rich. © 1986, 1976 by W. W. Norton & Co., Inc. Used by permission of W. W. Norton & Co., Inc.

for permission to reprint excerpts from "The Woman in Process in Angela Carter's *The Bloody Chamber*" from *Angela Carter and the Fairy Tale* edited by Danielle M. Roemer and Cristina Bacchilega. © 2001 by Wayne State University Press, with the permission of Wayne State University Press, Detroit, Michigan, 48201.

for permission to reprint excerpts from *Marvelous Geometry: Narrative and Metafiction in Modern Fairy Tale* by Jessica Tiffin. © 2009 by Wayne State University Press, with the permission of Wayne State University Press, Detroit, Michigan, 48201.

for the passages from *The Ice Puzzle* (http://anovelinpieces.catherynnemvalente. com, 2004) by Catherynne M. Valente, by permission of the author.

for permission to reprint the passages from *Daughtering and Mothering: Feminine Subjectivity Reanalysed*, edited by Janneke van Mens-Verhulst, Karlein Schreurs, and Liesbeth Woertman. © 1993 Janneke van Mens-Verhulst, Karlein Schreurs, and Liesbeth Woertman. Reprinted by permission of Taylor & Francis Books.

for excerpts from *Fairy Tale as Myth/Myth as Fairy Tale* by Jack Zipes (1994). By permission of the University Press of Kentucky.

for excerpts from *Relentless Progress* by Jack Zipes (2008). By permission of Taylor and Francis Group, LLC.

Chapter 4 appeared in a previous form as "Book as Mirror, Mirror as Book: The Significance of the Looking-glass in Contemporary Revisions of Fairy Tales," *Journal of the Fantastic in the Arts* 20.1 (2009). Grateful acknowledgment is made for the permission to reprint it here.

The cover image is created by and used courtesy of Tekla Benson.

Introduction:
The Mother's Looking-Glass

Tanith Lee's *White as Snow* offers a complex and fascinating answer to the question of how it is possible to represent feminine subjectivity using a language and stories implicated in patriarchal ideology. In her novel, a combined revision of the tales of Snow White and of Persephone and Demeter, Arpazia stands at her mirror. Her ignored daughter Coira watches worshipfully. Coira believes the mirror to be a window into another room, and her mother's reflection a miraculous enchantment:

> [S]tealing forward, gazing only upward now to the adult height, as the queen herself had done, Coira missed her own reflection as it entered the scope of the sorcerous mirror. She saw only the witch-queen facing the witch-queen, her wonder doubled.
>
> The child was now too moved even to need to be brave. "You're so beautiful—more beautiful—the most beautiful in all the world."
>
> … Arpazia … glanced over her shoulder and down in astonishment …
>
> "Am I?"
>
> "Yes—so beautiful. More beautiful than anyone. Like the goddess."
>
> "Hush," said Arpazia … Yet Arpazia looked back into the glass. She saw her beauty as if for the only time in her life. Her eyes darkened. "Yes. I am."
>
> And "Yes," answered the queen in the mirror, "you are." (81–2)

In Lee's retelling of "Snow White," the feminized magic, the witch-queen's power, is generated by a neglected daughter's adoration of her mother: the woman's power and beauty, even her sense of self is triggered by her daughter's desire. The powerful mother is not contained in one figure: she is distanced from herself, looking in the mirror; her reflection has the power of speech; her daughter looks in the mirror and sees only her mother. But Arpazia has been deeply damaged, driven insane, by the brutal misogyny of her life; surrounded by the same mirrors and fantasies of motherhood and daughterhood, Coira must find a way to integrate her mother's life without allowing herself to be similarly destroyed. Just so, Lee uses a story whose themes naturalize misogynistic notions of femininity (competition between women over beauty, the notion that there can be only one who is "fairest of them all," feminine power as evil witchcraft) in order to re-create it as a feminist tale. Lee is only one writer of many who use mother-daughter dyads and mirrors, vision and revision, to represent feminine subjectivity. This project will explore the significance of these figurations, and the relationship between the texts that employ them and theories regarding feminine subjectivity that were developed contemporaneously.

A common theme to the fairy-tale revisions and the theories under discussion here is a characteristic permeability of identity, a sense of fluidity between self and other, subject and object. This fluidity finds expression in the relationships between mothers and daughters as well as in the doubling inherent in mirror reflections. An interesting dynamic emerges, as the revisions and the theories play on the strengths of their respective genres to explore varying aspects of this greater connection and interchange through self and other. Feminist theorists often push back against the notion that a close mother-daughter relationship, even one in which the participants have permeable ego boundaries, must of necessity be unhealthy. The damage, if damage there be, lies in the destruction of the mother's self by patriarchy, and thus her inability to help the daughter construct a solid sense of self (an example of this concept can be found in Luce Irigaray's famous essay "And the One Does Not Stir Without the Other"). Many of the revisions, however, seem to focus on the dangers of such relationships; Toni Morrison's *Beloved* and Tanith Lee's *White as Snow* spring easily to mind. But even in texts that problematize the mother-daughter relationship to such a great extent as well as in revisions that portray a more beneficial relationship, such as the relationship between Helle and Ida Ten Brix in Kathryn Davis's *The Girl Who Trod on a Loaf*, the relationship is strongly associated with the project of story-telling and revision themselves. What kind of ambivalence about rewriting the fairy-tale tradition is being expressed in these texts?

Conversely, revisions often valorize the multiple selves generated by mirrors and/or doubles: Kelly Link's "The Girl Detective," Catherynne M. Valente's *The Ice Puzzle*, and Robin McKinley's *Deerskin* portray the doubled or multiplied self as something to be celebrated and/or appreciated, and as something that can provide space in which to heal. In stark contrast to the threatening "uncanniness" of the double that Sigmund Freud and Otto Rank found inherent in the concept, these writers portray the multiplied self as liberation, comfort, and power. While this sense of joy in multiplicity is often characteristic of postmodernism, it is no less striking that the theme is also found in theories of feminine subjectivity specifically, and it is absolutely necessary to understand how that theme functions in such a context. Over and over again, feminist theorists reject the notion of an atomized, walled-off individual as an insufficient model for women's sense of self, arguing instead of a relational understanding of feminine subjectivity. Further, it seems that in texts both postmodern (Angela Carter's "The Tiger's Bride") and not (*Deerskin*), doubling and multiplicity of identities generated thereby is closely identified not only with feminine subjectivity, but with the mode of the fantastic, the genre of fantasy, and with magic itself. Just as examining mother-daughter relationships tells us about how models of revision are operating in these texts, so too can examining the representations of multiple identities tell us about the use of the fantastic and the role of magic in these texts.

Feminist revisions of fairy tales and myths came into their own in the 1970s and 1990s, two decades that also saw a surge in feminist activism and theorizing. And, just as the foundational insights of second-wave feminist psychoanalytic theorists in the 1970s were extended and elaborated in the work of the clinicians at the Wellesley Stone Center during the 1990s, Anne Sexton's *Transformations* (1971), Olga Broumas's *Beginning with O* (1977), and Angela Carter's *The Bloody Chamber* (1979) served as inspiration to revisionists in the 1990s, such as Tanith Lee, Terri Windling, Kelly Link, and Catherynne M. Valente. Despite these similarities in timing and the shared focus on mother-daughter relationships and mirroring, this is the first project to consider the works of the revisionists and the works of the theorists in tandem, drawing out and analyzing the connections between the two genres. This is also one of the first projects to combine analysis of the mainstream, canonical writers, such as Carter, with that of the genre writers, such as Lee and Windling.

The considerations of literary revision contemporary with the texts under consideration have been deeply invested in the masculinist, Freudian/Oedipal struggle posited by Harold Bloom in *The Anxiety of Influence*. Even feminist critics such as Adrienne Rich, Rachel Blau DuPlessis, and Alicia Ostriker have taken as given the hostile relationship between originary tale and revision. More recent theories of intertextuality acknowledge that communication between texts is inherent in the language itself and not necessarily hostile, but not only do they fail to distinguish between allusions and echoes on the one hand, and deliberate revisions of a specific story on the other, but, as Nancy K. Miller points out, they have little to say about the specificity of texts written by women, let alone feminist texts. This is where my work comes in. In reading feminist fairy tale/mythic revisions from the 1970s and 1990s, I found that the themes they explore and conclusions they come to correspond most closely not with their contemporary theories of revision, but with contemporary feminist psychoanalytic theories. Both genres aim to make visible women's lived experiences, often using the metaphor/ symbol of the mirror; both explore relationships between women, *especially* the relationships between mothers and daughters; both attempt to present women's stories as central to our understanding of humanity. What, then, if instead of basing our understanding of the relationship between traditional tale and contemporary revision on a Freudian model of hostility and anxiety, we were to incorporate the insights of Nancy Chodorow, Jean Baker Miller, and the relational theorists of the Wellesley Stone Center? It is my argument that both genres, in the 1970s and 1990s, were grappling with the same problems and arriving at similar conclusions, and that thus we must read them together to fully understand the projects that either genre embarked upon. It is only by examining the theories of second-wave feminism alongside the expression of those same ideas in artistic form that we can fully understand the achievements of second-wave feminist thought. The second wave in this context has not been abjected, but rather, refined.

It is the position of this project that the confluence of focus between feminist fairy-tale revisions and psychoanalytic theory are not coincidences of timing, but that the feminist revisions of fairy tales and myths of the 1970s and 1990s are doing similar work to the concomitant feminist psychoanalytic theory, and that it is to that theory we must turn for a full understanding of the revisionary project, rather than to the literary theory of the time. Similarly, for a thorough nuancing of and elaboration on the themes identified and discussed by these theorists, we must pay close attention to the work of the revisionary writers, for it is my contention that these two genres, both of which bloomed in the 1970s and 1990s—feminist revisions of fairy tales and myth, and feminist psychoanalytic theory—are expressions of the same ideas and same goals in different forms. That is to say, the important political work of understanding feminine subjectivity on its own terms, rather than in comparison to a normative masculinity, was being accomplished in both genres, with a startling unity in themes. Both genres focus on the tropes of the mother-daughter relationship and the mirror, and by doing so, both trouble the boundary of self and other, I and not-I, subject and object. These two tropes express the permeable subjectivity and dual consciousness of feminine identity, regardless of genre. By studying both genres' uses of these two tropes, I hope not only to articulate a particularly telling case study of the relationship between theory and text, but also to discover why the field of fairy tale and mythic revision has been so attractive to writers working with feminist concerns.

Prior to the feminist interventions of the 1970s, psychoanalysis worked primarily on a deficiency model of the feminine psyche. This model took the masculine psyche as the norm for human development and mental/emotional health, and marked as inferior, pathological, or deficient the ways in which the feminine psyche deviated from that "norm." The second-wave feminist movement made profound changes in this entrenched paradigm. Jean Baker Miller's 1976 landmark book *Toward a New Psychology of Women* advocated instead an understanding of feminine psychology based on recognizing strengths in the previously devalued qualities of relatedness to others, emotionality, and nurturing, or aiding the development of others. Two years prior, Nancy Chodorow had published "Family Structure and Feminine Personality," the essay that she would expand into her 1978 book *The Reproduction of Mothering*. In both the essay and the book, Chodorow focused on the subjective experience of the mother in relation to her daughter as formative of women's personalities. While Chodorow's work has been rightly criticized, as has much second-wave feminist work, for its heteronormativity and focus on the experiences of middle-class white women, the importance, power, and enduring legacy of her models cannot be overestimated.

Based on the work of Miller and Chodorow, clinicians such as Judith V. Jordan and Janet L. Surrey developed a theory and practice of women's psychology known as relational psychology, or now, relational-cultural therapy. *Women's Growth in Connection: Writings from the Stone Center* was the first volume produced by the group of clinicians and theorists dedicated to this approach to mental health, and it appeared in 1991. Further books from the Stone Center were published throughout the 1990s. Thus, this important strain of psychoanalytic theory and practice, which bloomed in the 1990s and is still implemented today, was continuous with the work of 1970s second-wave feminist theorists and practitioners.

Combining close analysis of many primary texts with contemporaneous feminist and psychoanalytic theory, this book proposes a new model of understanding the project of feminist literary revision in the 1970s and 1990s by considering that project as a necessary partner to the psychoanalytic theories being advanced, nuancing and illustrating them. These two decades were a time in which both artists and psychoanalytic theorists were concerned with issues of how a woman's sense of self is constructed and how it develops; only by examining these texts in light of one another can we fully understand the answers they arrived at. Postmodern theory, as do many of the primary fictional texts under discussion in this study, rejects the notion of a singular, unified, authentic "self" in favor of a kaleidoscopic, constantly shifting set of identities that are always in the process of being constructed. But much psychoanalytic theory, much second-wave theory, and most popular culture continue to be fascinated by the search for/development of one's "true self." Certainly some of the great insights of second-wave feminism came out of consciousness-raising sessions that certain men of the New Left derided as "therapy" rather than political activism; in response, the slogan "The personal is political" was coined by feminists arguing that the "personal" arrangements and injuries women suffer under patriarchy are indeed the result of systemic and institutionalized disparities in power between the sexes. For the second wave, looking into the self and trying to distinguish between an "authentic," inner self and the corrosive effects of patriarchy was a powerful and meaningful political tool. It is no surprise that the theorists as well as the creative writers who came out of that wave engage with that process as well; it is intriguing to find the writers coming to value multiplicity in a way similar to postmodern theorists.

I consider mainstream literary revisions alongside of their genre counterparts in order to demonstrate the ways in which the common themes of these projects express concerns basic to the revision and feminism of their era. I find that revisions are not only reconsiderations of traditional tales, but are meditations on the nature of the revisionary project itself, especially as it relates to gender.

Why should these two genres, psychoanalytic theory and literary revision, go hand in hand? What do they have to offer each other? Psychoanalytic theory is, in many ways, the more direct and explicit medium, able to make direct political interventions into existing structures of power. Theory can directly advance new notions and explicate their importance. But it is in literature that the important work of nuancing those notions is done, of making those notions sufficiently complex as to illustrate human subjectivity. Thus, without the artistic production alongside the theory, the new ideas are neither nuanced nor complicated adequately—the bones lack flesh—and we risk selling second-wave feminism short, or caricaturing it. Thus, both genres are engaged in the same political project concerning a more accurate anatomy and depiction of the feminine sense of self as it has been understood in those recent decades.

The tropes of the mother-daughter relationship and of the magic mirror, I assert, are not merely themes within the texts; rather, they are ways that the texts are thinking not only about feminine subjectivity, but also about themselves. I develop a way of understanding revision based on the feminine subjectivity and relationality that emphasize women's flexible ego boundaries and more diffuse sense of self, and are so essential to the theoretical texts contemporary with the revisions under study. This way of understanding, or theory, I suggest, represents the relationship between traditional tales, or, as Vanessa Joosen terms it in her recent book on the relationship between fairy-tale scholarship and postmodern retellings, the "pre-text" and revisions as the revisors of the 1970s and 1990s may have understood it. I then examine the repercussions of this sort of subjectivity by analyzing the role of the doubled/multiplied self as highlighted by the mirror.

The book is divided into two sections. The first part of the book deals with the trope of the mother-daughter relationship in the texts under study. How is that trope represented and with what issues is it regularly connected? How does it relate to the process of literary revision itself? The second part deals with the trope of the magic mirror, asking questions about how it represents feminine experiences of the self in relation to other people. Each section begins with an analysis of the representation of the trope in question, proceeds to theorize that trope's relationship to larger issues of representation, and concludes by examining the implications of those issues to questions of revision and feminine subjectivity.

Foregrounding the mother-daughter relationship as central to the development of feminine subjectivity and identity was a significant project of second-wave feminism. Prior to the advances of that wave, Adrienne Rich could write, in *Of Woman Born: Motherhood as Experience and Institution*, "This cathexis between mother and daughter—essential, distorted, misused—is the great unwritten story ... Yet this relationship has been minimized and trivialized in the annals of patriarchy" (225). Prior to the work of Nancy Chodorow, Freudian theory had relegated the relationship between mother and child to the undifferentiated pre-Oedipal period, prior to the formation of any psyche worthy of the name, a sort of murky symbiosis in need of the Law of the Father to effect a full entry in human consciousness. In subsequent decades, mothers shouldered the blame for everything from inability to deal with color blindness to homosexuality to schizophrenia, but little work was done to examine how mothers actually experienced their children, and what effect those perceptions had on the developing psyche of the child. At best, Winnicott described the "good-enough" mother, whose children managed to glean enough support from her faulty care to develop into healthy beings, but the subjectivity of that mother was left unexamined.

Nancy Chodorow's work of the mid-1970s changed that. In her foundational essay "Family Structure and Feminine Personality" and her subsequent book *The Reproduction of Mothering*, she noted that mothers possess subjectivities of their own, and that these subjectivities strongly influence the developing psyches and personalities of their children. In particular, she is interested in the way women develop permeable ego boundaries and more diffuse senses of self in response to the strong, continuous identification a binary gender system produces between mother and daughter. Chodorow did not idealize this relationship; neither did she consider it inherently toxic. Her work, along with the work of Jean Baker Miller, provided the basis for the development of relational theory in the 1990s by the theorist/clinicians of the Wellesley Stone Center. These theorist/clinicians, including Judith V. Jordan, Janet Surrey, and others, took the experiences of women as normative; that is, rather than identifying permeable ego boundaries and a more diffuse sense of self as problematic deviations from a masculine, atomized, individuated "normal" psyche, they argued that psyches exist and develop only in relation to other psyches, and that identity formation and maintenance must be understood in the context of those relationships. Connection to others, they argued, was a psychic strength and a sign of maturity, rather than regression, as it had been identified by previous psychoanalysts operating within a paradigm that valorized individuation above all else. And the essential relationship that created a greater facility for these strengths in women was the relationship between mother and daughter. Indeed, Surrey writes that "Mothers and daughters often remain exquisitely open and sensitive to each other's feeling states" ("The Mother-Daughter Relationship" 119), and that the relationship between mother and daughter is the very model for relationships throughout life ("The Self-in-Relation" 53–9).

The significance of the figure of the mother was highly controversial within second-wave feminism. Shulamith Firestone denounced motherhood as barbaric in *The Dialectic of Sex*, and within two years, Adrienne Rich had fired back with *Of Woman Born*, in which she differentiated being a mother from patriarchal constructs of motherhood, and noted that denigrating a capacity possessed solely by women was a way of denigrating women. Nancy Friday's *My Mother, Myself: The Daughter's Search for Identity* blamed mothers for practically all internalized sexism their daughters carry and provided no vision of good mothering, while Judith Arcana's *Our Mothers' Daughters* provided a feminist analysis of mothers' situations under patriarchy, and their own desires. The fascination continued through the 1990s, with Paula J. Caplan's self-help book *Don't Blame Mother* going through two editions, and other books appearing throughout the 1990s on the topic of mother-daughter relationships.

Perhaps it is no surprise that a significant number of writers wishing to explore this hot-button topic would turn to fairy tales and classical myth. It is in fairy tales and classical myth, after all, that mother-daughter relationships often take center stage in the forms of Snow White and her (step)mother; Cinderella, her mother, and her stepmother; Persephone and Demeter; and others. But it is important to note that oftentimes, the characters in revisions enact and embroider on the relationships observed and theorized by Chodorow, Jordan, and their cohorts. Just as Chodorow and the Stone Center Theorists revise earlier psychoanalytic assumptions about the mother's role in the development of the daughter's psyche and the mother's own psyche, so too do the writers—Carter, Link, and Lee, for example—revisit traditional stories about mothers and daughters in order to more fully articulate and describe those relationships. After examining this dynamic in the first half of this book, I suggest that we can understand these particular writers' relationships to such traditional tales as a kind of mother-daughter relationship itself, and that we can best understand the revisers' project by examining it through the lenses offered by the contemporaneous theory that was another expression of that very project, as I contend here.

Chapter 1, "Mother-Daughter Relationships in Theory and Text," analyzes the many roles played by this trope in several key texts. I begin by paralleling the problematic nature of the relationships between mothers and daughters in traditional tales with the troublesome issues regarding motherhood raised by early second-wave feminists such as Adrienne Rich and Nancy Chodorow. I then proceed to use Angela Carter's "The Bloody Chamber" and "Wolf-Alice" as case studies in the importance of function of the relationship between mother and daughter to one of the foundational texts of the field under study. I then consider more recent texts in the light of work by Rich, Chodorow, and Luce Irigaray in order to highlight the ways the anxieties and fears regarding motherhood and daughterhood that permeated second-wave feminist thought have found expression in texts as diverse as Tanith Lee's *White as Snow* and Toni Morrison's *Beloved*. While highlighting the similarities between Lee's and Morrison's novels, I situate Morrison's work in the context of black feminists' work on mother-daughter relationships as well as the history of the relationship between African-American writers and the Greco-Roman classics.

Chapter 2, "Revisions of Motherhood and Daughterhood," explores the affinities between the mother-daughter relationship and the concept of literary revision. Through intensive close reading of several texts, I demonstrate that mother-daughter relationships are associated with story-telling itself. I then reverse the direction of that metaphor, and propose an understanding of feminist revision of the 1970s and 1990s that is based on feminist psychoanalytic theories of the mother-daughter relationship advanced by Chodorow, Irigaray, and the theorists of the Wellesley Stone Center. In order to do so, I analyze the primary texts mentioned above, and include other texts by writers as diverse as Kathryn Davis and Kelly Link.

How does this theory of literary revision fit into other theories of revision that would have been influencing writers during the 1970s and 1990s? That is the question that Chapter 3, "Revision and Repetition" seeks to answer. Using works as diverse as Sigmund Freud's "Creative Writing and Day-Dreaming," T. S. Eliot's "Tradition and the Individual Talent," Harold Bloom's *The Anxiety of Influence*, and Rachel Blau DuPlessis's *Writing Beyond the Ending: Narrative Strategies of Twentieth-Century Women Writers*, I argue that feminist revision as envisioned by the revisionists under study here in particular involves not a hostile or anxious relationship to the story tradition from which it draws inspiration, but instead a collaborative, affectionate relationship. I argue that far from seeking to replace or efface the original story, a revision incarnates the original tale and extends its influence and its "life." I conclude this chapter by differentiating revision from duplication by a close analysis of Terry Pratchett's *Witches Abroad*, a novel that explicitly grapples with and meditates on the power of repeated traditional tales and the importance of ringing changes on those tales.

The other trope this book takes up is that of the magic mirror. The mirror was a driving metaphor for Luce Irigaray, whose 1974 book (translated into English in 1985), the one that got her expelled from Lacan's circle, was entitled *Speculum of the Other Woman*, punning on the gynecological instrument but also on the medieval Latin use of the word "speculum" to mean "mirror." Irigaray continued to work with this metaphor in pieces such as "And the One Doesn't Stir without the Other" (1979; translated 1981), "Divine Women" (1987; translated 1993), and *This Sex Which Is Not One* (1977; translated 1985). With the rise to prominence, simultaneous with the rise of second-wave feminism, of Lacan's mirror stage and issues of the internalized male gaze described through the metaphor of the mirror by Sandra Gilbert and Susan Gubar in *The Madwoman in the Attic* (1979), the mirror became a highly significant issue during the 1970s. Similarly, with the publication of Naomi Wolf's *The Beauty Myth* in 1992, the question of appearance as a feminist issue took on new urgency, and so was the age-old relationship between women and mirrors interrogated anew within 1990s feminism. Like the permeable ego boundaries and diffuse senses of self found within the mother-daughter relationship, the mirror troubles the boundary between the subject and object, self and other, I and not-I. And so we find the mirror playing a major role in the fairy-tale revisions of Angela Carter, Tanith Lee, Terry Pratchett, and Catherynne M. Valente, where it often takes on a far greater importance than it had in the traditional tales.

By examining these writers' uses of mirrors in concert with the work of their theoretical counterparts, a significant pattern emerges. The mirror emerges as a potent source of self-creation, magic, and ultimately story-telling itself; the mirror is a figure for the very text being read, a fantastic tale closely identified with female power and creativity. How can we understand this connection? Again, I suggest we understand it through contemporaneous theory, arguing that the mirror becomes a symbol of telling stories through a feminine subjectivity that is characterized by permeable ego boundaries and connection with others, as well as with the alienation from the self under conditions of patriarchy, in a formulation going back to Simone de Beauvoir and W.E.B. DuBois. Ultimately, I argue that as the mirror cannot help but invoke the figure of the double, its importance can help us answer the question of why fantasy in general and fairy-tale revisions in particular held—and continue to hold—such appeal for writers dealing with feminist issues. The mirror's—and fantasy's—illusion of another world, identical and yet opposite to ours, creates a space for expressing the lived experiences of women and envisioning the feminist change necessary to improve those experiences.

In Chapter 4, "Through the Looking-Glass: Mirrors, Fantasy, and Reality," I examine the relationship between mirrors and fantastic literature, arguing that mirrors are an emblem of the fantasy genre itself. I then argue that the use of the mirror as an emblem closely identifies that genre with female power. I argue that rather than understanding the mirror as hostile to women, as do Irigaray and Sandra Gilbert and Susan Gubar, we must explore the way in which this symbol is being reclaimed by the feminist writers under study here, focusing in particular on the same Angela Carter stories that I analyzed in Part I. I find that like the mother-daughter relationship, the mirror is closely identified with the text itself, and often represents specifically feminine experiences and fantasies in a patriarchal world.

Chapter 5, "Double Vision: Women and Fantasy," asks why it should be that the magic mirror is so closely paralleled with women's experiences and fantasies in these texts. I examine the importance of one of the particular elements of fantasy the mirror invokes, that of the double, arguing that the fantasy of the double, evoked by the presence of the mirror, lays bare a particular correspondence between feminine subjectivity and these writers' chosen mode of fantasy. I begin by discussing the recurring motif in fantastic literature of the double, or *doppelganger*, its appearances in the texts under study, and its special relationship to feminine subjectivity. I then go on to examine the dichotomy between seeming and being, highlighted by the mirror. Ultimately, I argue that the mirrors and fantasies, illusions of another world, identical and yet opposite to ours, create a space for expressing the lived experiences of women and envisioning the feminist changes necessary to improve those experiences.

In many ways, by reconnecting myths and fairy tales to psychoanalytic theory and clinical work, I am rejoining genres that had been put asunder. Myths, fairy tales, and psychoanalytic theory have long occupied the same psychic space. These categories have been intertwined since the birth of psychoanalysis, when Sigmund Freud used the story of Oedipus Rex to illustrate and name his controversial theory about infant desire, and only became more so with the theories of Carl Jung. More recently, Jessica Tiffin, author of *Marvelous Geometry: Narrative and Metafiction in Modern Fairy Tale* (2009), notes that "[t]he recognition fairy-tale pattern ... becomes not only a structural recognition or an evocation of primitive ritual repetitions but also a psychological one: the patterns evoked by fairy tales are profoundly linked to human development and consciousness" (11). But what is the relationship among fairy tales, psychoanalysis, and human consciousness in this project? How do I justify applying theories about psyches to texts, which are, after all, merely words on pages?

Let us begin by discussing the differences between fairy tales and myths. The technical, definitional difference is that a myth is a sacred, unquestioned story, involving divine or semi-divine beings, which purports to be history and explains how the physical or cultural world came to take the form it has, whereas a fairy tale does not involve divinity and was never taken for truth. Obviously these differences are somewhat problematic. How can we claim, for instance, that a myth is sacred, unquestioned, and taken for truth, when so many classical myths have opposing variants? Do we honestly suppose that the ancient Greeks believed *both* that, for instance, Penelope was chaste and faithful, as in Homer's *Odyssey*, and that she had sex with all the suitors, as other versions of the story have it? Too, the level of belief is to be questioned; the ancient world spans thousands of years; do we suppose that all ancient Greeks and Romans literally believed every story they told about the gods?

[handwritten margin note: link to Bettelheim]

Besides these technical, definitional differences, however, there is a matter of canonicity, of high culture and low. Classical myth has traditionally taken on a much higher status within our culture than have lowly fairy tales, which are often assumed to be "simple," and to come from the simple folk. For hundreds of years, learning ancient Greek and Latin and concomitant familiarity with the stories that went along with them was the province of the upper classes—upper-class men, in particular. Fairy tales were associated with women and with servants, despite the fact that the editors who rose to fame through publishing such tales were usually upper- or middle-class men. In contrast, Alicia Ostriker writes about myth that it "belongs to 'high' culture and is handed 'down' through the ages by religious, literary, and educational authority" (*Stealing the Language* 212–13). This has hardly been the case for fairy tales, often attacked by educational, religious, and literary authorities. Fairy tales have long been the stuff of pop culture. Angela Carter, the revisionist *extraordinaire*, differentiates between myth and fairy tales/ folklore as follows: "I'm interested in myths—though I'm much more interested in folklore—just because they *are* extraordinary lies designed to make people unfree. (Whereas, in fact, folklore is a much more straightforward set of devices for making real life more exciting and is much easier to infiltrate with different kinds of consciousness.)" ("Notes" 380). Myth, she contends, is what Blake called "the mind-forg'd manacles" and attempts to shut down uncomfortable questions with its explanatory power and pose of ahistoricity, while folklore/fairy tales, orally transmitted traditional tales, as also argued by Jack Zipes, are stories of lower-class origin that can subvert or ridicule existing structures of power.

Given this perhaps more pressing difference, and the differentiation between myth and fairy tale on the part of my predecessors, it may seem strange that I have chosen to treat myth and fairy tale revisions together. In part, doing so is a political choice; I would like to undermine the hierarchical distinctions of canonicity that suggest certain types of magic are sacred while others are unimportant, that certain tales of magic are prestigious, while others are childish. But in even larger part, it is because I think that these distinctions are, currently, already almost entirely undone when it comes to classical myth and Western European fairy tales in contemporary culture. The era of classical myth as high culture is passing. Latin and Ancient Greek are no longer required subjects for college students, let alone the well-educated upper-class scion or arriviste. Young men are very unlikely to be able to answer that classic question, "Who dragged whom around the walls of what how many times?" In his fascinating essay "On Fairy-Stories," Tolkien noted that "fairy stories have ... been relegated to the 'nursery,' as shabby or old-fashioned furniture is relegated to the playroom, primarily because the adults do not want it, and do not care if it is misused." In this century, the same has happened with classical myth. Most contemporary encounters with these myths take place in childhood; perhaps the main source is *D'Aulaire's Book of Greek Myths*. Sheila Murnaghan and Deborah H. Roberts allude to this when they write, in their essay on Louise Glück's and Linda Pastan's poetic revisions of the *Odyssey*, that "Although she [Glück] does not self-consciously thematize, as Pastan does, her recollection and revision of the Homeric poem, *Meadowlands* plays freely with the story elements of the epic in a way that suggests that the *Odyssey* is itself a part of the world seen in childhood, and now only remembered" (3). Classical myths, just like fairy tales, have become children's stories. Zeus is no more sacred than Snow White—and no less.

But what of their relationship to psychoanalytic theory? In my opinion, this is a question about how to responsibly use psychoanalytic theory in literary studies—how can one justify treating texts as psyches?

Consider what Patricia White in "Lesbian Minor Cinema" and Teresa de Lauretis in *The Practice of Love* have to say about Freud's "A Child is Being Beaten." In this essay, Freud finds that several of the small girls to whom he speaks have a fantasy about a little boy being beaten by his father (Freud is at a loss to understand this fantasy, in my opinion because he is unable to understand patriarchy as anything but natural and right; it seems fairly clear to me that the fantasy portrays a desire to punish the dominant gender class, coupled with an inability to associate the authority and power needed to punish that class with anyone *but* a stronger member of that class). Freud is particularly taken aback by the fact that the little girls in question do not seem to play a role in this fantasy themselves, and when he presses one child to say where *she* is, she finally comes out with "I suppose I am looking on." (This essay has been very influential on film theory for obvious reasons.) De Lauretis and White cite LaPlanche and Potalis in suggesting that the girl does not need to be *anywhere* in the fantasy, because she is what they call the *syntax* of the fantasy; that is, the entire thing is an emanation of herself, and thus she is not only the boy and the man, but she is also the setting, the action, the entire dynamic. What LaPlanche and Potalis suggest, and de Lauretis and White elaborate on, is the idea that a fantasy is a *holistic* expression of the psyche.

It seems fairly conventional to think of texts as fantasies. Obviously, they are informed by phantasy (subconscious as opposed to conscious fantasy), created as fantasies, and then edited and refined artistically. If a fantasy is a holistic expression of the psyche, and the editing and refining process represses some elements and highlights others, it creates a structure that can be, in my opinion, usefully analogized to a psyche, unless one rejects the notion of a psyche with a conscious and an un/subconscious altogether. Once we think of a text as a subspecies of fantasy, a kind of holistic representation of the psyche, its connections to other texts/fantasies/representations of psyches become relationships, and relational theory, as well as the theories advanced by Irigaray, Chodorow, and others, can be brought into play to understand those connections.

It is my contention that we have not understood those connections sufficiently. Intertextuality posits that all texts are essentially created of allusions and echoes of prior texts in an endlessly circulating language, and certainly this is the case. All language is always already in use, or it would be unintelligible. And most, if not all, texts make reference to other texts. But surely we must recognize a difference between texts that make allusions to other texts, and/or recycle phrases that derive their meaning from prior use ("Once upon a time"), and/or rework a general idea, such as the marriage plot, on the one hand, and, on the other hand, texts that are deliberately rewriting and revivifying specific stories. That difference deserves, or rather, demands, a specific theorizing and critical lens. I accept that in making this distinction, I am, in some part, hearkening back to authorial intent ("deliberately" rewriting and revivifying). But revisions are indeed a case of authorial intent. A revision is only a revision insofar as the author sets out to rewrite a specific story. It is nearly impossible to revise by accident on the one hand, or for a specific story to be a revision only in the eyes of the reader, on the other. As many of my students note, *Jane Eyre* may allude to both "Cinderella" and "Bluebeard," but it would be a far stretch to argue that the novel is a revision of either story; on the other hand, it is impossible to understand Tanith Lee's *White as Snow* as anything *but* a revision. In a culture that had no tradition of either Snow White or Persephone and Demeter, it would be a meaningless novel. It is the job of this project, however, to, among other things, pay tribute to the ways its many meanings continue to resonate.

I am not the first scholar to note the intertwining of fairy-tale revisions and scholarship/theory. Most recently, Vanessa Joosen's *Critical and Creative Perspectives on Fairy Tales: An Intertextual Dialogue between Fairy-Tale Scholarship and Postmodern Retellings* (2011) examines creative and critical interactions with three key, highly influential pieces of fairy-tale scholarship: the feminist debate on fairy tales between Alison Lurie and Marcia K. Lieberman, Bruno Bettelheim's *The Uses of Enchantment*, and Sandra M. Gilbert and Susan Gubar's *The Madwoman in the Attic*. Stephen Benson, in *Contemporary Fiction and the Fairy Tale* (2008), describes the relationship between fairy-tale fiction and fairy-tale scholarship as an "extraordinary synchronicity" and "fascinatingly close" (5). Jack Zipes, one of the most influential fairy-tale scholars of the past few decades, notes in the recent *Relentless Progress* that in the past 30 years, "there has been an inextricable, dialectical development of mutual influence of *all* writers of fairy tales and fairy-tale criticism" (122).

This project diverges from the those of the above-mentioned scholars in its choice of scholarship on which to focus; for fairly obvious reasons, Joosen, Benson, and Zipes describe the relationship between fairy-tale revisions and fairy-tale scholarship/theory, with feminist revisions and analysis as a subsection of their work. I reverse that focus, considering the relationship between feminist fairy-tale revisions[1] and feminist theory, and, interestingly, find that the level of engagement with similar concerns is just as high as that identified and analyzed

---

[1] The decision concerning whether or not a given revision is feminist is, of course, one that is open to a great deal of debate. For this project, I have tried to err on the side of inclusivity. Thus, while, I would argue, all of the revisions discussed in this book are feminist, they are certainly not all feminist in the same way. Consider, for instance, the brutality of Tanith Lee's *White as Snow*, which highlights women's struggles for autonomy within a patriarchal system, as opposed to the woman-dominated world and power-structures of Terry Pratchett's *Witches Abroad*, which takes older women as complex central characters whose concerns are of great significance. Each illustrates an aspect of feminist thought, though neither is all-inclusive.

by Joosen, Benson, and Zipes. Joosen writes of her book that "[t]he underlying hypothesis ... is that retellings and criticism participate in a continuous and dynamic dialogue about the traditional fairy tale, yet they do so on different terms" (3). I would rephrase that hypothesis with respect to my own project in order to say that feminist revisions of fairy tales and myths and feminist scholarship/theory participate in a continuous and dynamic dialogue about feminine subjectivity, and yet they do so on different terms. In this book, I explain and explore those terms, illustrating fairy-tale/mythic revisions' capacity to engage in multiple theoretical dialogues at once.

A word on terminology: in this book, I follow Jack Zipes in *Fairy Tale as Myth/Myth as Fairy Tale* in differentiating between two types of fairy-tale retellings: "duplicates," which reaffirm and support the values, structures, and norms of traditional tales, reasserting "the deeply entrenched modes of thinking, conceiving, believing that provide our lives with structure," and "revisions," which articulate new values and beliefs, "incorporat[ing] the critical and creative thinking of the producer [of the revision]" and "alter[ing] the reader's views of traditional patterns, images, and codes" (8, 9). I have limited my primary texts to these latter writings, the revisions, as well as to texts intended for adults, not because literature directed at children and adolescents is any less complex, or, indeed, any less bound up in the same concerns, but in order to make manageable my sample size.

Chapter 1
Mother-Daughter Relationships in Theory and Text

In fairy tales and classical myth, the relationship between mother and daughter is rarely untroubled. The overwhelming impression of mother-figures given by the most recognizable versions of our culture's most popular fairy tales and myths is of evil, absent, or unpleasant mothers.[1] Snow White's (step)mother tries to kill her; Cinderella's stepmother forces her to be a servant; Hansel and Gretel's (step) mother convinces their father to abandon them in the forest.[2] Then there are the dead or absent mothers: the 12 dancing princesses have no living mother who can advise them; the Little Mermaid's mother is equally absent and unable to help; Beauty does not have a mother to protect her from her foolish father and his dealings with the Beast; the death of Donkeyskin's mother sets off the disturbing events of the story; Little Red Riding Hood's doting grandmother gets eaten. As Kelly Link writes in "The Girl Detective," "This is another thing about … fairy tales … The mother is usually missing. The girl detective imagines, all of a sudden, all of these mothers. They're in the same place … What are they up to, all of these mothers" (246)? What, indeed?

In *Of Woman Born: Motherhood as Experience and Institution* (1976) Adrienne Rich noted the absence of the mother-daughter romance from the canonized works of human tragedy. But traditional fairy tales do have a history of contemplating the mother-daughter bond. It is true that mothers are wicked or absent in the most popular contemporary versions of the best known fairy tales, such as Disney's versions of Cinderella and Snow White, or the Grimms' version of Hansel and Gretel. But it is not true of the genre as a whole, which contains a number of fairy godmothers, helpers who reincarnate a dead mother in order to protect her orphaned child, and clever mother-daughter duos. Just a little research on the part of a reader can unearth a treasure-trove of mother-daughter dyads, acrimonious, loving, or both. I would suggest that it is precisely because the mother-daughter relationship in fairy tales has been so conflicted over the past century that feminist writers seized upon it; it is a site of tension in a genre of tales that constitute and are constituted by the culture around them. As Rachel Blau DuPlessis notes

---

[1]   There are a number of less well-known tales and variants on well-known tales that do represent mothers in a positive light. See for example many of the tales collected in *The Virago Book of Fairy Tales* and *Strange Things Sometimes Still Happen*, both edited by Angela Carter and *Mirror, Mirror* edited by Jane Yolen.

[2]   I put "step" in parentheses here because within this project I am using the word "mother" to denote all maternal figures in fairy tales and myth.

about revisions of myth, revisions of fairy tales involve an intervention at a site of great power—familiar stories of childhood, fairy tales encode social and political ideologies that influence the way we look at the world. To rewrite such tales is to re-examine a world-view entrenched from childhood, and thus to intervene at a highly charged source of our ideological outlook.

The mother-daughter relationship was a primary site of attention for both 1970s and 1990s writers of fairy-tale and myth revisions; such writers fastened on the mother-daughter relationships in Rapunzel and Snow White, exploring and often recuperating them. They even create pivotal mother-daughter relationships in retellings of tales that did not originally contain such a relationship, as in "The Bloody Chamber," Angela Carter's revision of Bluebeard, and *Deerskin*, Robin McKinley's revision of the tale of Donkeyskin.

Motherhood in general, and mother-daughter relationships in particular, have been highly charged sites in feminist thought, especially in the feminisms of the 1970s and 1990s, so it is not surprising to find them playing such a large role in that era's literature. Second-wave white feminists inherited a tradition of mother blaming and mother pathologizing from the surrounding culture. Betty Friedan observed that by the middle of twentieth century, mothers were being blamed for the unhappiness of every "troubled child; alcoholic, suicidal, schizophrenic, psychopathic, neurotic adult; impotent, homosexual male; frigid, promiscuous female; ulcerous, asthmatic, and otherwise disturbed American" (189). Janet Surrey lists the various ailments that mothers have been and still are held responsible for in their children: "sleepwalking, ulcerative colitis, hyperactivity, peer avoidance, delusions, poor language development and inability to deal with colour blindness" (115). Perhaps then, it is not surprising, though it is disappointing, to find similar tendencies in classics of early second-wave feminist thought.[3] However, there were some books published during the 1970s that worked toward a more sympathetic understanding of mothers, motherhood, and mother-daughter relationships (*The Reproduction of Mothering* by Nancy Chodorow [1978], *Of Woman Born* by Adrienne Rich [1976], *Our Mothers' Daughters* by Judith Arcana [1978]) and it is the feminist theories of mother-daughter relationships outlined in these texts that best express the dynamics of those relationships that are at the center of feminist revisions of fairy tales published contemporaneously.

Black feminists were also articulating and theorizing their experiences of the mother-daughter relationship, and strongly arguing against the all-too-prevalent assumption on the part of white feminists that they and their experiences could speak for women as a whole. Whereas white feminism had spent some years mired in the mother-blaming endemic to Western culture as a whole, black feminists emphasized the admiration they felt for their mothers, the strength they drew from them, and the way that mothering and loving black children was a form of empowering resistance to a racist culture that seeks to denigrate and devalue black culture, black children, and black mothers. Black feminists looked to their mothers

---

3   See, for example, Nancy Friday's *My Mother, Myself.*

Adaptation

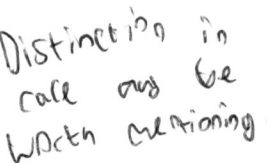

Distinction in
colo aws be
worth mentioning.

as models of both resistance and creativity, perhaps most famously articulated in Alice Walker's essay "In Search of Our Mother's Gardens."

Before proceeding to textual analysis, however, it is necessary to define certain terms. Within this project I am using the word "mother" to denote all maternal figures in fairy tales and myth. While stepmothers and mothers may seem to serve very different purposes in fairy tales, I consider them to be different aspects of the same figure. The evil stepmothers in several tales, such as "Snow White" and "Hansel and Gretel," were originally evil *mothers*. The Grimms altered such mothers to stepmothers in order to make the tales conform to nationalist and gender ideologies. Bruno Bettelheim and other psychoanalytic theorists have argued that "stepmothers" are the result of children's natural "splitting" of their image of the mother into "good" and "bad" in order to maintain the feelings of security, safety, and love they feel regarding the mother in the face of the mother's anger and disapproval. Marina Warner and other more historicist critics have argued that the ubiquity of the stepmother in fairy tales represents the higher mortality rate of women in childbirth prior to the twentieth century.

Given my interest in psychoanalytic theory, I am unsurprisingly inclined toward the first hypothesis. Linda Pollack notes that although fear of death in childbed was widespread, demographic evidence indicates that far fewer women died in childbirth during the Renaissance in England than is often believed. Indeed, she cites R. Schofield's work on maternal mortality from 1650 to 1850 in stating that the likelihood of a woman dying in such a way was probably around 1 percent during each birth, and so perhaps 6–7 percent over the course of a woman's lifetime, no greater than the many other ways one could die in the eras before antibiotics and good hygiene (Pollack 47). Irvine Loudon agrees, noting that "as maternal mortality was declining faster than mortality from other causes in the eighteenth century, the relative risk of dying in childbirth decreased." He too cites Schofield's work among other studies and writes that "taking all these estimates together, there is broad agreement. It seems there was a continuous and substantial decline in maternal mortality in England from the second half of the seventeenth century to the first half of the nineteenth" (160). He posits that the credit for this statistic lies mainly in an increased number of skilled midwives "who took pains and pride in their work" (161). He also quotes Schofield in observing that "women will have known of others who died giving birth to a child, but they may also have considered it such a rare event that there was little risk that the tragedy would befall them" (163–4).[4] In other European countries associated with fairy tales, rates were even better. The main point I am making is that risk of maternal mortality and therefore the potential for the appearance of a stepmother in a family in pre-industrial European cultures not only varies by nationality but also may well be much lower than we commonly suppose.

---

[4]   Pollack disagrees, and uses extant letters to argue that women's fear of death in childbirth in pre-industrial England was much higher than the actual risk itself would warrant.

Returning to the question of motherhood in fairy-tale revisions, we must ask what it means to be a maternal figure. Surely such a complex question cannot be reduced to biology, and several of the second-wave feminist theorists whose work is at issue in this project, such as Adrienne Rich and Nancy Chodorow, grappled with the issue. For the purposes of this project, I consider a mother to be an older female character responsible for the welfare of and with power over a younger character, or an older female character who has borne such responsibility and power in the past. Note that such a definition does not demand any specific emotional response or action on the part of the mother, and thus it is not a prescriptive definition of a "good" mother. It is rather a description of a participant in a literary situation that produces a literary mother. As we shall see, in Angela Carter's fairy-tale revisions, this production is necessary both for survival and for the production of human consciousness in the subject.

Mother-Daughter Relationships in Angela Carter's "The Bloody Chamber" and "Wolf-Alice": A Case Study

Angela Carter's *The Bloody Chamber* is the inspiration for many of the revisions that flourished some 15 to 20 years later. With respect to Carter's posthumously published story "Ashputtle, or, The Mother's Ghost," Michelle Ryan-Sautour notes that the "reader of Angela Carter cannot help but observe ambivalence about the mother figure in her writing," but Carter is better known for her explorations of female sexuality, its revolutionary potential, and its wounds under patriarchy than for the mother-daughter relationships she depicts, but this collection is bookended by stories heavily invested in the importance of the bonds and permeable ego boundaries that second-wave feminist theorists contend can be found between mothers and daughters. Carter begins and ends her collection with stories that demonstrate the importance of the mother-daughter relationship to survival and full participation in the human experience. Her first story emphasizes the strength of the mother-daughter relationship in the face of a murderous patriarch, while the final one finds a twice-orphaned girl bringing herself and her companion into humanity by taking on the qualities of motherhood. What I hope to demonstrate in this section, then, is the centrality of the mother-daughter relationship as described in texts by foundational second-wave feminists to the foundational feminist revisions of fairy tales.[5]

More than one story in Carter's collection opens with a father sending his daughter to a beast, but the collection begins with and is named after a story in which a mother tries to dissuade her daughter from going to a monster and then arrives to save her when she insists on going anyway. "The Bloody Chamber" is a revision of the fairy tale Bluebeard, which is about a wealthy man who weds and

---

[5]   Angela Carter was a highly controversial figure within academic second-wave feminism; for a thorough overview of scholarly feminist responses to and analyses of her work, please see Jessica Tiffin's *Marvelous Geometry* (69).

murders a succession of young women. Carter's version is set in early twentieth-century France, and tells the story of an impoverished piano student who marries a much older, very rich Marquis (the allusion to the Marquis de Sade is no accident). The unnamed protagonist has always been in awe of her mother but also mocks "the antique service revolver that my mother, grown magnificently eccentric in hardship, kept always in her reticule, in case—how I teased her—she was surprised by [a tiger's] footpads on her way home from the grocer's shop" (*Bloody* 111–12). Even in eccentricity her mother is "magnificent," according to her daughter, but that daughter believes that it is she herself who is worldly and realistic, and thus she marries to "banish the spectre of poverty from its habitual place at our meagre table" (111). But what does it mean to be worldly and realistic? As the story unfolds, we find that the protagonist is in a Gothic world, and that her mother's assessment of the need to prepare for—rather than hide from or sacrifice oneself to—violence is far more astute.

The protagonist's mother is a force to be reckoned with, larger than life: "My eagle-featured indomitable mother; what other student at the Conservatoire could boast that her mother had outfaced a junkful of Chinese pirates; nursed a village through a visitation of the plague, shot a man-eating tiger with her own hand and all before she was as old as I" (111). It is the mother about whom we should be reading, the daughter implies, her stories are the more interesting, rather than the daughter and her story. Indeed, in contrast to her tales of the heroic mother's exploits, the overshadowed daughter refers to herself only as a "student" and a "poor widow's child" (117, 114). She effaces herself again when she refers to her suitor coming to visit "my mother's sitting room" (112). The sitting room belongs to her mother; in the wake of such an overpowering figure, how can her daughter find a place of her own? Even her musical ability is in some way a debt to her mother: "I ... whose mother had sold all her jewelry, even her wedding ring, to pay the fees at the Conservatoire" (117). The daughter's music is another testament to her mother's heroism. At the beginning of the tale, the daughter cannot begin to hold her own in comparison to her mother. Unable to match her mother on the mother's own terms, the daughter changes them from romantic heroism to worldly status: "Are you sure you love him?" the mother asks regarding the Marquis, the protagonist's wealthy but disturbing fiancé. "I'm sure I want to marry him," her daughter answers (111). But in altering the terms of success to ones by which she can establish herself, she cuts herself off from her mother: "I felt a pang of loss as if ... I had, in some way, ceased to be her child in becoming his wife" (111).

It seems likely that part of the Marquis's allure derives from the girl's desire to separate herself radically, as described by Adrienne Rich in *Of Woman Born* only two years earlier, from her indomitable mother, but that separation pits birth and motherhood against death and the husband. Her fiancé first usurps the mother's role in providing his bride's trousseau, and he then sends the protagonist's mother a black dress to wear to the wedding—her daughter's wedding is her occasion for mourning. In sending her the black dress, the Marquis is also forcing the mother to be the jinx, the figure of ill fortune, at the wedding, displacing his own responsibility for the inevitable violence he does his wives. The daughter's escape from overpowering mother to unguessable husband is illusory; she is welcomed to "*his* castle" (emphasis added) by the "amniotic salinity of the sea"—a maternal metaphor that threatens to annihilate her as the sea cuts the castle off from all aid for half of each day (116). This threatening sea pervades the castle, as "No room, no corridor ... did not rustle with the sound of the sea and all the ceilings ... were stippled with refracted light from the waves" (117). The Marquis's home re-creates the most threatening of maternal aspects: engulfment and omnipresence. However, it is in this threatening setting that the girl finds a small place that is hers ("my music room" [134]), and comes into her own as a woman who incarnates and is connected to her mother.

Her mother returns in spirit, infusing the daughter with courage and determination after she has discovered the corpses of her husband's previous wives in his secret chamber. In the bloody chamber she also discovers herself not as "a poor widow's child" but as her mother's daughter, just as it is from her mother's bloody chamber that she was originally dis-covered: "Until that moment, this spoiled child did not know she had inherited nerves and a will from the mother who had defied the yellow outlaws of Indo-China. My mother's spirit drove me on, into the dreadful place, in a cold ecstasy to know the very worst" (131). The narrator's "ecstasy" comes as she takes on the attributes of her own mother. In this moment, the daughter becomes herself by experiencing a deep connection with her mother; no longer a mere "student" without an identity commensurate with her mother's, she has "inherited nerves and a will" *from* that mother. After this point, the protagonist reclaims her identity as her mother's daughter and associates that identity with courage. She says of the blind piano tuner that "he looked far more terrified of me than my mother's daughter would have been of the Devil himself" (134). Thus courage and strength of character, instead of separating her from her mother as they did early in the story, form a bond between them, a legacy or dynasty that stands up to and defeats the Marquis's traditional, feudal powers.

That psychic bond is the daughter's salvation, as "*maternal telepathy* ... send[s] [her] mother running headlong from the telephone to the station ... I never heard you cry before, she said, by way of explanation. Not when you were happy" (143). At the same time as the daughter is partaking of her mother's nerves and will, so too does the mother take in her daughter's distress. The mother arrives in the nick of time and puts down the Marquis just as she had the man-eating tiger, with the antique service revolver her daughter had mocked—but only after the daughter springs up to open the castle door and let her mother in. The mother's power is dependent upon her daughter's action. Mother and daughter are not separated again; they keep enough money to live on and retire to a quiet life with the daughter's new husband, a shy piano-tuner, and the daughter notes that "I do believe that my mother loves him as much as I do" (143). Thus mother and daughter are joined in this shared love where romance had before divided them, and the daughter re-embraces her mother's choices by "beggar[ing] herself for love" (111). Having established her own bravery, the daughter no longer feels confined; she shares ownership in her own right rather than being a tenant in her mother's rooms ("I felt I had the right to retain sufficient funds to start a little music school" [143]) and the closing references to material comfort belong to all three: "We do well enough" (143). The protagonist's bond with her mother allows her to thwart the repetition of spousal murder that the Marquis insists on re-enacting; that bond is also the essence of the difference between Carter's tale and the original: in Perrault's version, the heroine is saved by her brothers, and the moral admonishes women for their curiosity.

Thus Angela Carter's opening salvo in her feminist project of fairy-tale reclamation is one in which salvation comes about through the psychic joining of mother and daughter ("*maternal telepathy*") and the happy ending is not of a woman abandoning the family of her childhood in order to live happily ever after with a man, but of a woman able to maintain her connection with her mother while also loving a man who is able to appreciate the artistry and musical skill of the daughter. The indivisibility of mother and daughter at first generates rebellion, a desire to perform what Adrienne Rich calls "radical surgery" in separating oneself completely from one's mother, then a reincarnating of the mother in the daughter, and finally a reunion based on the psychic fluidity between mother and daughter.

The book ends with a story that similarly emphasizes the importance of mother-daughter relationships to the possibility of becoming human. In the final tale of Carter's collection, identification with motherhood transforms the beastly into the human; becoming human is synonymous with becoming a mother. "Wolf-Alice" is the tale of a girl raised by wolves who has been taken from her wolf-mother by the hunters who killed that mother.[6] She is trained by nuns to perform simple tasks and placed as a servant in the castle of a duke who is a composite of a werewolf and vampire. The short story combines aspects of "Little Red Riding-Hood," "Cinderella," and Lewis Carroll's two novels *Alice's Adventures in Wonderland* and *Through the Looking Glass and What Alice Found There*. At the beginning of the story, neither the girl nor the Duke is fully human. Carter's Alice begins her story as a beast; raised by wolves, she is without any consciousness of herself as a human being. Wolf-Alice learns to recognize herself in the mirror and then re-enacts the scenes of her adoption by her wolf-mother as well as that mother's death. The Duke, through her ministrations, also becomes identified with her mother, and this identification finally brings him into the realm of the human. Mirroring and mothering become two aspects of the same process, the creation of human subjectivity.[7] This human subjectivity is a feminine subjectivity; it comes through multiple identifications with others, especially with mothers. But at the beginning of the story the Duke is not human; he does not cast a reflection—he "passed through the mirror and now, henceforward, lives as if upon the other side of things" (*Bloody* 222). Thus the Duke begins the story as lacking the ability to mother.

---

6   We never learn how she lost her first, human mother.

7   Carter is very clearly drawing on Lacanian models of psychological development, an issue I will explore in more detail when I discuss the significance of the mirror in Chapter 5.

The Duke is on the wrong side of the mirror but Wolf-Alice is fascinated by the object, and has not quite grasped the purely imitative, two-dimensional nature of the glass. She initially understands her reflection to be a playmate: "She rubbed her head against her reflected face, to show that she felt friendly towards it, and felt a cold, solid, immovable surface between herself and she" (225). Carter's confused cases reflect Wolf-Alice's own confusion about the nature of her reflection and thus about her own identity. When Wolf-Alice finds that her playmate is only a reflection, "A little moisture leaked from the corners of her eyes, yet her relation with the mirror was now far more intimate since she knew she saw herself within it" (226). She then puts on a wedding dress that "the Duke had tucked away behind the mirror" and knows that she has "put on the visible sign of her difference from them [the wolves]" (226). Wolf-Alice becomes human, or at least unbeastly, when she understands the nature of mirrors and finds what is hidden behind them.

The connections among mirroring, mothering, and marriage culminate in a final scene in which Wolf-Alice and the Duke take on aspects of maternality. For Carter, mutual connection, empathy, the ability to shift among identities and especially to assume the position of the mother as an active, desiring subject is necessary in order to fully realize one's humanity. Shortly after the girl dons the wedding dress, the Duke is shot and comes home injured:

> She prowled round the bed … Then, she was pitiful as her gaunt grey mother; she leapt upon his bed to lick … the blood and dirt from his cheek and forehead … As she continued her ministrations, this glass, with infinite slowness, yielded to the reflexive strength of its own material construction. Little by little, there appeared within it … as if brought into being by her soft, moist, gentle tongue, finally, the face of the Duke. (227–8)

The Duke has been shot, and we find that he is only a man after all as he is forced to rise up on two legs and run. The multiplicity of roles that Wolf-Alice and the Duke take on in this ending allows them both finally to enter the realm of the human. Wolf-Alice is her foster-mother, taking pity on a wounded creature, but this scene also echoes one described early in the story; she had been found "in the wolf's den beside the bullet-ridden corpse of her foster mother" (221). Once again she is in a den in the company of an older being injured by bullets, but this time she can help. She is not only her mother; she is also an older, more competent version of herself. In his turn, the Duke is not only an infant Wolf-Alice being tended by a pitiful creature; he is also Wolf-Alice's bullet-riddled wolf-mother, and Carter notes that he "howls like a wolf with his foot in a trap or a woman in labour, and bleeds" (227). Wolf-Alice is able to bring herself into humanity by putting on human clothing in the same evening that her care brings the Duke back into the world reflected by the glass, and it is no accident that their rapprochement comes when each is able to occupy a maternal subject positions.

How can we account for the healing and generative permeable ego boundaries between mother and daughter depicted in these stories? We can only do so through the feminist theories of motherhood and daughterhood contemporary with them, which do not pathologize the connection between mother and daughter, but do acknowledge the ways in which the bond can become distorted. In the following section, I will use Adrienne Rich's *Of Woman Born* as a lens through which to understand many of the revisions under study in this project.

Blurred Identities and the Mother-Daughter Bond

Adrienne Rich's *Of Woman Born* is one of the earlier second-wave feminist texts on mothering to discuss the blurring of identities between mother and daughter, a blurring that is an essential aspect of the mother-daughter relationships delineated in revisions of fairy tales and classical myth of the period under discussion. *Of Woman Born* is a moving book on the personal, historical, psychological, and mythical experience of mothering as well as on the patriarchal institution of motherhood, by which Rich means the ways in which women have been forced to mother children under ideological and material conditions that reinforce female subjugation. Motherhood, Rich tells us, does not have to be that way—women do not have to feel "bad" about resenting children, do not have to give up all else in their lives, do not have to annihilate themselves for the sake of their children.

Rich considered her chapter on mothers and daughters to be "the core of [her] book" (218). For her, the reclamation of the mother-daughter bond is essential to any feminist project, insofar as patriarchy fragments women and devalues bonds between them: "Women are made taboo to women—not just sexually, but as comrades, cocreators, coinspirators. In breaking this taboo, we are reuniting with our mothers; in reuniting with our mothers, we are breaking this taboo" (255). Yet this conclusion comes at the end of a chapter about the difficulties and dangers of uniting with a person from whom one has never truly separated, whom one has never truly understood as different. Rich eloquently describes a constant identification between mother and daughter, hazy ego boundaries that provide a more fluid sense of self but can also threaten to overwhelm that self; these elements are essential to many feminist psychoanalytic understandings of feminine personality through the 1970s and 1990s. She describes the confluence of identification and anger, the extraordinary identification as a source of anger:

> I find myself divided, slipping under her skin; a part of me identifies too much with her. I know deep reservoirs of anger toward her still exist … Psychic osmosis. Desperate defenses. The power of the bond often denied because it cracks consciousness, threatens at times to lead the daughter back into "those secret chambers." (231)

Rich combines an analysis of the social constraints of mothering with an analysis of the psychological impact of those constraints and their effects on the mother-daughter relationship in order to explicate exactly why the mother-daughter relationship can threaten its participants: "Our personalities seem dangerously to blur and overlap with our mothers'; and, in a desperate attempt to know where mother ends and daughter begins, we perform radical surgery" (236).[8]

The metaphor of surgery makes it clear that in Rich's view the blurring and overlapping of daughter with mother is as essential and seamless as the naked body about to go under the knife: in this metaphor, the emotional merging of mother and daughter is made flesh. Surgery is sometimes necessary, but it is always traumatic.

In "And the One Doesn't Stir Without the Other," (1978) Luce Irigaray explores the hatred, fear, and blame of a mother by her daughter. In this essay/ prose-poem, the daughter blames her loss of self on a mother whom she cannot tell from herself. The milk flowing from her mother turned to poison, and both mother and daughter exist in a state of paralysis, either overwhelming or turning away from each other. One sentence has no adequate English translation; it can mean "You give me yourself to eat," "You give yourself something to eat," and "You give me something to eat" (61). The multiplicity of meanings and the inability to distinguish among them comprise a microcosm of the relationship and play of identities between Irigaray's daughter and mother. But this play is not benign; the narrator has lost herself: "You look at yourself in the mirror. And already you see your own mother there. And soon your daughter, a mother. Between the two, what are you? What space is yours alone? ... Of the two of us, who was the one, who the other" (73)? The mother and daughter have effectively annihilated each other by becoming only reflections without selves.

The danger of annihilation through imagined fusion, or the threat of such deep identification, runs throughout much of the literature that is in the scope of this project. One case in point is Gregory Frost's "The Root of the Matter," a revision of the tale of Rapunzel. The story is told in the first person, first by Mother Gothel, then by Rapunzel, and then finally by the prince. Mother Gothel is presented as a victim of childhood sexual abuse by her father. She runs away and eventually achieves complete independence from the larger world, first making money as a dominatrix and then learning magic and retreating from civilization. She views Rapunzel as another self, a younger self untainted by the violence and abuse of her past, and that view leads her to deny Rapunzel's individuality and thus to abuse her, even while she believes herself to be protecting and caring for her adopted daughter.

The language of Gothel's mother-love is sexual. When Gothel describes her longing for a daughter, she says that "I began dreaming about you, my love," and tries masturbation and orgasm in order to alleviate this physical longing (166). She dehumanizes Rapunzel's birth mother while alluding to future abuse: "No man will ever lay a hand on you. Only I, because I know how to touch your heart as you touch mine, you beautiful girl. I know what pleases you best because it pleases me the same. Never to strike you, to harm you, as that horrid creature who bore you would have done" (170). This ominous promise comes to fruition in Rapunzel's bath; Gothel bathes Rapunzel well into the girl's adolescence and Rapunzel tells

---

[8]   Carter alluded to this maternal bondage by comparing a woman in labor to a wolf with a paw caught in a trap (*Bloody* 227).

us that "Mother Gothel spends a great deal of time washing between my legs, and I've always let her" (182). Gothel molests Rapunzel in her bath just as she herself was raped by her father during her bath. Gothel's inability to distinguish between herself and her daughter leads to disastrous cruelty and the replication of abuse, because she is unable to understand that Rapunzel is a separate person, that what pleases herself does not necessarily please Rapunzel, is not necessarily best for her daughter. Rapunzel knows this only too well:

> I don't even exist for her, not really. She keeps this image of me in her head, of what I am ... she's talking to the illusion ... The false-me can't get into trouble, no matter what I do. But then I'll have my monthly flow and she'll start screeching at me as if I did it to vex her. The image again—the image doesn't bleed. (175)

Rapunzel's menstruation, her maturity and sexuality, destroys Gothel's fantasy of a pure childhood self, a fantasized self that has obscured the actual daughter. The mother in this destructive union, despite her avowed hatred of men, is closely identified with patriarchal ideologies of disgust at the mature, sexual female body. Gothel refers to the woman who physically bears Rapunzel as a "creature," attacks and vilifies Rapunzel for menstruating—even her molestation of Rapunzel takes the form of "a great deal of time washing between [her] legs," as though Rapunzel's vulva is dirty. Gothel becomes her own abusive father, and she is also briefly identified with a male, patriarchal god. Rapunzel's narrative takes the form of a diary that is cut off in mid-sentence as Gothel uses magic to punish her. The sentence that is cut off began with "Mother Got"—Mother Gott, or mother God (187). By identifying Mother Gothel with the deity of the major patriarchal religions, the mother's abuse of her daughter is related to the mother's role in socializing the daughter into patriarchy.

Of course, within second-wave thought, it is not only daughters who risk losing themselves in an annihilating, abusive fusion. Earlier in *Of Woman Born*, Rich discusses the loss of self feared and experienced by many women who become mothers and are expected to deny themselves all self-expression, ambition, and pleasure in caring for their children. Such utter, literal self-lessness is of course not only nightmarish and impossible, but also utterly undesirable, and attempts to achieve it result in the anger and subsequent guilt found in the diary entries Rich quotes regarding her feelings as the mother of young children:

> Sometimes I seem to myself ... a monster of selfishness and intolerance. Their voices wear away at my nerves, their constant needs, above all their need for simplicity and patience, fill me with despair at my own failures, despair too at my fate, which is to serve a function for which I was not fitted. And I am weak sometimes from held-in rage. (21)

Rich wrote in her diary that she experiences "Anger, weariness, demoralization. Sudden bouts of weeping. A sense of insufficiency" (30). Rich experiences the loss of self that so enrages Irigaray's daughter-narrator in "And the One Does Not Stir

Without the Other." That narrator is an angry daughter, and she is angry, at least in part, because her mother has no self: "Your function remains faceless ... And never having known your own face, didn't you nourish me with lifelessness? ... Each of us lacks her own image; her own face, the animation of her own body is missing ... Trapped in a single function—mothering" (63, 64, 66). An unhealthy fusion, based in self-lessness and helplessness, can be as dangerous to a mother as it is to her daughter. And due to the identification of a daughter with her mother, such selflessness in a mother is often identified with womanhood and reproduced in and by the daughter, as I will now explore in two revisions of the Persephone-Demeter myth, one from 2001, and the other from 1989.

Tanith Lee's *White as Snow* is a simultaneous revision of Snow White as well as the story of Persephone and Demeter. The novel is set in a fantasy world in which the story of Persephone and Demeter is a legend, ritual, and belief from an old pagan religion that survives in secret, having been displaced by a particularly violent and oppressive version of Christianity. The political representative of Christian Empire in this novel is Draco, a barbarian king who destroys the kingdom of Arpazia's father, rapes her, and forces her into marriage. Within a year a daughter, named Candacis (White) and called Coira (Kore, a name for the maiden Persephone before her abduction) is born, and thus begins the distortions, distances, despair, and hostility that mark the relationship between Arpazia and Coira, who take on the roles both of the wicked (step)mother and Snow White as well as Demeter and Persephone.

In *White as Snow*, Arpazia experiences her daughter's birth as her own death, even as she, like Frost's Gothel, understands her daughter to be her former, purer self. Arpazia goes into labor on her fifteenth birthday. During the pregnancy, from the rape onward, Arpazia has been completely dissociated from her surroundings, experiencing nothing, understanding nothing, feeling nothing. Indeed, the gestation of her daughter is her own gestation as well: "Like herself, though taking sustenance and sometimes moving, it [the not-yet born infant] had been asleep. Now Arpazia saw it had woken, and this in turn had woken her"(56). Arpazia is her own unborn daughter, unconscious, and developing. Unlike Gothel, though, who desires and seeks out this young, pure self in order to "protect" it, Arpazia experiences her daughter's existence as a *loss* of the self she once was, as a death. "*Kill it*," she screams silently during labor, "*kill it as it kills me*" (56). The relation between mother and daughter becomes a life-or-death struggle between Arpazia and her daughter. Once the infant is born, "they thrust the thing ... into her arms and somehow now she did hold it. It sucked on her, hurting her ... this tiny, milking grub. She had no more stamina to resist. Oh, let it murder her then. That was all it wanted to do. To eviscerate and drain her" (57). The physical connection between mother and daughter, nursing, is pain and destruction to Arpazia—in giving her daughter sustenance, she is dying. Mother and daughter are one (the identical birthday, the mutual gestation, and, as we later find out, the identical looks), but unlike the more healthfully connected mother and daughter in Carter's "The Bloody Chamber," they are playing a zero-sum game with identity. For one to survive the other must die. This connection is made even clearer later on when Lee adopts free indirect discourse to explore Arpazia's thoughts and understanding: "She [Arpazia] *had* died, was *dead* ... The embryo, dividing her from herself on entering, had left her in two pieces. Her childhood had run out with the parturition blood, and become another being: obviously, a child. And the woman remained, crazy, in her hollow fortress" (76). Coira is Arpazia's own childhood, and motherhood has killed Arpazia: Arpazia has lost her self.[9]

Toni Morrison's *Beloved* is another novel in which a parasitic, blurred relationship between a mother and her daughter results in a loss of self for the mother, and perhaps not coincidentally, it is also another revision of the myth of Persephone and Demeter. Morrison's portrayals of black motherhood are multilayered and complex enough to be the subject of a book, and indeed Andrea O'Reilly's *Toni Morrison and Motherhood: A Politics of the Heart* takes up that challenge nicely. She situates Morrison's work in the tradition of black feminist work on motherhood. Black feminist writers, such as Alice Walker, emphasize that in contrast to the inhuman idealization to which white middle-class mothers have been subjected, black mothers in the United States mother children in the context of a society that continually devalues and insults their love and work for their children, from the selling away of children from their mothers under slavery to the Moynihan Report's blaming the problems of a community beset by racism on the community's mothers. Despite these assaults, black women have continued to mother their children, and that work has been valued and honored within black communities as the source of strength and resistance to racism that it is. Black motherhood, rather than being conceived of as "an individual act undertaken in the privacy of one's home, separate and isolated from the public, political, and social realm," is a site of social activism and a political act (O'Reilly 30). Jean Wyatt examines the role of maternality in Morrison's more recent novel, *A Mercy*, and finds that the formal structure and language of the novel represent the rupture between the mother and daughter whose separation lies at the heart of its story. I find a similar encoding of the relationship between mother and daughters in *Beloved* in that novel's story-telling techniques.

Beloved concerns a Sethe, a young mother who escaped with her small children from the brutal life of slavery, only to be hunted down again by slave-owners. Rather than see her returned to a life of dehumanizing misery, she murders her baby daughter (the daughter's age is unspecified, but as Sethe is surprised to find that she is "crawling already" and is six months pregnant, I assume she is somewhere around eight months old) and tries unsuccessfully to do the same to her two sons and her newly born infant girl, named Denver. Close to 20 years later,

---

9   Arpazia's experiences fit all too well into the models of anger described by the theorists of the Wellesley Stone Center, which I will discuss below. In short, her experience and understanding of reality have been completely dismissed and negated: she grew up ignored by father and nurse, she was raped (relegated to objecthood completely), and she is unheard during her own labor (she screams "silently").

a young woman called "Beloved," who may or may not be the murdered daughter, returns to find Sethe, still living at the same house with Denver. This loss of a beloved daughter to death and the daughter's subsequent return opens up space for a reading of the novel as a revision of Persephone and Demeter. After the murder, the previous bounty of the farm on which Sethe lived is gone and Sethe retreats into social isolation, much like Demeter's mourning, during which she withdrew the earth's bounty and mortals starved. Sethe can also be read as a successful Demeter, one who keeps her daughter safe from the grasp of the slave-owners, who are rapists just as was Hades, and this is certainly how Sethe understands her own actions. Sethe's violent actions force the white power structure to alter its actions, just as Demeter's brutal famine forces Zeus to change his plans. There are numerous other correspondences as well, one as specific as Stamp Paid, an older man who ferried Sethe and her children across the river to safety during their first escape, celebrating that safety by slipping a blackberry into the infant Denver's mouth despite the protests of the surrounding women that she's far too young for such a treat; such a move seems a direct reference to Hades in the realm of the dead slipping a pomegranate seed into Persephone's mouth to prevent her unconditional return to her mother. The blackberry symbolizes a special connection between Denver and Stamp Paid, and it is no coincidence that unlike Beloved, Denver is able to separate herself from her mother enough to seek help from the outside world. Denver is able to seek help from the other women of the town, leaving her mother's property for the first time in years to do so. In making those connections, she appeals to the community's women as other mothers.

Patricia Hill Collins writes that "othermothers—women who assist bloodmothers by sharing mothering responsibilities—traditionally have been central to the institution of Black motherhood" (178). For the biological mother, such a network of women provides a resilient resource of aid and support. For the daughter, the othermothers may be even more important, for, as Rosalie Riegler Troester writes, not only do othermothers relieve the intensity of the mother-daughter relationship during times of great stress, such as adolescence, but "sometimes othermothers live different lives and exemplify values widely divergent from the biological mother. Othermothers provide a safety valve and sounding board and release the teenage girl from the confines of a single role model … And sometimes they give gifts mothers find hard to give" (163–4). Rather than being trapped in the exclusive symbiosis described by Chodorow, then, black feminist theorists writing shortly after her suggest that black daughters have a multiplicity of mothers to turn to. Such a theory of motherhood works nicely with the theory of the relational self delineated by the Stone Center theorists described in Chapter 2, as it posits that the black daughter develops her sense of self as a being in relationships.

In *Beloved*, Sethe loses her self in her children, but just as black women are far less likely to reject an identification with the mother, for Sethe, motherhood has a far more complex and positive valence than it does for Lee's Arpazia. Her understanding of herself first and foremost as a mother has preserved her life.

Prior to having escaped slavery, she was viciously raped by nephews of the plantation-owner; her then-husband had been forced to witness this act and as a result loses his mind. Sethe fantasizes about having gone mad along with her husband, but understands motherhood as having precluded that option for her:

> Other people's brains stopped ... which is what must have happened to Halle. And how sweet that would have been: the two of them back by the milk shed, squatting by the churn, smashing cold, lumpy butter in to their faces with not a care in the world. Feeling it slippery, sticky, rubbing it into their hair, watching it squeeze through their fingers. What a relief to stop it right there ... But her three children were chewing sugar teat under a blanket on their way to Ohio and no butter play would change that. (70–71)

Sethe's sense of being needed by her children draws her away from the desired paradise of insanity and relief from worldly responsibility. Motherhood is what makes Sethe decide she has to free herself from Sweet Home, the plantation on which she is a slave, as she realizes that her children's future is slavery as well: "[The children] tagged after me the whole day ... For now. For now" (197). Motherhood is a spur to action, a call to life, but it is also a great burden. Sethe knows that she can lose herself in motherhood, that at times she must lose herself in motherhood: "She was frightened by the thought of having a baby once more. Needing to be good enough, alert enough, strong enough, *that* caring—again ... Unless carefree, motherlove was a killer" (132). Sethe's love for her children causes her to kill her baby girl and to try to kill her other three children to save them from slavery. It also comes close to destroying Sethe herself.

Sethe understands herself only as a mother. She has been ostracized by the Bluestone community due to her killing love for her children; she has sacrificed the community's acceptance, her own happiness to her identity as a mother ("Those twenty-eight happy days were followed by eighteen years of disapproval and a solitary life" [173]). In the process of being a mother, Sethe loses her self, her understanding of herself as a separate person. When she sees the four white men who have tracked her down ride up to the home of her mother-in-law, Baby Suggs,

> she heard wings. Little hummingbirds stuck their needle beaks right through her headcloth into her head and beat their wings. And if she thought anything, it was No. No. Nono. Nonono. Simple. She just flew. Collected every bit of life she had made, all the parts of her that were precious and fine and beautiful, and carried, pushed, dragged them through the veil, out, away, over there where no one could hurt them ... where they would be safe ... "I stopped him ... I took and put my babies where they'd be safe." (163, 164)

Like Gothel and Arpazia, Sethe understands her children as the "precious and fine and beautiful" parts of herself, the parts of herself as yet unhurt, unscarred by slavery and cruelty: preserving them as such is a way of preserving herself, selves untainted by the mossy teeth of the boys who took her milk and split open her back. Her decision to kill her children is intimately connected to her having been the one to give them life in the first place: she "collected every bit of life she had made." As creator, she also has the power, even the right, to put them back on the other side of life, where they would be unreachable, safe from the slave-owners' cruelty. They are parts of her.

This fusion has obviously been dangerous, murderous to the children, but it has cost Sethe her sense of self as well. When she tells her story to Paul D, he recognizes her loss of boundaries: "This here new Sethe didn't know where the world stopped and she began" (164). The haziness of Sethe's ego boundaries is intimately connected to her motherhood—she made these children, these children are pieces of herself. The hummingbirds that invade her head just prior to her actions also demonstrate how Sethe's sense of self is continuous with her sense of the world around her. The beating of the hummingbird wings is echoed when the cart taking Sethe to jail is heading west: "They waited till the cart turned about, headed west to town. And then no words. Humming. No words at all" (152). It is as if Sethe's experience of the hummingbirds beating all thoughts from her mind has expanded to the entire community, the humming driving out the coherent thoughts and words of the town. Despite the community's disapproval and shunning of Sethe, there is no clear delineation between her experiences and theirs. Neither Sethe nor the reader knows where the world stops and Sethe begins. Where is Sethe's self? And what is Sethe's self?

Sethe doesn't know where the world stops and she begins, she doesn't know where her children stop and she begins. Ultimately, her inability to locate herself causes her to lose herself. The last time we see her in the novel, she has retired to the room of the late Baby Suggs, and seems to be preparing to die. Paul D returns to help Denver, who is now working outside the home, take care of her and offers to bathe her. Having been abandoned by Beloved, Sethe feels that "There's nothing to rub now" (272). She experiences the loss of her returned daughter as a destruction of her own body, and just as she had earlier thought of her children as "all the parts of her that were precious and fine and beautiful," she now wonders: "If he bathes her in sections will the parts [of her body] hold?" (272). She finally begins to cry as she tells Paul D that Beloved has left: "'She left me.' 'Aw, girl. Don't cry.' 'She was my best thing.'" Paul D "leans over and takes her hand. With the other he touches her face. 'You your best thing, Sethe. You are.' His holding fingers are holding hers. 'Me? Me?'" (272, 273). Throughout the novel Paul D has evoked an identity for Sethe beyond that of mother. He has helped her to remember her past, before she had children, and helped return her to a relationship in which she does not have to be responsible for all; she can lay her burdens, her body in his hands and be relieved of the weight of motherhood, the need to nurture others, and the pain of her rape. With Paul D, she could entertain the hope of being "relieved of the weight of her breasts ... Maybe this one time she could ... trust things and remember things because the last of the Sweet Home men was there to catch her if she sank?" (18). At the end of the novel he tries to return Sethe to herself, to help her understand herself as a woman with a life beyond motherhood. O'Reilly notes that time and again in Morrison's work, she, like Irigaray in "And the One," "emphasizes the need for the parent to have a strong sense of self so that he or she may nurture the same in the growing child" (33). By subsuming her whole self in mothering, Sethe saves herself and her children from slavery, but her sons run away, one of her two daughters is dead, and she herself is unable to conceive of a life after mothering. The joys and achievements have been great, but so too has been the costs.

The brutality and violence of Arpazia's and Sethe's worlds as well as the exclusivity of their relationships with Coira and Beloved have required and resulted in pathological and dangerous bonds, but those pathologies and dangers can illuminate a healthy subjectivity and way of being in the world that was described and theorized in detail in the 1990s by clinicians whose work is strongly based on and continuous with the work of the major second-wave feminist theorists regarding motherhood. In the following chapter, I will discuss a way of understanding mother-daughter relationships that is significantly more nuanced than the pathological identity-blurring observed here, but is still beholden to analyses of that pathology.

Chapter 2
Revisions of Motherhood and Daughterhood

What if the connection between these texts and the theories of the mother-daughter relationships they portray is important not only on the level of content, but also on the level of genre? That is to say, as feminist revisions of fairy tales and classical myth are so heavily invested in mother-daughter relationships, and their portrayal of those relationships dovetails so beautifully with the second-wave feminist theory regarding those relationships contemporary to the revisions, can we conceive of revision itself, as enacted and reflected upon by these texts, as participating in mother-daughter relationships? What would a theory of revision based on the theories of mother- and daughterhood portrayed in these novels, poems, and stories look like?

Daughterly Revisions

Let us begin by thinking of the relationship between these revisions and the traditional tales out of which they grow in a way based on Nancy Chodorow's theories of the mother-daughter relationship, relational models of feminine psychic health, and the centrality of these relationships to feminine subjectivity.[1] Not only do these revisions portray the contemporaneous concepts of feminine subjectivity by their characters' feelings, experiences, and actions, but we can also consider the revisions themselves as case studies in second-wave mother-daughter relationships. These revisions enact between texts, between themselves and their

---

[1]   Michael Awkward presents a similar argument regarding the relationship of African-American female writers to one another in *Inspiriting Influences: Tradition, Revision, and Afro-American Women's Novels* when he writes that

> the Afro-American woman writer attempts to establish with her female predecessor the type of positive symbiotic merger which, according to Gardiner, Nancy Chodorow, and others, characterizes the patterns of female identity formation ... the female, who has been taught to "develop capacities for nurturance, dependence, and empathy" in her relationship with her mother, views the creation of fiction as an occasion for cooperative textual interactions with maternal figures. (7)

Similarly, Gilbert and Gubar note that the nineteenth-century female writer "can begin such a struggle [to write] only by actively seeking a *female* precursor who, far from representing a threatening force to be denied or killed, proves by example that a revolt against patriarchal literary authority is possible" (49). However, Awkward and Gilbert and Gubar are discussing the relationships between authors who serve as inspiring and authorizing forces for one another. My theory is more concerned with the relationships between *texts* than with women writers' relationships to each other.

traditional sources, the permeable boundaries, shared identity, and fluid sense of self that Chodorow, Nancy K. Miller, Irigaray, and the Stone Center theorists argued are characteristic of feminine subjectivity as well as the mother-daughter matrix generative of that subjectivity. Revision not only incarnates prior versions of the tale, but it is also identified with those versions by looking toward its own revision, just as Chodorow argues that a mother of a daughter usually experiences a simultaneous identification with her own mother as well as with her infant daughter. Insofar as a revision both requires and embodies its older version, the revision does not destroy its mother-story, but instead re-creates and prolongs its life just as Vanessa Joosen argues when she notes that the "ever-growing corpus of fairy-tale retellings … help[s] to keep the interest in the old tales vibrant" (2).

The author reads and incorporates the mother-story, and out of that experience, creates a daughter-story, a revision, which both is and is not the mother-story. Just as the mother-daughter relationship is often characterized by permeable ego boundaries, a revision and its traditional tales of origin will also have permeable boundaries. The movie *Company of Wolves*, for instance, both is and is not the fairy tale "Little Red Riding Hood." Where does the fairy tale leave off and the revision begin? Once a revision is created, is there any way of definitively and completely separating out what belongs to the daughter story and what to the mother story? Is it possible to fully appreciate *Company of Wolves* without knowing the fairy tale? Conversely, after seeing the movie, is it ever again possible to read the fairy tale without its being inflected by the revision? I would say no: daughter-story and mother-story are simultaneously the same and not the same, just as, in second-wave thought, mother and daughter learn to understand each other as being simultaneously self and not-self. The daughter-story is continuous with the mother-story, incorporating those traditional stories as a vital part of its identity, necessary for full understanding, and the mother-story contains the daughter-story *in potentia* or *in utero*, as it were.[2]

Chodorow writes, almost in passing, that the desire to mother often re-creates itself within daughters who experience that mothering. Similarly, I would argue that often implicit in revisions contemporaneous with Chodorow and her intellectual heirs is the potential for future revisions: all revisions look toward their own daughter-stories. By its very nature, revision destabilizes and debunks the idea of a single authoritative version of a tale, thus opening space for future revisions. Elizabeth Wanning Harries makes a similar observation when she writes that "recent storytellers tend to stress the subjective unreliability of their narrators. Each new tale is only one version of the many possible versions. They encourage the reader to see the new telling as a *version*, as one, but not the only, way to tell

---

[2]   This way of understanding a given tale as containing the potential for its future revisions is not entirely unlike the implications of the etymology of "author," which comes from the Latin meaning "to grow or to increase." However, the word "author" is also deeply bound up with the cultural cache of "authority," a concept which oral folklore in general, as well as literary revision, rejects.

the tale." Similarly, a daughter who experiences the identification with her own mother attendant upon herself becoming a mother looks toward her incorporation into her own daughter. Patricia Hill Collins writes of black mothers that in teaching their daughters "how to survive in interlocking structures of race, class, and gender oppression while rejecting and transcending those same structures … mothers demonstrate varying combinations of behaviors devoted to ensuring their daughters' survival … to helping their daughters go further than the mothers themselves were allowed to go" (184). Feminist revisions, which themselves are manipulating structures or stories that had often encoded oppressions in order to "reject and transcend" those oppressions, bear their own revisions, revisions which themselves can go further.

The mother-story is incorporated by the author and reborn as the revision, the daughter-story, in the same way that Chodorow argues that mothers reproduce themselves in their daughters, and experience themselves as doing so, and daughters reproduce their mothers in themselves, and experience themselves as doing so. Chodorow writes that the production and reproduction of girls as women and women as mothers is a cyclical process, a constant revision of prior experiences of girlhood, womanhood, and motherhood. Mothering a daughter, then, is a way of living the past in the present and extending the effect of the past to the future, as each mother extends the effect of her own mother's care to her daughter while at the same time revis(it)ing her own childhood.[3] Just as the reproduction of mothering is not conceived of as mere replication, literary revision is not merely repetition. An unrevised story loses its meaning: as time moves on, persistence changes a story's nature, demanding revision to continue to be what once it was. Just so, mothering requires revisiting one's own past, one's own mother, and that revisiting generates change, a revision of one's own mother in oneself, and of oneself in one's daughter. Here, especially for revisions of fairy tales, myths, and folklore, the concept of othermothers becomes highly significant. There is no one original version of Cinderella, for instance; our most cherished tales and myths have significant numbers of variants. While one version may hold a particular fascination for a given writer, and act as a main mother, other variants consulted by the writer come into play as othermothers, providing relief from the main variant as well as alternative role models for the revision to follow or draw upon, transforming replication to revision.

Other scholars have alluded to certain aspects of this theory already. Michelle Ryan-Satour writes about Carter's identification of motherhood with authorship in "Ashputtle, or, The Mother's Ghost," and Kimberly Lau conceives of Carter's revisions as implying "an infinite chain of infidelities beginning with infidelities to her own tales" (79). But Ryan-Sautour does not generalize this insight to the project of revision, and Lau uses the metaphor of erotic infidelity rather than feminine genealogy to discuss the generative nature of revisions.

---

[3]   Of course, this process can be dysfunctional as well as healthy, and is often what is meant by the phrase "the cycle of abuse."

Emma Donoghue provides evidence for a theory of revision as a mother-daughter relationship by refiguring the process of revision as series of linked storytellings between mother-figures and daughter-figures. In the stories that make up *Kissing the Witch*, her book of revised fairy-tales, many of which seek to undo the normative heterosexism of the earlier tales, the stories are joined by the mechanism of the female protagonist of each tale asking a significant female character who *she* was before she became involved in the protagonist's story. The question is always the same: "Who were you?" (9, 23, 39, 57, 77, 95, 109, 123, 135, 155, 171, 191). Not "What did you do," or "Where did you come from?" In this sense, the tale, which is always the character's answer, becomes the identity of the teller, and significantly, the various tellers are usually linked in series of mother-daughter permutations. Out of 13 tales, nine linkages are through mother-figures. Donoghue would probably take issue with this statement; her characters repeatedly disavow the relationship of mother and daughter. Cinderella says of her fairy godmother that she knows the woman is not her mother, a statement that is vital given that the happy resolution of this tale is a romance between the daughter and the godmother. Given the erotics of the mother-daughter relationship outlined first by Jeanne Lampl-de Groot, and then by Adrienne Rich and Nina Lykke, I do not think that sexual desire precludes such associations (psychoanalytically speaking, one might argue that a mother-daughter relationship *requires* such desire), but more importantly, I do not think it is possible for Donoghue to simply write away the history of the tale, in which Cinderella's benefactress is a fairy god*mother*, and in other versions is clearly the spirit of the dead mother herself. There is another explicit disavowal of the mother-daughter relationship between Rapunzel and Gothel, but this one is even less tenable, given that Gothel has raised Rapunzel. The disavowal serves only to highlight the traditional relationship between the characters in question, as every denial contains within it the language of acceptance—it is after all impossible for any revision, no matter how skillful, to simply wipe out the memory of an earlier tale, just as no tale can pre-emptively destroy or prevent any revisions. Other linkages between Donoghue's stories are made by a younger protagonist asking an older woman who has mentored or protected her for her story.

In her article on intergenerational relationships in *Kissing the Witch*, Ann Martin takes pains to contrast Donoghue's revisions of fairy tales to those written by second-wave feminists, but in order to do so she quite clearly simplifies the creative projects of the second-wave, claiming, for instance, that "Through the oppositional nature of their projects, the authors implicitly reiterate the social, linguistic, and generic norms that they explicitly critique," never interrogating her own assumptions that such reiteration is unintentional, that second-wave writers are unaware of it, and that it is not part of the revisionary project. She also claims that for second-wave writers "praxis arises from specific and identifiable political platforms"; again, such a statement denies complexity and nuance to Donoghue's second-wave predecessors in the field of fairy-tale revisions, and so of course makes the complex, collaborative interactions between younger and older women in her stories, and between the stories and the fairy tales they are revising, seem newly born. What I am contending, however, is that the complexity of intergenerational relationships within fairy-tale revisions, and the resemblance between those relationships and the complexity of the interaction between revision and fairy tale/myth, have been present in feminist revisions all along.

Textual Representations of Mother-Daughter Relationships and Revision

As a thought-experiment, the theory proposed above may be interesting ... but does it hold water? Is there compelling textual evidence associating mother-daughter relationships with the acts of story-telling and revision themselves? There is. The complex, interwoven psychic relationship between mother and daughter as imagined by second-wave theorists is often depicted as being mirrored in the relationship between a traditional tale and its revision, and the connection between the two kinds of relationships is implied in the content and language of the revisionary texts themselves. In this section I will be discussing the representation of mother-daughter dyads in these works and the connection between those representations and revisionary story-telling. The mother-daughter relationship is closely allied with the literary representation of the process and concept of revision and with revisionary tales (folklore, for example, is dependent on the retellings and revisions of generations of story-tellers); daughters in this literature are often represented as revisions of their mothers.

In revisions of fairy tales and myths, portrayals of the mother-daughter trope illustrate the issues of fusion, identification, and violent desire for individuation that inform so much 1970s and 1990s work on the relationship. These mothers and daughters have hazy, permeable ego boundaries, often not knowing where one leaves off and the other begins. Mothers such as Sethe from *Beloved* and Arpazia from *White as Snow* often treat their daughters as bodily extensions; daughters such as Beloved and Coira desire to become their mothers or they simply desire their mothers; mothers desire to become their daughters; mothers desire their daughters while simultaneously wishing them dead. These dynamics of the second-wave mother-daughter romance are closely associated with folklore, story-telling, and revision.

These links are perhaps most clearly demonstrated in Kathryn Davis's *The Girl Who Trod on a Loaf*. Davis's novel concerns Helle Ten Brix, a Danish opera composer and lesbian feminist who attempts to write an opera revising Hans Christian Andersen's tale. In Helle's version, the girl who steps on a loaf of bread meant for her impoverished mother so as not to dirty her shoes is not sucked into Hell as punishment (the pun on Helle's name is ever-present) but travels there as a conscious choice, stepping on the bread as a way of rejecting the domestic labor women have historically been forced into. Inger travels to the underworld of the bog, sustained by the life-giving element of water, to serve an apprenticeship with the Bog Queen, a feminine divinity with whom she will eventually lead an attack on the patriarchal God.

Davis crystallizes the connections among mothering, consumption,[4] destruction, and creativity when Helle tells Fran Thorn, the narrator, that "I guess I'm like one of those birds ... who's always finding an unfamiliar egg in its nest left there by a cuckoo. Who wouldn't hatch it—or else crack it open and make an omelette?" (92). Here the act of mothering and the destruction/incorporation of the object to be mothered are two sides of the same coin. But that destruction is in itself an act of creativity, and the product of that creativity is destined to be consumed and (re-)incorporated. The cyclically destructive and creative energy of maternity is, in this novel, tied closely to revision, to creating an object anew.

Helle's mother Ida is deeply associated with the revision that fuels Helle's opera and Davis's novel. In speaking of Helle, Fran says, "Never mind her persistent urge to revise history," a statement that is echoed later in the novel as Helle's father says of her late mother, "*Her* passions had been fueled merely by a foolish need to repeat history" (9, 133). Helle understands this desire of her mother's as a desire to "be more powerful than he [her father] was. Thus the weak could strike at the root of the strong. They could learn to exist in history; they could learn how to inflict pain" (134). Helle's father uses the term "repetition" to describe Ida's interventions in history, but Helle clearly understands her mother to be *revising* history, changing the story, intervening in it, to "learn to exist in history." Revision is a way for power imbalances to be righted. Fran even suggests that Helle's stories of Ida are themselves revisions, for Helle's story of her mother as a wild gypsy is inconsistent with the recorded facts; Fran writes that "Women, she [Helle] would say, were the world's inventors ... The act of invention was basically lawless ... Looked at through this lens, wild Ida, perched on her hillock, could be seen as the inevitable result of a daughter's need to invent a mother consistent with her vision of the truth" (38). Thus Helle invents her own mother, and Helle and Ida take on a reciprocal relationship. Ida creates Helle, both physically and artistically, as Helle finds her creativity suffused and permeated by her mother's desires, spirit, and music; in turn Helle recreates Ida, a (re)vision of the mother she needs to fuel her art and her feminism. Thus for Helle, revision is a maternal, feminist tool.

Ida is the source of Helle's creativity in general as well as the inspiration for her revision of "The Girl Who Trod on a Loaf" in particular. The origin of Helle's musical artistry is a vision of herself as her mother's puppet. Ida gives Helle music lessons, "refus[ing] to let Helle touch the keyboard until she'd proved that she could curve her fingers in the proper position around an apple ... reminding her to think of herself as a puppet, her arm suspended from the ceiling on wires" (45). The use of the apple in these mother-daughter sessions suggests an occasion of female disobedience and sin, but Helle is refiguring female sin and fall as a positive apprenticeship in female power and divinity. Furthermore, these music lessons take place in a room overlooking the bog into which the fall that Helle is

---

4   Helle's mother Ida, whom I will discuss at length below, dies of consumption, lending a further dimension to the traditional connection between pregnancy/motherhood and "consumption."

writing about and revising takes place. Ida's musical influence pervades Helle's work, and "Some of her earliest compositions … had been inspired by her mother's extensive repertoire of bedtime songs" (36). The conjunction of Ida's music with Helle's sleep is not coincidental. Later on, Helle speaks of her mother's music: "Like a dream, Helle said; no matter what else you might say about her, my mother played like a dream" (46). Ida's music enters Helle's mind as she falls asleep and is like a dream; it becomes part of Helle's subconscious, part of her art, part of her revision. Helle's artistic creativity and revisionary impulse is informed by her mother's artistic skill and thwarted desires to make a musical career of her own: she revises her mother's life in her own.

Ida's art inhabits Helle's subconscious, and perhaps it is not surprising to find that Fran and Helle both describe Helle as a revision of her mother. Helle attends her mother's old conservatory, and even uses the same practice room her mother had spent hours in. In this practice room, Helle, masquerading as a boy, begins composing her second opera. Helle thus echoes and surpasses her mother, who attained no artistic recognition, and grasps more power by stepping up in the gender hierarchy. Helle says of her mother: "She was serious enough … but she lacked nerve. That was why her pedagogy was so rigorous: nerveless mothers couldn't abide nervelessness in their daughters" (46). Ida's desire and achievement was to make her daughter not in her own image, but in the image she desired to achieve: Helle is not a replica of her mother, rather she is a revision, incorporating her mother in a more vigorous, more aggressive, braver, more talented form.

Helle's titular opera, *The Girl Who Trod on a Loaf*, is both inspired by her mother and concerns mothers and daughters. Very early in the novel Fran tells us of a formative memory, real or imagined, concerning Helle and Ida. Ida, who has frightened her daughter with tales of the terrifying Bog Queen,[5] taker of unwary travelers who make a misstep in the bog, is dragging a young Helle through the bog as she goes to meet her lover.[6] There is tension in the bog between two sets of mothers and daughters: Ida and her daughter Helle, on the one hand, and the Bog Queen and her three daughters on the other. Ida's subsequent abandonment of Helle in the bog infuriates the girl, whose expression of desire for her mother and her need for her mother's attention has been rejected by that mother. Helle hurls Ida's similarly abandoned boot off the path into the bog and her anger calls up the Bog Queen and her daughters:

> while she watched, terrified, the Furies began to stir within the deep peat of the bog … There were, as Ida had predicted, three of them in all. "Little girl," the first of them called out, "we accept your offering." And then the second asked, "But shouldn't we tell her the price?" "No one ever believes it," the first replied … Helle stood looking down at them. "Mother," she said as one at a time they

---

[5]   Incidentally and interestingly, "hag" means both "bog" and "crone." The word comes up often over the course of the novel.

[6]   In another example of Helle's assumption of her mother's being, Helle will later find support and funding from this lover.

submerged themselves, each one releasing, as she went under, a wide, viscid bubble (56).

Is "Mother" the price Helle must pay, or is it another name for the furies, who most famously scourged Orestes for killing his mother? Perhaps it is both. Ida dies shortly after, and the young Helle blames herself, attributing her mother's illness and death to her own anger. Helle seems haunted by her mother throughout her life. In her operatic retelling of "The Girl Who Trod on a Loaf," the protagonist Inger collaborates with the Bog Queen and her daughters in an attack on a masculinist, rationalist God (this is the language Fran and Helle herself use to describe the opera's dynamics). Such an attack replays Helle's conspiracy with her artistic, romantic mother against her rationalist, doctor father, who likened his wife and daughter to the witches of *Macbeth*.

The narrator of this novel, Fran, has two daughters of her own, Ruby and Flo,[7] and functions as both an object of desire and as a daughter to Helle. Helle desires her sexually, but is rebuffed. Later, she leaves her unfinished opera to Fran to complete, placing her in the position of a daughter and heir, but Fran finishes the opera in a way inconsistent with Helle's original vision. Fran does not replicate Helle, but incorporates her own experiences and vision into the artistic project, revising the unfinished opera even as she completes it. Fran's daughter Flo has also collaborated with Helle on this opera, and after Helle's death, takes "to wearing her lank brown hair in a tight little knob at the nape of her neck [like Helle], who refused to believe that anyone else's grief equaled her own" (271). Flo tries to resurrect the artistic mentor/mother-figure in herself, making herself into a revision of the lost one.

Just such a complex and fluid sense of identity pervades second-wave feminist writing about mother-daughter relationships. In "Family Structure and Feminine Personality," Nancy Chodorow provides an explanation for the hazy ego boundaries that often exist between mothers and daughters. She argues that because women have been and continue to be children's primary caretakers, girls' and boys' developmental paths diverge sharply. She writes that mothers experience a dual identification when caring for their infants: they identify with their own mothers as well as with their children. But due to socially constructed gender binaries, mothers experience their daughters as "like," and sons as "unlike" themselves. Therefore mothers enter more fully into infantile symbiosis with daughters, and continue in it for a longer period of time. This significant, qualitative difference in the relationship with the mother leads girls to experience themselves as continuous and unindividuated, to develop flexible, permeable ego boundaries, and to experience primary object-boundary confusion. Female maturation is marked by continuity: girls are expected to identify with the same figure from infancy onward, while boys must make a break between infantile identification

---

[7]   Their names are clearly a reference to menstruation and thus female reproductive power. Female fluidity is associated with creativity throughout the novel.

and symbiosis with their mothers and an identification with masculinity as they mature. Chodorow writes that "[g]irls are thus pressured to be involved with and connected to others," and that "feminine personalities [are] founded on relation and connection, with flexible rather than rigid ego boundaries" (254, 256). This sense of the self as having permeable, hazy ego boundaries, not being sharply differentiated from others, and of defining the self primarily in relation to others is what Nancy Chodorow refers to as "feminine personality," what the theorists of the Wellesley Stone Center, writing in the 1990s, call "the relational self," and what I am terming "feminine subjectivity." Chodorow argues, and many clinicians and theorists have followed her lead, that these qualities are based in the mother-daughter matrix and its blurring of selves in early symbiosis. Due to the length and quality of this symbiosis,

> [g]irls emerge from this period with a basis for "empathy" built into their primary definition of self in a way that boys do not. Girls emerge with a stronger basis for experiencing another's needs or feelings as one's own (or of thinking that one is so experiencing another's needs and feelings). Furthermore, girls do not define themselves in terms of the denial of preoedipal relational modes to the same extent as do boys. Therefore, regression to these modes tends not to feel as much a basic threat to their ego. From very early on, then, because they are parented by a person of the same gender ... girls come to experience themselves as less differentiated than boys, as more continuous with and related to the external object-world and as differently oriented to their inner object world as well. (*Reproduction* 167)

Furthermore, this emphasis on continuity in maturation and with the external world is reinforced by social role-training: girls are expected to mature into women, and

> femininity and female role activities are immediately apprehensible in the world of her daily life. Her final role identification is with her mother and women, that is, with the person or people with whom she also has her earliest relationship of infantile dependence ... Because her mother is around, and she has had a genuine relationship to her as a person, a girl's gender and gender role identification are mediated by and depend upon real affective relations ... Feminine identification is based not on fantasied or externally defined characteristics and negative identification, but on the gradual learning of a way of being familiar in everyday life, and exemplified by the person ... with whom she has been most involved. It is continuous with her early childhood identifications and attachments. ("Family" 250)[8]

---

[8]   "Negative identification" refers to the process of identifying with a role based on what it is not. As boys are raised mostly by women and fathers are too often absent or do not engage in primary care, boys often have to develop a sense of masculinity based on being *not* like their mothers/women.

Thus female experience is characterized by continuity of identification throughout development and continuity with others. Rather than taking the mother as a static object, as Irigaray notes that prior theorists of the self have done and Angela Carter critiqued the Marquis de Sade for doing, Chodorow theorizes the creation of feminine subjectivity by tracing it to maternal experience, the mother's experience of her child. Such experiences generate the hazy, permeable ego boundaries and greater sense of connectedness to others often found in women.

Writing 10 years before Chodorow, at the beginning of feminism's second wave, in *The Magic Toyshop*, Angela Carter uses the uneasy identification between mother and daughter to mark the moment when the guiding myth of the novel appears. *The Magic Toyshop* describes the life of a teenage girl and her younger brother and sister in 1960s London after they are orphaned and sent to live with their tyrannical and abusive uncle, taking the myth of Leda and the Swan as a leitmotif. The novel opens with Melanie's mother out of town and alive. One evening, Melanie attempts to incorporate her absent mother in herself by wearing her clothing. When Melanie puts on her mother's wedding dress (feeling "like a grave-robber" as she does so [15]), she is putting on her mother. Melanie remembers her mother as clothing: "Her mother … was an emphatically clothed woman, clothed all over … Her mother must have been born well-dressed" and the narrator notes that "[o]n her mother's wedding day [Melanie's mother] had an epiphany of clothing" (10). The mother dies the night Melanie inadvertently destroys the wedding dress, prematurely replacing her mother in it, and tearing it to ribbons as she climbs a tree. As the boundary between Melanie and her mother blurs with the assumption of the wedding dress, the dress itself takes on the role of the Swan in the first allusion to the story of Leda that forms the leitmotif of the book: the white dress "had scooping sleeves, wide as the wings of swans," and as Melanie climbs the apple tree to return to her child-bedroom, the dress "opened out, flapping white wings in her face" (11, 22). The dress figuratively ravishes Melanie, first nearly smothering her in its veil, which she discards, and then leading her out into a night that overwhelms her. Thus the very first revision of the guiding story of the novel casts Melanie as Leda and her mother's wedding dress as the swan, and is intimately connected to the blurring of identity between Melanie and her mother.

But Melanie and her mother are not the same person and Melanie cannot fit into her mother's dress. When she unfolds her mother's veil, she realizes that she cannot cope with it. It "blew up around her, blinding her eyes and filling her nostrils. She turned this way and that but only entangled herself still more. She wrestled with it, fought it and finally overcame it" (15). This scene prefigures Melanie's later struggle with the puppet-swan that tries to rape her; that attack results in a temporary loss of self. The veil, fabric that obscures women's sight and the sight of women, is hostile; the dress itself is too big and Melanie "was bitterly disappointed" (16). Venturing out into the magical night, she finds that the sky "was too big for her, as the dress had been. She was too young for it … She panicked … Too much, too soon" (18). Melanie's desire to become her mother overwhelms her own identity; she has lost sight of her own self, her own size, her own needs. Her mother is then destroyed by her daughter's attempt at incorporation and supplantation. Melanie's mother dies in a plane crash that night, and the wedding dress is shredded. The destruction of Melanie's mother's wedding dress and the subsequent death of her mother begins with Melanie's emerging sexuality, as her cut feet leave "little flecks of blood, black in the moonlight, on the hem of her mother's dress" (18–19). The juxtaposition of blood and a wedding dress suggests both menstruation and defloration; Melanie's nascent sexuality thus taints the purity of her mother's fully blooming sexuality (symbolized by the wedding dress, a memento of the beginning of a long-since consummated marriage).

The next day, after Melanie's re-entry into the safe childhood of her home and her own identity as a child, she finds that "the dress was in ribbons" (22) and shortly afterwards receives word of her mother's death in a plane crash. Melanie instantly associates the destruction of the dress with the death of her mother: "It is my fault because I wore her dress. If I hadn't spoiled her dress, everything would be all right. Oh, Mummy!" (24). Like young Helle and like Sethe, Melanie lacks the ego boundaries that distinguish herself from the world around her, her desires and feelings from the events of that larger world. And in the Gothic world and logic of the fantastic, she may be right. Melanie feels that her desire to replace her mother by taking on her dress has killed her mother, even though she found that the mother's dress still needed a mother to fill it. By trying to take on her mother's identity rather than using her mother's identity to create one of her own—taking over rather than revising her mother's life—Melanie has displaced her mother.

Melanie is not the only girl among Carter's characters to try and invoke her mother by use of her wedding dress. "The Lady of the House of Love" is Carter's revision of the tale of Sleeping Beauty, in which a vampiric girl is trapped in her role as a monster. The vampiress has only one dress, her mother's wedding dress. When the virgin hero sees her, "he thought of a child dressing up in her mother's clothes, perhaps a child putting on the clothes of a dead mother in order to bring her, however briefly, to life again" (*Bloody* 202). By wearing her mother's wedding dress, the Countess materializes her mother in herself, but she is also trapped in the ancient series of events that isolates her, leads her to suck the blood-life out of every possible source of love, including pets. When she pierces her finger on a broken piece of glass, the hero breaks her curse by "put[ting] his mouth to the wound. He will kiss it better for her, as her mother, had she lived, would have done ... How can she bear the pain of becoming human?" (207). Like a mother making and bearing a child, the hero of the tale creates the Countess as human. The hero finishes the mothering that the Countess's late mother was forced to leave undone, but he also positions himself as the Countess's baby, enacting the way in which Talia's infant woke her up in one of the earliest known versions of "Sleeping Beauty," "Sun, Moon, and Talia."[9] In this version, collected by Basile

---

[9]   Carter, who edited two collections of fairy tales and translated the tales of Charles Perrault, was surely aware of Basile's work as well.

in 1636, Talia sleeps through the prince's discovery of her, his necrophiliac rape of her, her pregnancy, and labor. She is awoken only when one of her nursing infants sucks the splinter out of her finger. Thus the hero combines mother and infant in one, allowing the Countess to be both daughter and mother and thus to break free from the mere repetition of her ancestor's monstrous, soul-destroying ways. As in "Wolf-Alice," incarnating oneself *and* one's mother is the key to humanity. Being only one's mother is repetition instead of revision. To incarnate one's mother and then to incorporate other aspects of being is revision.

Kelly Link too ties mother-daughter relationships to revision via clothing in her story "Flying Lessons," which is about a teenaged girl, June, who falls in love with a boy who turns out to be one of Zeus's bastard children, hidden and protected from Hera by Venus, Ceres, and Minerva. During a re-enactment of the choice of Paris, June stands shivering on a dream golf course while wearing "her nightgown, an old one that had belonged to her mother" (86). As she does so, Rose Read, the goddess Venus, instructs her on the importance of story-telling and revision over true events: "It doesn't really matter whose ball it is, little thief," she tells June, "just whose ball you *say* it is" (88). The event, Rose Read explains, means far less than the retelling of the event. By calling June "little thief," she alludes to June's earlier actions whereby she stole a bottle of scent and a revisionary hardcover book (a retelling of the events in Ancient Troy) as gifts for her mother, linking her mother's birth(day) to revision and story-telling. Rose Read later points out the parallels between June's loss of her boyfriend and her mother's loss of her father. June notes that she herself is the difference: "She didn't go after him!" she shouts. "She had to stay here and look after me" (97). June wears her mother's passed-down clothing while revising a myth and then revises her mother's story with her own actions. Again, June does not merely re-enact her mother's story, treading the same paths with no volition, but incorporates her mother's past as an aspect of her own, producing a revision.

Link explores the connections among revision, mothers, and daughters most thoroughly in "The Girl Detective," in which she revises the tale of the 12 dancing princesses, incorporating a riff on the girl-detective genre as well (e.g., Nancy Drew, Trixie Belden, Judy Bolton). This story is formally an innovative masterpiece; its narrative is difficult to explain, mosaic-like in form. It is made up of several sections with bold headings, some digressions on the nature of food or the underworld, some lists of characteristics of the girl detective, some descriptions of the exploits of a group of 12 female tap-dancing bank robbers. Interwoven with the tale of the 12 dancing princesses/bank robbers is the tale of the girl detective's search for her mother. "The girl detective's mother has been missing for a long time," we are told, and furthermore, "The girl detective won't eat her dinner … If only her mother were still here, the housekeeper will say, and sigh" (241, 242). In the absence of her mother, the originator of her body, the girl detective refuses to incorporate anything further into her body—to a certain extent, her growth and physical well-being are inextricably linked to her mother's bodily presence and absence. Instead of the traditional quest of the tale, in which a soldier follows the 12 dancing princesses and finds a wife, this story follows the girl detective as her investigation of the 12 dancing bank robbers leads her to her mother. The girl detective relates herself to fairy tales via the trope of the absent mother: "This is another thing about fiction, fairy tales in particular. The mother is usually missing. The girl detective imagines, all of a sudden, all of these mothers. They're in the same place. They're far away, some place she can't find them. It infuriates her. What are they up to, all of these mothers?" (246). Here the girl detective expresses the anger of an abandoned child, highlighting the lack of attention paid to the effect of a mother's death or absence on the various protagonists of fairy tales. More significant for this analysis, she makes a conscious link between her relationship with her mother and the genre of the fairy tale, a genre dependent on traditions of retelling and revision.

Where *is* the girl detective's mother? Well, she seems to be incarnated in her daughter: "The girl detective has been looking for her mother for a long time. She doesn't expect her mother to be easy to find. After all, her mother is also a master of disguises. If we fail to know the girl detective when she comes to find us, how will the girl detective know her mother?" (251). In this passage, the narrator and the reader become associated with the girl detective in our bafflement. Just as we have difficulty recognizing the girl detective, so too does the girl detective have difficulty recognizing her mother. They are both masters of disguise— blurring their identities is a characteristic they share. I would contend that the unknowability of the girl detective's mother is akin to the unknowability of the story itself. The narrative structure is so very unusual, elliptical, and non-linear, that it is difficult to know where in the story one is. Thus the girl detective's mother becomes a metonym for the revisionary text itself.

The girl detective is a revision of her mother. They may share the same name: "No one ever speaks of her mother. It causes her father too much pain even to hear her name spoken ... Possibly the girl detective was named after her mother and this is why we must not say her name" (260). The mother becomes one with her name, as the mother's absence causes her name to be absent as well. The name, word, text, embody both the mother and her absence. Even the girl detective's title marks the mother's absence, as "perhaps" we use that title rather than her name because she shares a name with her mother.

Eventually, the girl detective arrives at a Chinese restaurant that advertises "DANCE WITH BEAUTIFUL GIRLS" (263), and we find that the mother is the girl detective's most desired escort. But as the reunion between mother and daughter takes place, identity and ego boundaries are elided: "Someone says 'Mom?' Someone embraces someone else. Everyone is dancing. 'Where have you been?' someone says. 'Spring cleaning,' someone says" (263). Identity is not completely effaced; given the prior text of the story, we can identify the speaker of the first question as the girl detective. But nonetheless, in this reunion, as in Demeter and Persephone's reunion in "The Homeric Hymn to Demeter," mother's and daughter's minds are "as one," and further identification or separation becomes unnecessary. The narrator becomes unsure as well: "Is that the girl detective or is it her mother? One looks back at the other and smiles. She doesn't say a thing, she just smiles" (264). In their happiness and satisfaction, the girl detective and her mother confound any attempt to separate them.

In these three tales, *The Magic Toyshop*, "The Lady of the House of Love," and "Flying Lessons," the primary focus is on the daughter's identification with the mother. It is from this perspective that Luce Irigaray writes in "And the One Doesn't Stir Without the Other," discussed in the previous chapter. She explores the frustrations of a blurred self, a boundless self, a self in endless fusion and confusion with her mother. Significantly, the mother's own subjectivity and experience of the relationship is largely effaced by her daughter's anger and sense of betrayal. But this angry daughter does not long for greater separation or more fixed delineations between her self and her mother. She does not write of the connection between herself and her mother as though it were necessarily pathological; rather she desires a connection or union based on vivacity, fulfillment, and self-realization. "I'd like you to remain outside" the narrator tells her mother (61). "Keep yourself/ me outside, too ... I would like both of us to be present. So that the one doesn't disappear in the other, or the other in the one. So that we can taste each other, feel each other, listen to each other, see each other—together" (61). On the one hand, this daughter is certainly asking for her mother to remain "outside," but the desire behind that request is a desire to fully and mutually behold and experience each other. The narrator bemoans the "disappearance" of her mother into herself and herself into her mother, but her fantasy is not one in which the mother goes away and leaves the daughter whole, but one in which the mother and daughter are mutually whole. The daughter's desire for a healthy connection with her mother is emphasized again later in the essay: "And never having known your own face, didn't you nourish me with lifelessness? ... Of necessity I became the uninhabitable region of your reflections ... And what I wanted from you, Mother, was this: that in giving me life, you still remain alive" (64, 67). Irigaray's daughter understands that her mother's lack of self reproduces itself in the daughter, and her desire is for a mother who, in maintaining her own self, can generate a self in her daughter. The wish is not for a more distant mother but for a mother who can fully, mutually connect with her daughter as both subject and object, without disappearing.

The desire for healthy intimacy and ego-fluidity is described in more detail throughout Irigaray's work in the 1980s. She develops a theory of female subjectivity[10] based on a feminine sense of fluidity and volume. Irigaray begins by writing that previous theories of selfhood based on the sharp distinction between "self" and "other" have served to disempower women. She argues that

---

[10]   Irigaray's theory seems to me to construct a view of feminine subjectivity that is largely based in the idea that women, as a sex, have an innate subjectivity different from that of men. For that reason, I use the term "female" when discussing Irigaray's work on subjectivity. While I find Irigaray's descriptions and analyses insightful and inspiring, I disagree on this point.

the subject-object split, so essential to sharp distinctions between self and other, is always inherently misogynous, always inherently matrophobic, for the primary fixed object that the subject is defining himself (and for Irigaray, any theory of the subject has always been appropriated by the masculine) against first and foremost is the mother, that figure so disturbing to the binary of self and not-self: "The ban upon returning, regressing to the womb, as well as to the language and dreams shared with the mother, this is indeed the point, the line, the surface upon which the 'subject' will continue to stand, to advance, to unfold his discourse" (*Speculum* 140). In other words, the subject is necessarily defined against a stable, objectified other, and the other being so used is always implicitly the maternal figure from whom the subject must make his first break. Thus when a woman participates in such a definit(iv)e split, she is of necessity undercutting her own sense of self, "renouncing the specificity of her own relationship to the imaginary" (133).[11]

What, in Irigaray's view, is the nature of that specific "relationship to the imaginary?" Boundlessness and androgyny are the characteristics Irigaray argues are part of (the/a) woman's unique relationship to the imaginary in her essays "Volume without Contours" and "Any Theory of the Subject Has Always Been Appropriated by the Masculine." Irigaray celebrates the idea of feminine boundlessness even while the earlier "And the One Doesn't Stir Without the

---

[11]   Irigaray is here referring to the Lacanian "imaginary," which refers to one's internal psychic understanding of the world, based on visual images and brought into being by the Lacanian mirror stage, which I will discuss in more detail in future chapters, Lacan disparages the "imaginary" as enclosed and solipsistic, but, in the words of Jane Gallop: "The symbolic is politically healthy; the imaginary is regressive. That is a classic Lacanian ethical hierarchy. But like all hierarchies, it can be oppressive. One of the effects of this hierarchy ... is to support the valuation of men over women. The symbolic is linked to the Law of the Father, to the Phallus; whereas the imaginary is linked to the relation to the Mother. There have been some thinkers who have questioned this valuation of the symbolic at the expense of the imaginary. Two of the most eloquent in their questioning are Jean Laplanche and Michèle Montrelay ... [I]t is possible to see the Lacanian devaluation of the imaginary as related to a hatred of the flesh, of woman and of pleasure" (149).

I would take issue with the primacy Lacan gives to the visual; research on infant development suggests that sight is in fact the least essential of senses to the baby: touch, smell, and hearing are all more vital. Irigaray has developed a feminist theory of infant development based on touch as the primary way of understanding the world (Angela Carter touches on the dichotomy between touch and sight in the film *Company of Wolves* when, faced with a human hand that had once been a wolf's paw, Rosaleen's father says "Seeing is believing." Rosaleen reaches out her hand toward the severed hand and asks "What about ... touching?" Donald P. Haase, in his article on the language of proverb in the film, notes that Carter is working with an English proverb, of which only the first half has remained popular: "Seeing is believing but touching is truth," and that Rosaleen's resistance to the phrase "seeing is believing," which is spoken by men throughout the film, becomes "a leitmotif that marks ... the progress of Rosaleen's maturation" [94, 100, 95]).

I have read of no evidence that suggests that prior to seeing his/her image in the mirror, a child understands his/her self to be incapable and fragmented, as Lacan claims.

Other" reaches toward a more complex understanding of the nature of boundaries and fluidity. Irigaray understands the destruction of boundaries and collapse of distinctions described above as inherent in maternity and thus inherent in our understanding of femininity. But for Irigaray, the dynamic, maternal fluidity's threat to the masculine subject is not inherent in the creation of any subjectivity; rather the threat has been created by the gendered, hierarchical construction of masculine subjectivity. Irigaray suggests that the threat of women's boundlessness, which cannot be enclosed, possessed, or captured, is a threat to gendered hierarchy rather than to an inherent psychological well-being, and that maintaining this fluidity or excess is an act of gendered resistance: "Woman is neither closed nor open. Indefinite, unfinished/in-finite, *form is never complete in her*. She is not infinite, but nor is she *one* unit ... But that excess is (not) nothing: the abeyance of form, the fissure in form, the reference to another edge where she retouches herself" (*Speculum* 55, 56). Irigaray, like the theorists at the Wellesley College Stone Center, conceives of psychological development as largely relational in nature, and like Nancy Chodorow, describes women as having a greater ability and tendency to conceive of themselves in relational terms: "For the/a woman, two does not divide into ones. Relations preclude being cut up into units" (63). Similarly, no single term is sufficient to enclose female desire: "No singular form(s)—form, act, discourse, subject, masculine, feminine—can complete the becoming of the desire of a woman" (55). Irigaray's vision of ecstatic boundlessness is seductive, and was an important corrective to a psychology that had too long based its assessment of emotional health on isolation and rigid ego boundaries, but it fails to address the dangers of boundarylessness.

The boundarylessness and boundlessness taken to pathological extremes by Sethe in *Beloved* and Arpazia in *White as Snow* are, in an Irigarayan formulation, qualities inherent in feminine subjectivity and inextricably linked with maternity. But Sethe's and Arpazia's obsessions and exclusivity of focus create pathology (Arpazia isolates herself in her madness; Sethe's need to unite with Beloved winds up excluding even Denver, Sethe's younger daughter). Irigaray might argue that such pathology is the result of artificial limits being placed upon the mothers' passions ("the risk of maternity is that of limiting (herself and her desire) to the world of *one* child ... Whereas what happens in the jouissance of women exceeds all this" [*Speculum* 229]), but in my opinion, such a reading sidesteps the issue that Irigaray addresses so brilliantly in "And the One Does Not Stir," that lack of boundaries actually precludes mutual understanding, replacing empathy with incorporation.

In both *Beloved* and *White as Snow*, the bound(ary)less mothers are also figures of folklore and stories: Arpazia the witch-mother knows her own mother, who died in childbirth, only from tales. She bears a child after being raped and in her turn, becomes a figure of tales to her ignored, unwanted daughter Coira: "The witch made no effort to commune with her child, and had borne no others—it was said she had refused even to suckle the baby, and that imps had feasted on her milk. Coira's attendants now began to tell her such stories" (61). Arpazia becomes a figure of folklore, tales that exist only in telling and retelling. Coira and Arpazia's relationship is absorbed by folklore as they become bound up in the myth of Demeter and Persephone, which Lee transposes to their world as one of its own myths. This lack of primary connection for Coira is deeply painful and damaging, as Coira internalizes her lack of effect on her mother so that it becomes a lack of efficacy in the world: Coira spends much of the novel passive and apathetic, and her ability to make genuine connections is only fully restored at the end of the novel when she becomes pregnant.

In *Beloved*, the relationship between mother and daughter is also mediated through story-telling; Barbel Hottges notes that the novel itself "bears resemblance to a storytelling session" and that "oral traditions obviously have been an important aesthetic and stylistic model for Morrison" (147). Chiji Akoma, in an examination of the use of African folklore and oral traditions in non-African black fiction, argues that Morrison's use of myth and traditional African oral arts is a way of constructing a counter-discourse to the European, literacy-based tradition that has tried to write black subjectivity out of existence, and to create "counter-memories," the histories of those excluded by legitimized, dominant narratives.

Morrison negotiates the relationship among African, African-American, and classical myth/Western European fairy tale carefully. White women and black writers have a vexed relationship with classical myth and with Western European fairy tales; white women contend with a mythic tradition in which almost all of the significant female characters are raped and a set of fairy tales whose contemporary best-known variants valorize female passivity and helplessness. Black women writers face not only those challenges but also must grapple with what it means to work with a cultural tradition belonging to a society that enslaved and continues to oppress African Americans. Indeed, the classical tradition was used to justify the enslavement of black people in the United States, as slaves had been an integral part of ancient Greek and Roman society, and classical culture was held up as inherently superior to the historical and mythic traditions found in Africa. As charged as the stories informing western European culture are for white women, those stories are doubly charged for black women writers.

Toni Morrison has stated that she deliberately works African-American mythic traditions into her novels, and more than one scholar has traced out the African roots of such traditions. But what do we make of her use of classical myth? In an interview with Cecil Brown, Morrison notes that when her characters find themselves in the middle of a myth from the Western European tradition, they are generally in deep trouble—Western European myths (and interestingly in the context of this project, the example Morrison uses is of "Hansel and Gretel," again underlining the confluence between myth and fairy tale in contemporary culture) signal dire wrongness. But classical myth is only one aspect of the story-telling tradition explored in *Beloved*.

Beloved first manifests her consuming love for her mother by desiring stories from and about Sethe. Like Arpazia, Sethe becomes a figure of folklore to her daughters: "It became a way to feed her ... Sethe learned the profound satisfaction

Beloved got from storytelling" (58). Sethe's living daughter, Denver, finds that "the more fine points she made," in her stories about her mother, "the more detail she provided, the more Beloved liked it" (78). Sethe's own mother is irretrievably tied to a forgotten language, a language that we later learn holds the secret of Sethe's own daughterhood. Sethe's memory of her mother and her mother's language is embedded in her own maternal relationship to Denver and Beloved. Sethe is combing Denver's hair (an act of female intimacy with a long history in both fairy tales and African-American culture). Beloved asks her, "Your woman she never fix up your hair?" (60). Sethe responds by telling stories of the mother she barely knew. At the end of her story something strikes her:

> She had to do something with her hands because she was remembering something she had forgotten she knew ... Nan [the woman assigned to take care of the children of slaves on the plantation where Sethe had grown up] ... used different words. Words Sethe understood then but could neither recall nor repeat now. She believed that must be why she remembered so little ... What Nan told her she had forgotten, along with the language she told it in. The same language her ma'am spoke, and which would never come back. (62)

Sethe's relationship to her mother and her maternal caretaker is mediated by a first language, a mother tongue she no longer remembers or understands. Her distance and separation from her mothers is reflected in her distance from her first language. She then remembers Nan telling her that Sethe's mother "threw away" all the babies that had resulted from repeated rape by white men; Sethe is the only child she kept and raised, Sethe's father was a black man, and she was created through love rather than rape. Despite the barriers of lost language, Sethe finally remembers her own origin, rediscovering it as if it were a lost oral tradition, told to her as if it were folklore, and in this discovery, she finds that she has re-enacted her mother's story in killing a child, though for different reasons.

This telling and retelling of stories as a trope for the mother-daughter relationship and its elision of identities occurs in the very form of both texts: the story of Sethe's daughter's murder is told three times, in different voices providing different shadings and information, and a few pages later Sethe's, Denver's, and Beloved's voices and selves merge and the identifying pronouns are lost: "She smiles and it is my own face smiling," "Will we smile at me?" "You are my face; I am you. Why did you leave me who am you?" (214, 215, 216). It is this very intensity that requires the intervention of the town's othermothers; Denver is able to save herself and her mother only when she ventures out of her mother's house and seeks the literal nurturing of other older women who provide food for her and her family, as well as an alternative way of being in the world, one that it is not inward-looking to the exclusion of all else.

Lee's novel expresses a similar confusion of selves when Arpazia, older and completely mad, finds Coira, now grown to a woman's estate. The narrative moves into free indirect discourse: "Arpazia saw herself. There she was, walking on the hill's ridge in a plain dress ... Her name though, was not Arpazia any more ...

What was her name, up there, walking along the hillside? Coira. That was it"
(247). Arpazia loses any sense of difference between herself and her daughter:
"She had found herself. Naturally herself would return, to be found again …
She did not expect her younger self to know herself" (248). As she draws near,
Arpazia confuses her daughter with the memory of her own youthful reflection
in the mirror: "But Arpazia had seen. It was herself right enough. The mirror had
lessoned her in this body and this face" (269). The homophone of "lessoned/
lessened," suggests Arpazia's early feelings of diminishment, which are indeed
reflected in the novel: when Arpazia becomes a hag-like old woman, Coira comes
into the full flower of her beauty, beauty that is identical to Arpazia's own. Arpazia
and Coira are thus locked into the zero-sum game that Arpazia experienced during
labor, as if they are the same person with only one body and one life between them.
When Arpazia and Coira do find each other, they confuse—and fuse—the roles of
mother and daughter:

> Her mother would not let her go. *She's smothering me*, Coira thought … *I can
> hardly breathe* … Coira would not let Arpazia go … *Let her smother me. I want
> her to …* Arpazia held her as if to press her back inside her body into the warm
> oven of her womb. And as if to press herself inside the womb of Coira. (273)[12]

Here Coira's and Arpazia's roles become entirely interchangeable; they
are simultaneously gripping each other and losing themselves in each other—
it is unclear even whether Arpazia's womb would contain Coira or vice versa.
Both Arpazia and Coira embody each role. Finally Coira "held tighter still, but
now her fingers had no grip. She did not realize, for Arpazia held her so close,
tighter, tight as any loving, clinging child" (273). Coira cannot differentiate
her own grip from her mother's, and Arpazia's grip is likened to a child's grip:
daughter is simultaneously mother and mother is simultaneously daughter.
Never communicating, never achieving empathy, only worshipping, merging, or
rejecting, Arpazia and Coira never experience mutual recognition and knowledge.
After her mother's death, Coira says "She meant no harm. No, she meant harm.
But she was mine" (317). Coira never gains insight into her mother and vice versa,
but nonetheless the desire, possession, and love endure, however distorted. Their
shifting identities combine into "The goddess three-in-one, who might be Coira
the Maiden, or Demetra-Arpazia the Woman, or Persapheh (or Granny) the Crone"
(247).[13] Mother and daughter become one in folklore, one in narrative style, one in
maternal delusion, and one in daughterly desire. Even embedded in such a close
identification, however, Coira is able to revise her mother's story—while the story
of her life mimics her mother's to a certain extent (both are the sole legitimate
daughters of kings; both are tended to by their father's other daughters; both are

---

[12] Note here the proximity and similarity between the words "mother" and "smother."

[13] Arpazia and Coira each take on the name "Persapheh" at different points in the
story.

abducted; both are raped by kings), Coira is ultimately able to choose a different path from her mother's.

Ultimately, the escape from the misery of bound(ary)lessness in both novels is not one of the "radical surgery" that would require complete and utter separation. Coira is able to reunite with her lover, and will bear a child whose paternity is uncertain but who, unlike either Coira or Arpazia, will be raised in a family characterized by love and connection. Denver has forged connections with the women of Bluestone and maintained her connection to her mother, and Paul D offers Sethe another avenue of relationship. It is not separation, but complexity in connection that is sought. But what would that kind of connection look like?

The theorists of the Wellesley Stone Center, whose work came to fruition in the 1990s and some of the most prominent being Judith V. Jordan, Janet Surrey, Jean Baker Miller, and Irene Stiver, acknowledge their debt to Chodorow and her ground-breaking work but are critical of the some of the assumptions and language informing her theories. Prior models of the self presuppose a linear development from undifferentiated symbiosis toward greater and greater separation, independence, and self-sufficiency—psychic health was measured in distance from others, need for relationships was considered "regressive" or weak, and ego-boundaries were to "protect" the discrete self from influence, input, and stimuli, rather than provide sites of connection.[14] The Stone Center theorists note that traditional models and theories of the self, like traditional models and theories of morality, always produce a deficiency model of women; that is to say, previously established understandings of what produces a healthy mature self and what sort of morality is the most sophisticated and mature have consistently ranked women as lower and lacking—woman is by nature "deficient" in these models, so that the flexible, permeable ego boundaries described by Chodorow are seen as signs of weakness and regression rather than signs of health, complexity, and growth. Even the language of "object-relations theory" assumes a sharp differentiation between subject and object that implicitly valorizes an understanding of the self as separate and bounded. Jordan and the other Stone Center theorists instead put forth a paradigm of the self based on women's experiences as studied and observed in a clinical setting, arguing that the "deepest sense of one's being is continuously formed in connection with others and is inextricably tied to relational movement," that the purpose of development is the achievement of greater complexity and articulation *within* relationships, that empathy is a complex cognitive and affective process, that such empathy and relatedness blur the difference between self and other, and that the need for "connection and essential emotional joining" is the foremost human emotional need (Jordan "The Relational Self," 137, 142).

---

[14]   While discussing the roles of Plato and Freud in promoting such models, Jordan et al. do not neglect to make connections between such theories and "the socio-political context in Western, democratic societies, where the sanctity and freedom of the individual greatly overshadowed the compelling reality of the communal and deeply interdependent nature of human beings" ("The Relational Self" 135).

The primary feature of a mature self is not "structure marked by separateness and autonomy," but rather "increasing empathic responsiveness in the context of interpersonal mutuality" (137). The theory of self constructed in this paradigm is called variously "the relational self," "relational subjectivity," or "the self-in-relation" to emphasize the inextricability of self from relationship, and "being-in-relation" to emphasize that the self under discussion is constantly in process, a verb as well as a noun. Like Irigaray, Jordan notes the difficulty of adapting a language built on the discrete distinction between subject and object to the task of describing a different paradigm of the self: "Our language does impose limits on our ability to delineate modes of being ...; we quickly resort to reifications, making solid that which is fluid, changing, and ongoing" ("A Relational Perspective" 30). The close association of relationality with women's ways of being in the world suggests that Jordan would agree with Irigaray that language as it is traditionally employed cannot contain or accurately express women's experiences or subjectivity.[15]

Super [margin annotation]

Due to the aforementioned gendered differentiations, Janet Surrey has asserted that the "best realm available" through which to understand the development of the relational self is via the mother-daughter relationship, which is central to many of the theorists' earlier publications ("Self-in-Relation" 53). For reasons similar to those described by Chodorow, girls are encouraged in their relational capacities while boys are not. Indeed, Surrey writes that into adulthood, "mothers and daughters often remain exquisitely open and sensitive to each others' feeling states" ("Mother-Daughter" 119). This does not mean that mothers and daughters are merged or fused. Jordan argues that empathy is a complex and psychologically intricate process that by its very nature precludes fusion, as it "rel[ies] on a high level of psychological development and ego strength ... In order to empathize, one must have a well-differentiated sense of self in addition to an appreciation of and sensitivity to the differentness as well as the sameness of another person" ("Women and Empathy" 29). Empathy combines affective arousal with cognitive understanding, "affective surrender" and "cognitive structuring." As such, it requires the subject to hold two different frames of reference in her consciousness at once:

> Empathy begins with the basic capacity and motivation for human relatedness that allows the perception of the other's affective cues ... followed by a surrender to affective arousal in oneself—as if the perceived affective cues were one's own—thus producing a temporary identification with the other's emotional state. Finally there occurs a resolution period in which one regains a sense of ... self that understands what has just happened ... There is a momentary overlap of self and other representations as distinctions blur experientially. (29)

---

[15] Most relational theorists agree that although the separate-self models are not sufficient, accurate, or desirable models of men's development, because male capacities for empathy and nurturing are discouraged and stunted from an early age, men are more likely to make a better fit with such models of separation than women.

Rather than representing a "regression" into a state of infantile symbiosis, fusion, or merging[16], empathy is a sign of maturity that requires the recognition of difference before affective arousal; otherwise no true insight into the other's affective state can be obtained.[17] It is precisely this kind of complex mutual recognition that Irigaray's narrator in "And the One Does Not Stir Without the Other" longs for, and which her merging with her mother and subsequent loss of self-mother distinction has prevented her from finding; thus the theorist/clinicians of the 1990s, whose work grew out of the advances of second-wave feminism, are able to provide solutions to the problems their foremothers posed. Jordan observes that the paradox of empathy is that "in the joining process one develops a more articulated and differentiated image of the other and hence responds in a more accurate and specific way, quite the opposite of what regressive merging would lead to" ("Empathy and Self Boundaries" 73).

In these writings daughters often function as revisions of their mothers. They are not replicas, trapped into repeating the same acts and thoughts; they are revisions, based in an earlier being, closely connected to her to the extent of not necessarily defining a clear boundary at which one leaves off and the other begins, sharing areas of merged subjectivity, but incorporating new, unique, individual experiences.

Second-wave theorists have acknowledged the link between mothering, daughtering, and revising, sometimes in their own choice of metaphor. Gilbert and Gubar write that "the female artist makes her journey into what Adrienne Rich has called 'the cratered night of female memory' to revitalize the darkness, to retrieve what has been lost, to regenerate, reconceive, and give birth. What she gives birth to is in a sense her own mother goddess and her own mother land"[18] (99). The use of the metaphor of childbirth to describe the process of artistic creation is an old one, often used, curiously enough, by male artists. Søren Kierkegaard wrote that "he who is willing to work gives birth to his own father" (56); although the attempt to masculinize birth does marginalize female reproductive power, the inversion of the relationship between parent and child is suggestive of Rich's description of

---

[16]   The existence of which state even in infancy has, as noted above, been called into serious question by more recent research. See for example Daniel Stern's *The Interpersonal World of the Infant*.

[17]   Think, for example, of the pre-schooler who presents her father with stuffed animals for a birthday present; the desire to please is there, but the ability to understand the difference between herself and her father, and thus the difference between what pleases her and what would please him, is not. Nevertheless it is an endearing trait in small children; less so in adults. It behooves us all to mature into a capacity for empathy.

[18]   I personally agree with Angela Carter when she writes that "Mother goddesses are just as silly a notion as father gods," and that "if women allow themselves to be consoled for their culturally determined lack of access to the modes of intellectual debate by the invocation of hypothetical great goddesses, [we] are simply flattering [our]selves into submission" (*Sadeian Woman* 5). Nonetheless, the metaphorical links among mothering/creation-myth/revision are important to this project.

an artist giving birth to "her own mother goddess." Second-wave poet and critic Alicia Ostriker points us back to the concept of the partially merged self in her study of women poets and revisionary myth-making. She writes that "the private-public distinction is one that contemporary women poets tend to resist and attempt to dissolve in favor of a personal-communal continuum … the tacit assumption in women's myth poems is that the self in its innermost reaches is plural. The 'I' is a 'we'" (*Stealing* 235). The self is plural, the self is always in relation, the I is a we. My analysis here is in part an attempt to more thoroughly know the workings of this "we" as it was conceived of and elaborated on by Ostriker's generation of feminists and those who carried their ideas further in the following two decades.

They didn't though!

Chapter 3
Revision and Repetition

In the previous chapters, I traced the connections between mother-daughter relationships and revision in the feminist fairy-tale/myth revisions of the 1970s and 1990s, and suggested a way of understanding those revisions based on psychoanalytic models of the mother-daughter relationship contemporary with those texts. How does this understanding of revision fit into prior critical formulations of literary revision, influence, and the importance of past stories to present writing? In this chapter, I place the model proposed in the previous chapter not in the context of its contemporaries, but of its tradition. Drawing on this tradition, I discuss the need traditional stories have for radical rewriting, arguing that a story's artistic and cultural power can reach or return to its full effect *only* in a revision. In making this argument, it is vital to distinguish revisions from duplicates, not only for the sake of aesthetic quality and artistic achievement, but also in order to avoid thoughtlessly recycling stories or propaganda whose messages have caused great harm; rewriting stories so as to expose and/or transform underlying misogynies is one of the tasks of feminist revisionism. Revision has the potential to expose the ideological underpinnings of the stories that shape our lives, not in order that we surrender to them, but in order that we can shape them in turn.

While the relationship between the texts of revising authors and their traditional sources has not before been represented in terms of the mother-daughter relationship, it has very commonly been figured as a process of communicating with, or even reviving, the dead. T.S. Eliot asserts that the poet must experience all literature as if he were contemporaneous with it, because all literary work is of the same time, and that his meaning as an artist can only be found in "his relation to the dead poets and artists … you must set him, for contrast and comparison, among the dead" (15). I will discuss the historical sense of Eliot's poet in greater detail in the next section, but here I would like to note that Eliot implies that the poet is always simultaneously among the dead and living, the past and present.

Indeed, this metaphor of writing and revision as talking to the dead seems to be more pervasive in literary criticism about revisionary work than it is in the revisions themselves. Most obviously, Rich associates the project of feminist revision with that of the speaking dead through the title of her famous essay, "When We Dead Awaken: Writing as Re-Vision." Her use of this title in some ways encapsulates the position of revisionary work: even while arguing for new eyes and vision and what seems to be a hostile stance toward earlier work, she relates herself to a privileged literary heritage through her use of Ibsen's play about the position of women in art. This use is anything but hostile; Rich's essay elucidates the themes in Ibsen's play. The "dead" here are women, who have been "killed" literally and literarily by their subjugated position under patriarchy; their speech constitutes revision. However, at the end of the essay, Rich argues that patriarchal, masculinist creativity is self-destructing, and that it is up to women-as-revisers to create and rejuvenate art. Thus "the dead" become not the women-artists, but the texts and authors those artists must revise. We find this metaphor in other works of literary criticism as well: as cited above, Gilbert and Gubar write that "the female artist makes her journey into what Adrienne Rich has called 'the cratered night of female memory' to *revitalize* the darkness, to retrieve what has been lost" (emphasis added) and Alicia Ostriker writes that "the outrageous rewritings of Biblical narrative by women poets, far from destroying sacred Scripture, are designed to *revitalize* it and make it sacred indeed to that half of human population which has been degraded by it" (emphasis added) (*Feminist* 31). Gilbert and Gubar's and Ostriker's use of the word "revitalize" suggests that the stories being revised are, in some sense, dead, in need of the revivification revision can provide—that "the outrageous rewritings ... by women poets" are in fact a way of communicating with and resurrecting the dead.

[margin handwriting: Only some (limited) are valid]

Gilbert and Gubar's work is a response to Harold Bloom's influential book on what he terms the anxiety of influence; the process whereby a writer copes with the influence of his predecessors is, according to Bloom, divided into six stages. The sixth and final stage of Harold Bloom's theory of influence/revision is termed "apophrades," or the return of the dead, and it is named for the ancient Greek days in which ghosts come back to the houses they once inhabited. Bloom describes this stage as being one in which the later poet,

> in his own final phase ... holds his poem so open again to the precursor's work ... and the uncanny effect is that the new poem's achievement makes it seem to us, not as though the precursor were writing it, but as though the later poet himself had written the precursor's characteristic work. (15–6)

In a book as thoroughly invested in Freudian theory as is *The Anxiety of Influence*, I find the use of the word "uncanny" telling. Freudian theory suggests that "uncanny" refers to a simultaneous sense of familiarity and strangeness, a sense that he connects, in a footnote, to our common origins in our mother's bodies and our passage through her vagina. The connections here, among sex, birth, and death, echo Bloom's initial effacement of motherhood in his assertion that poets are originally "in the father," a biological absurdity that points toward patriarchal anxiety about the biological fact that we all, actually, originate in the body of the mother.[1] Might, then, Bloom's return of the dead poet, rather than being the overtaking or surpassing of the father by the son, not be the resurgence and reincorporation of the mother by the daughter—the dual identification discussed by Nancy Chodorow?

---

[1]   Were Bloom's own book not intensely based on an elucidation of Freudian sexual theory, this reading of his use of "uncanny" might be too tenuous; however, I feel that his work it is far too invested in Freudian theory to disavow such a reading at this late date.

In *The Sadeian Woman*, Angela Carter argues that "the curious resemblance between the womb and the grave lies at the roots of all human ambivalence towards both the womb and its bearer" (108).[2] Certainly Gilbert and Gubar evoke this resemblance when they write that the female artist makes the journey analyzed above "to regenerate, reconceive, and give birth. What she gives birth to is in a sense her own mother goddess and her own mother land"—her own mother (99). The revitalization of revision, then, in second-wave texts and their heirs, is a process of rebirthing the dead as simultaneously one's own mother and one's own daughter. No wonder, then, that Bloom notes the "uncanny" effect of a poem which seems to make its precursors its own children: the result of revision is a joining of the powers of the mother and the daughter.

The need for an artist to be both created by and the creator of her parents appears in Davis's *The Girl Who Trod on a Loaf*. Let us return to a few quotations discussed in the previous chapter. As noted before, Helle defines creation as a female act:

> Women, she would say, were the world's inventors; it was only after the fact that men came along and discovered whatever it was that women had already invented. The act of invention was basically lawless, whereas the act of discovery required the making of laws, an endless cataloguing, describing, judging, and ultimately dismantling of the thing discovered. (38)

In one version of her life story, she tells Fran that her mother, Ida, was a wild gypsy found in the moors by her father. Fran finds documentary evidence suggesting otherwise, and reconsiders Helle's tales of her mother (revealed to have come from a book of short stories) in light of Helle's dichotomy between invention and discovery, female and male: "Looked at through this lens, wild Ida, perched on her hillock, could be seen as the inevitable result of a daughter's need to invent a mother consistent with her vision of the truth" (38). Ida dies when Helle is still a child; Helle becomes an artist, a great composer, and, as discussed in the previous chapter, her art is thoroughly imbued with the influence and spirit of her mother—but which mother, the fictional, romanticized figure of the wild gypsy, or the real daughter of a respectable burgher? Here Davis suggests that as much as Ida has influenced Helle, Helle in turn has created Ida as the figure from which she needs to be descended.

Further, Helle is convinced that she has killed her mother: when Ida leaves her in the bog in order to rush off and meet her lover, Helle, furious at the abandonment, throws Ida's boot into the water, and the Furies arise. Furies have

---

[2]   She cites the goddess Kali, "who stands for both birth and death" (115) and goes on to discuss Sade's Juliette, who is fertile (unlike her suffering sister Justine) and deadly; as Justine is the ancestress to those "heartstruck, tearful heroines of Jean Rhys, Edna O'Brien and Joan Didion who remain grumblingly acquiescent in a fate over which they believe they have no control" (56), perhaps Juliette is the ancestress of the femme fatale, desirous, desirable, and deadly.

long been identified with maternal anger (witness their punishment of Orestes for his matricide) and their presence suggests an interesting Freudian twist. Do they represent Helle's anger at her mother, turned instead through projection into maternal anger at herself? Helle's vision of the Furies is the result of Ida's tales and legends, told with the effect of frightening the little girl, and Helle uses them to, as she understands it, kill her mother in return.

Ida returns from her assignation and develops consumption soon after. She is dying, and

> Helle also knew who it was who'd thrown her mother's boot into a peat hag; she knew on whose body the raveling thread of her mother's soul had been snagged. How cautiously she'd enter the sickroom, how fearfully she'd accept each kiss and hug! … Sometimes [Ida] would ask Helle to brush her long brown hair and pin it up with tortoiseshell combs … "Don't leave, darling," Ida would say, and Helle would back out the door. (76)

"Hag" can mean both "bog" and "crone," and Helle blames herself for consigning her mother to both. As Ida dies, there is a reversal of care: where we have previously seen that Helle's friend Inger has her hair braided and put up by her mother, here Helle does the same *for* her mother. Helle is taking over her mother's role in a capacity which will culminate in her (re-)creation of her mother. The experience of creation and abandonment between mother and daughter, artistic and otherwise, is mutual. Helle uses a re-visioning of her past in general and of her mother in particular in order to create a truth about herself—her change in the story explains or illustrates her relationship to the world in a way that the documentary truth of that story never could, and given that Fran is attempting to discover the story of Helle's life, the revision ends up being more revealing—more truthful—than the documents.

Carter, who was not only a fascinating revisionist but a thoughtful critic as well, expresses agreement with Roland Barthes on the subject of mythology; both argue that myths are non-living. Barthes writes that "Myth … is a language which does not want to die: it wrests from the meanings which give it its sustenance an insidious, degraded survival, it provokes in them an artificial reprieve in which it settles comfortably, it turns them into speaking corpses" (33). Barthes states that myth does not want to die, but he describes its effect on meaning as positively vampiric: myth may not want to die, but it does not have a full life either, and it turns other meanings into empty, corpse-like minions, like Dracula's Renfield. Barthes's vision is of myth as undead, and perhaps it is this association that Carter drew on when she wrote "The Lady of the House of Love," in which a young vampiress is trapped in "the timeless Gothic eternity of the vampires, for whom all is as it has always been and will be" (199). Unusually, "the timeless Gothic eternity of the vampires" is passed along through the generations: the vampire girl has inherited her vampirism, linked to the generational, though not the gendered, aspect of the mother-daughter model. The young soldier's maternal nurturing and care allow the girl to free herself in true death. Barthes writes that

If you're trying to destroy Myth…

the best weapon against myth is perhaps to mythify it in its turn, and to produce an *artificial myth*: and this reconstituted myth will in fact be a mythology. Since myth robs language of something, why not rob myth? All that is needed is to use it as the departure point for a third semiological chain, to take its signification as the first term of a second myth. (135)

Shrek?

I suggest that this is exactly what revision does: transforms myth, a signification that makes meaning into form, into the form itself out of which meaning is drawn. A revision of a myth consciously invokes the symbols and regalia of that myth, while transforming the meaning or signification of those symbols and regalia. In doing so, a revision disrupts the naturalization or obfuscation of historical/ cultural specificity that Barthes claims is so integral a part of the ideology of myth. However, I would argue that revisions also thereby revivify their undead mythic predecessors, and that this is a positive thing. When the symbols and regalia of myth (the glass slipper, the pomegranate seed, the magic mirror) are rethought and imbued with different meanings, they retain those new associations when read in their earlier, mythic context, providing new layers of meaning to the older myth as well as to the newer revision. With respect to "The Lady of the House of Love," then, I wonder if we understand the reversal of roles between vampire and victim, when the young man puts the girl's bleeding finger to his lips, as way of breaking the grip of the undead myth by using the myth itself "as the departure point for a third semiological chain," which allows the girl freedom and true death (Barthes 135).

In her fiction, then, Carter seems to agree with Barthes's representation of myth as an undead, killing force, but a force that can be disrupted. In an interview, she elaborated on her views of myth[3] as "ideas, images, stories that we tend to take on trust without thinking what they really mean." Being undead, or not living, with respect to tales and stories seems to mean being taken for granted, being uninterrogated, accepted without thought. In that case too, revision is a form of revivification for myth, as revisions force the reader to rethink previously accepted tales using different perspectives and to come to consciousness of the cultural and material forces that had generated the earlier interpretation of the myth. Thus traditional tales not only give life to their revisions, but revisions re-imagine and revitalize their traditional tales, engaging in the same kind of mutual creation and conflict that Davis, in *The Girl Who Trod on a Loaf*, portrays between generations.

A revision does not replace the traditional tales from which it springs, but rather it revivifies them, gives them new life, both incarnating the original tale in itself and re-animating it by providing new perspectives, new understandings, and thus forcing an old tale back into consciousness and making it once more the subject of thought. Revisions derive their effect partially through the invocation and disruption of earlier tales; therefore they *require* the persistence of the earlier

---

3   As noted above, Carter had in previous work differentiated between myth and folklore. I am not as comfortable with the division as she seems to have been, and I will be using her thoughts to develop my own analysis of both myth and fairy tale/folklore.

tales in order to achieve their full effect. Angela Carter's *The Bloody Chamber* would lose a great deal of its meaning if read by someone who had never before heard of Bluebeard, Beauty and the Beast, Sleeping Beauty, Snow White, or Little Red Riding Hood. Kirsty Gunn's *The Keepsake*, a beautifully written, disturbing, and elliptical re-imagination of Donkeyskin, was not a commercial success, and that can be partly attributed to the failure of the publishers to market the book to a fairy-tale revision audience who would have been more invested in and familiar with the novel's guiding stories (it makes use of Bluebeard as well). Indeed, as of Spring 2005, none of the reviews on Amazon.com's website even mentions the novel's use of Donkeyskin. Despite Rich's contention that we must rewrite old stories in order to break their hold over us, revisions require the continued knowledge, popularity, and life of their origin-tales, and they help to provide those tales with new life, in the ways discussed above. Revision does not banish or vanquish the undead; rather revision renews the undead, is a process of talking to the undead, and in that process, gives the undead new life. Revision makes new and extends the life of older stories; revisions and traditional tales exist in symbiosis, intertwined, like the mother-daughter relationship described by second-wave feminists and the Stone Center adherents. The daughter's new blood gives aspects of her mother a longer life as well. As Joosen writes of fairy-tale revision, "at the same time it criticizes and reinforces the target text; it is simultaneously negative and affirming, desacralizing and resacralizing, rebellious and conservative" (16).

Revision throws the power of the undead over us into sharp relief, releasing us from the psychic slavery of a Renfield. For those of us in the academy, of course, theory can be as powerful a master narrative as any fairy tale, a form of myth itself, which, if we use it too bluntly, can drain us of our originality, to say nothing of our writing skills. By revising theorists' estimation of their projects of revision, by talking back to the academy, Davis and Carter place those theories firmly in the realm of the undead, reminding us that a Renfield-like devotion to, say, Foucault, is no more radical than a blind belief in the narrative given us by Disney's *Cinderella*.

Revision and Theories of the Early Twentieth Century

> Nothing / is always the answer; the answer / depends on the story.
> —Louise Glück (9)

> Do not all the achievements of a poet's predecessors and contemporaries rightfully belong to him? Why should he shrink from picking flowers where he finds them? Only by making the riches of others our own do we bring anything great to being.
> —Goethe (quoted in Bloom 52)

Goethe's analogy with flower-picking suggests that revisionists are not only poets but protagonists: Persephone and Little Red Riding Hood with pens. In doing so, he elevates their desire for beauty and sexual exploration to the level of art. Both girls suffer for their appropriation of the beauty around them, but perhaps this too is necessary to "bring anything great to being." Glück's observation about the individuality of answers and stories comes in *Meadowlands*, a collection of poems in which she writes about the various figures and situations of the *Odyssey*. She notes that answers and stories are never stable. There are two ways of reading the first clause, of course. One suggests that the only stability is absence of meaning; the only reliable answer is "nothing." But, according to the other meaning, for an answer to be meaningful, to fit the story, it has to change.

In the previous section, I discussed the ways in which revision brings new life to old stories. In this section, I will explore the necessity for those revisions. As Glück writes, nothing is always the answer; in other words, there is no such thing as a stable, unchanging, eternal meaning. As a given story persists in its original form, it actually changes its meaning as its context changes, and revision is a way to create new vitality, immediacy, and meaning for a tale. Changing the meaning and form of a given tale, revision is in fact the only way to keep a story a living part of the culture around it. I have discussed above Barthes's characterization of myth as undead—not living, but not quite dead either—and Carter's incorporation of that concept in "The Lady of the House of Love." I would argue that the kind of immobility and unchangingness described by Barthes and Carter produces meaninglessness: stasis is unable to convey any kind of human or artistic meaning. Bloom, in Joyce's *Ulysses*, muses on the fake, metal flowers placed on graves: "Rusty wreaths hung on knobs, garlands of bronzefoil. Better value that for the money. Still, the flowers are more poetical. The other gets rather tiresome, never withering. Expresses nothing. Immortelles" (93).[4] If the immortelles are meaningless, that is because they are unable to change; beauty, withering and the need for replenishment express the dynamics of life and death. Immortelles imitate this expression but cannot enact it. It is the very timelessness of the immortelles that makes them "tiresome" and expressive of nothing. Metal flowers express nothing; so, too, a story that is static seals itself off from the changing world.

When it comes to stories, persistence creates a kind of change, though not necessarily a positive one. As the larger cultural context surrounding a story changes, an unchanging, hermetically sealed story no longer has the same meaning it did when it first evolved out of an earlier cultural context. The impact and freight of a story changes because it does not respond to the changes going on around it. Thus, in Carter's "The Lady of the House of Love," the vampire-girl's mother's white wedding dress is seen by the hero as "a hoop-skirted dress of white satin draped here and there with lace, a dress fifty or sixty years out of fashion" (202). The dress has not changed; it is the same dress it was when the Countess's mother married. But several decades later, it has acquired a new meaning *because* it is unchanged.

---

4   Bloom does not contemplate the Jewish custom of placing stones rather than flowers on a gravestone in order to show that it has been visited. I am not sure whether this omission is intentional or not, or what it may signify, but a stone does not pretend to be anything other than that which it is, whereas immortelles mimic living and dying flowers.

Similarly, in *Meadowlands*, Glück's Telemachus muses on his parents' lives, and thinks, "When I was a child looking / at my parents' lives, you know / what I thought? I thought / heartbreaking. Now I think heartbreaking, but also / insane. Also / very funny" ("Telemachus' Detachment" 13). Odysseus's and Penelope's life stories have not changed; what has changed is Telemachus's understanding, and so those lives have taken on new meanings. Immortelles express nothing through their unchangingness while the unchangingness of the wedding dress and Telemachus's parents' lives create new meanings beyond the control of the dress's wearer or Odysseus and Penelope. What they have in common, however, is that their stasis makes them artifacts rather than living expressions: they are not responding to or interacting with their current cultural context. Immortelles and lives already lived, unlike tales, are not *capable* of change; tales can change, through the process of revision.

Revision pulls a story into the present, changing it in order that the old story can be experienced once again as fresh and immediate, allowing it to shuck some of the layers of mediation that come with the weight of history. Revision becomes a way of revealing a prior truth and clarifying meaning. Glück's Circe tells us that "I never turned anyone into a pig. / Some people are pigs; I make them / look like pigs" ("Circe's Power" 37). Circe reads the men as pigs, more than that, as *having been pigs all along*. Circe's transformation of Odysseus's men is conceived of here as returning them to their true state, as putting their original meaning, the identity obvious to a woman such as Circe, into meaningful dialogue with the world around. Revision can provide exactly the same kind of revelation, especially when approached from the point of view of a previously silenced reader. A meaning or reading of the story that had previously been ignored or dismissed can be preserved and brought to full blossom via the revelatory, transformative power of revision. Doing so, however, has yet a further implication: there is an implicit acknowledgment of the likelihood that future revisions will be needed to more fully render the unnoticed impact and meaning of *these* revised tales. Thus, revision condenses within itself the past, present, and future as simultaneous experiences: the difference of the past is experienced at the same time as present revision preserves and/or reveals a current meaning, and in doing so opens the story to further changes in the future. "Political," one of Rita Dove's poems in *Mother Love*, her collection of poems about the myth of Demeter and Persephone, contains the line, "It is becoming the season / she was taken from us" (55). In this sentence, Dove condenses past, present, and future in two lines: the action, "is becoming," is a present tense, but the verb she chooses, "to become," always carries within it the expectation and contemplation of the future, and here, it is becoming the past—a season that has already occurred. Thus the cyclical nature of revision encompasses all tenses. The story-cycle, then, by which I mean the various narratives we draw on in memory when thinking of a tale, is ongoing, and indeed, Dove ends *Mother Love* by writing that "Only Earth—wild / mother we can never leave ... / ... —knows / no story's ever finished; it just goes on, unnoticed in the dark that's all around us" ("Her Island" 77).

Sigmund Freud and T.S. Eliot considered the question of literary creativity and its relation to different perceptions of time from psychoanalytic and historical perspectives, respectively. Freud specifically disavows, and I choose that word with all its psychological weight advisedly, the possibility that his theories on creative writing, described in "Creative Writers and Day-Dreaming," could have anything to do with the revision of popular myth or folklore: "We must begin by making an initial distinction. We must separate writers, who, like the ancient authors of epics and tragedies, take over their material ready-made, from writers who seem to originate their own material. We will keep to the latter kind" (9). I would argue against that kind of artificial distinction when it comes to the processes of creativity.[5] The reasons for taking over existing material and the choices that must be made in reworking it require as great a creativity and art as does "seeming" to originate one's own material, and comes from the same conscious and unconscious processes. Freud himself recognizes the falsity of this division at the end of the essay, when he writes:

> We must not neglect, however, to go back to the kind of imaginative works which we have to recognize, not as original creations, but as the re-fashioning of ready-made and familiar material. Even here, the writer keeps a certain amount of independence, which can express itself in the choice of material and in changes in it which are often quite extensive. Insofar as the material is already at hand, however, it is derived from the popular treasure-house of myths, legends, and fairy tales. The study of constructions of folk-psychology such as these is far from being complete, but is extremely probable that myths, for instance, are distorted vestiges of the wishful phantasies of whole nations, the *secular dreams* of youthful humanity. (12)

Freud does not elaborate on what he means by the final statement; presumably that work is left to Jung. In any case, for the reasons acknowledged by Freud as well as for reasons that I will more fully elaborate after a discussion of the relevant theories, I feel as confident in considering the application of those theories to revisionary works as I would to works less dependent upon "the popular treasure-house of myths, legends, and fairy tales."

Freud stresses the unique relationship of daydreaming to time:

> The relation of a phantasy to time is very important. We may say it hovers, as it were, between three times—the moments of time which our ideation involves. Mental work is linked to some current impression, some provoking occasion in the present which has been able to arouse one of the subject's major wishes. From there it harks back to a memory of an earlier experience (usually an

---

5   The effect and resonance of a text, once created, in the larger world is an entirely different matter, and I would support recognizing such a division between revisions and non-revisions in that case—I could hardly do otherwise without undermining the entire basis of my project!

infantile one) in which this wish was fulfilled; and it now creates a situation related to the future which represents a fulfillment of the wish. (7)

Freud compares creative writing to daydreaming, and argues:

> In light of the insight we have gained from phantasies, we ought to expect the following state of affairs. A strong experience in the present awakens in the creative writer a memory of an earlier experience (usually belonging to his childhood) from which there now proceeds a wish which finds its fulfillment in the creative work. The work itself exhibits elements of the recent provoking occasion as well as of the old memory. (11)

Thus creative writing encapsulates both past and present. But what of the future? The piece of writing is itself an expression of a possible future, to continue Freud's analogy with day-dreaming. With respect to such phantasies, Freud writes, "The past, present, and future are strung together, as it were, on the thread of the wish that runs through them" (8). Freud's paradigm of linear time demands that past, present, and future be "strung together." But given the merging of experience and identity implicit in the consideration of certain revisionary texts as occupying the mother- and daughter-positions articulated by second-wave feminism, and with respect to the irrationality of the unconscious, we might come to the conclusion that the past, present, and future are not so much strung together as they are bleeding into one another through the medium of writing/phantasy.

One of the most salient differences between applying Freud's theory of literary creation to revisionary works and to non-revisionary works is that "the popular treasure-house of myths, legends, and fairy tales" itself constitutes a childhood memory, often associated with strong feelings of contentment, envy, or other such emotions, that the writer can be reminded of by a present-day stimulus. It is for this reason that I find Freud's theory, despite his own misgivings, particularly interesting with respect to revision: revision implies the centrality of narrative to the construction and experience of self. Otherwise, why would writers feel the desire to revise earlier stories, and why would there be such a dedicated audience for their work? If we consider the early pleasure or displeasure found in the childhood experience of our common treasure-house as occupying the place of the earlier experience in which a desire was fulfilled, Freud provides a very productive framework for considering how and why temporality may become simultaneous in revisionary works.

Freud writes that phantasy/writing is "linked to some current impression, some provoking occasion in the present ... [that] harks back to a memory of an earlier experience in which this wish was fulfilled" (7). In the context of revision, I would suggest that this current impression is a new understanding that transforms the way the writer thinks of a well-known story. Reconsidering the well-known tale reminds the writer of the previous pleasure in or dissatisfaction with the narrative—the lost childhood emotion. The desire to recapture that pleasure, or, alternatively, to amend that dissatisfaction, by writing a more fulfilling version of the story impels the writer to revise, and that revision represents a future wish, in the sense that the revision is an appeal to future readers, to whom it can serve as the present impetus or the past memory.

With respect to the feminist revisions of the 1970s and 1990s in particular, this process takes on an added poignancy, as many feminist writers and readers bear deep affection and took great pleasure in tales that they later find contain poisonous ideologies. Insight into the history and condition of women gives us a new understanding of the values encoded in the many tales of rape in classical mythology, or the idealization of female passivity found in popular versions of tales such as "Sleeping Beauty." Some of us critique the ideology of those tales; some of us seek out earlier versions of these tales, which are often far more complex in their depictions of gender and power than more current popular versions; some of us remake the tales of our childhood into what we wish they had been or into a version that explores the complexity of our relationship with those tales; most of us do all of these. Sheila Murnaghan and Deborah Roberts discuss in their study of women's poetic revisions of the *Odyssey* the link between memory and (re)creation in both Glück's and Linda Pastan's use of the epic. Pastan's work is a cycle of poems about re-reading the *Odyssey*, in which

> the accidental transformations of memory serve as an unstated paradigm for a process of more deliberate reinterpretation and revision … [Glück's] *Meadowlands* [on the other hand] plays freely with the story elements of the epic in a way that suggests that the *Odyssey* is itself part of a world seen in childhood and now only remembered (Murnaghan and Roberts 3).

In all revision, "the wish makes use of an occasion in the present to construct, on the pattern of the past, a picture of the future" (Freud 11). That picture, the revisionary work itself, contains the past story, the present occasion, and the desired future. By "desired future," I do not mean to imply that all feminist revisions are utopian projects; many highlight with varying degrees of complexity the distress and suffering inflicted on women under an essentially patriarchal cultural and political system. However, the revision depicts that predicament in the way *desired by the writer*, so that the depiction, the fantasy, is desired, even though what it depicts may not be.[6] Freud writes that "a happy person never phantasies,

---

[6] Freud himself touches on this seeming paradox: we often fantasize and write avidly about events which, if they were to happen, would be truly terrible. He notes that

> The unreality of the writer's imaginative world … has very important consequences for the technique of his art; for many things which, if they were real, could give no enjoyment, can do so in the play of phantasy, and many excitements which, in themselves, are actually distressing, can become a source of pleasure for the hearers and spectators at the performance of a writer's work. (4)

Terry Pratchett makes a sharp distinction between fantasy and what we would truly want to happen in *Witches Abroad* when he writes "In Genua, stories came to life. In Genua, someone set out to make dreams come true. Remember some of your dreams?" (147).

only an unsatisfied one" (6). This statement leaves open to interpretation the question of what it means, then, to be happy. Does happiness require the absence of imagination? Of desire? I think not. In this context, I believe that fantasy and revision, desired futures that depend upon a lost past and an unsatisfactory present, are expressions not merely of personal discontent, but also of political unhappiness with an unjust, imperfect world, and so of the human will to better our condition.

T.S. Eliot discusses the trans-temporal nature of literary creation in aesthetic and historical rather than psychoanalytic terms, and he comes to an understanding of the role of time in writing very similar to Freud's. In "Tradition and the Individual Talent," he argues that the relationship between present and past is mutual, and that as past literature influences and informs the present work, so too does the present work inflect and inform all future readings of earlier work. In effect, he argues that each writer *creates* the tradition that influences him: "Tradition … cannot be inherited, and if you want it you must obtain it by great labor" (14) (we see the specter of motherhood in the term "labor"). Thus the writer is not merely a passive recipient of the past, but rather obtains it by "great labor"—whether this labor involves creating the past, the interpretation I favor, or gaining access it to it, or both, is almost immaterial: what matters is that the writer and his work must encompass the past as well as the present. Eliot goes on to describe how he must do so:

> [Tradition] involves, in the first place, the historical sense … and the historical sense involves a perception, not only of the pastness of the past, but of its presence; the historical sense compels a man to write not merely with his own generation in his bones, but with a feeling that the whole of the literature of Europe from Homer and within it the whole of the literature of his own country has a simultaneous existence and composes a simultaneous order. This historical sense, which is a sense of the timeless as well as of the temporal and of the timeless and temporal together, is what makes a writer traditional. And it is at the same time what makes a writer most acutely conscious of his place in time, of his own contemporaneity. (14)

In Eliot's formulation, then, past and present are not the same, but they share areas of merging—for the writer they are and must be both simultaneous and sequential.

An artist must consider the work of his predecessors as contemporary interlocutors to his own, but that is not sufficient; he must do so while maintaining "an awareness of the past in a way and to an extent which the past's awareness of itself cannot show" (16). In the awareness and the work of Eliot's writer, the past and the present exist in mutual, active relationship to each other, and the present affects the past as much the past affects the present:

> When a new work of art is created … something … happens simultaneously to all the works of art which preceded it. the existing monuments form an ideal order among themselves, which is modified by the introduction of the new … work of art among them. The existing order is complete before the new work

arrives; for order to persist after the supervention of novelty, the *whole* existing order must be, if ever so slightly, altered; and so the relations, proportions, values of each work of art toward the whole are readjusted ... the past [is] altered by the present as much as the present is directed by the past. (15)

I believe we must understand the concept of an "ideal order" literally—it is a complete order that exists only in the ideation of readers, and thus when a new piece of literature is incorporated, it casts its shadow not only forward, as a reference for the reader to come back to in the future, but also backward, as it inflects and informs considerations of past works as well. Eliot is of course speaking of literature in general, but he notes that "the poet who is aware of this [reciprocal relation between past and present] will be aware of great difficulties and responsibilities" (15). Surely the writer who takes on the task of re-distilling and re-elaborating tales that have worked their way down through the centuries is most fully aware of his or her relation to the past.

In Eliot, as in Freud, the genesis of writing is the confluence of past, present, and future into a fantasy that refuses to order these temporal aspects of experience linearly while simultaneously preserving the distinctions among them. I have argued that while both theorists were discussing the genesis of literary creation in general, their theories have special relevance to the process of revision. I believe that a better understanding of this relationship between revision and time can provide an answer to the dilemma in which Telemachus finds himself in one of Glück's poems: "I can never decide / what to write on / my parents' tomb ... one does not / honor the dead by perpetuating / their vanities, their / projections of themselves. / My own taste dictates / accuracy without / garrulousness; they are / my parents, consequently / I see them together" ("Telemachus' Dilemma 33). How ought Telemachus to represent the stories that have passed? To write what his parents would have written would perpetuate their biases, deny that the past is past, and abjure that awareness of the past that the past's awareness of itself could not encompass. And yet to impose his own taste upon the past without consideration for its own awareness of itself flattens out the famously separate lives of Odysseus and Penelope into joined parenthood. Further, what would their vanities or biases mean to readers at a remove? What would Telemachus's limited view mean to such readers? Telemachus is attempting to represent the past to the future while taking himself, the present, into account. While the final line of the poem suggests that he has reached a decision ("they are / my parents, consequently / I see them together"), the tense of his statement ("I can never decide") makes his dilemma eternal.

I would argue that revision allows a writer to achieve both ways of representing past stories. By invoking, embodying, and preserving the traditional stories, as I have argued that revision does, while simultaneously ringing changes on those tales, revision both reminds the reader of the past's perspective and marks the differing perspective of the present. Indeed, one is only meaningful with the other. Telemachus's statement that he sees his parents together is moving precisely because he has acknowledged the great separation between Odysseus and Penelope, noting that his father's preferred epitaph, "Beloved," is certainly accurate if it is in reference to the many women Odysseus encountered in his travels. Telemachus may be forever caught in his dilemma, but Glück is not. Thus revision brings past and present together in a way that acknowledges their merging, their difference, and the tension involved in both.

Conceiving of Story in the Age of Revision

In her entry on revision in *The Encyclopedia of Fantasy*, Roz Kaveney distinguishes between straight revisionism and what she refers to as "twice told stories." In true revisions, she writes, "the retelling of stories or elements of stories is less a polemical revision than a way of meditating on Story itself." I wonder if Kaveney's distinction is one of quality rather than one of type, insofar as all thoughtful revisions, consciously or not, provide a way of thinking about the nature of Story and storytelling itself, and that a revision that fails to do so is weak at best. Kaveney notes the importance of revisionism with respect to social justice, noting, for instance, "The thoroughgoing programme of revisionism that followed on from Second Wave feminism … was both a necessary piece of common human decency and a productive force," but she does not neglect such revisionism's implications for future writing: "When revisionist fantasy deals with traditional and folkloric material, particularly when it is aimed at children, it is further at risk of patronizing the past, and takes the consequence of being criticized in similar terms by a putatively more enlightened future." I would suggest that any well-made revision does not run such a risk, but rather, *requires* such future revisionism. Having purposefully disrupted the supposed authority of a received story, a revision inherently looks toward future retellings and helps to generate them, in the same way its own traditional tale or set of tales generated it. In her poem, "Little Red Riding Hood," Olga Broumas's heroine says, "I grow old, old / without you, Mother, landscape / of my heart. No child, no daughter between my bones / has moved, and passed / out screaming, dressed in her mantle of blood / as I did / once through your pelvic scaffold" (67). The speaker's isolation comes from her lack of a daughter, which signifies her estrangement from her mother, separates her from the landscape of her heart. Reproduction, continual revision, keeps stories alive, and revisions are even more invested in such reproduction than completely original works of literature. Kaveney notes that "In almost all revisionist genre fantasy … there is a strong element of complicity with the thing disapproved of … this [can] produce a useful creative tension between moral programme and imaginative sympathy," and in doing so puts her finger precisely on the process of synthesizing present desire, past memory, and future fantasy essential to the writing of revision. For example, we love the trope of the wicked stepmother; we are disturbed by its ideological implications; we write out of this tension. Future tension, revision, and correction is not a risk; it is a necessary promise.

Story as Stasis: When Revision Is Necessary

> "Things have come to an end, see," said Granny. "That's how it works when you
> turn the world into stories. You should never have done that. You shouldn't turn
> the world into stories. You shouldn't treat people like they was *characters*, like
> they was *things*. But if you *do*, then you've got to know when the story ends."
>
> "You've got to put on your red-hot shoes and dance the night away?" said Lily.
>
> "Somethin' like that, yes."
>
> "While everyone else lives happily ever after?"
>
> "I don't know about that," said Granny. "That's up to them ..."
> — Terry Pratchett, *Witches Abroad* (270)

In *The Girl Who Trod on a Loaf*, Kathryn Davis's composer Helle acknowledges
the great harm that stories can do in one of her operas, in which a nightingale
requires other birds to destroy themselves, animals, and people, in order to fulfill
her vision:

> The birds were setting upon the people on the beach, tearing them apart,
> providing Nightingale with bits and pieces of their bodies—the valet's shiny
> black hair and eyebrows, one scullion's pretty lips, the other's nimble fingers,
> the downstairs maid's perfect breasts, the cook's long white thighs, the master's
> prick, the mistress's cunt, the twins' little red hearts. *Fuglespil*, [Helle] said,
> was a dark opera, an opera born out of her need to define, once and for all, the
> monstrous nature of the artist. (364)

Here, art and re-creation/revision become a monstrous set of murders, as the
Nightingale's vision forces all around her to submit to it. Davis touches on this
theme earlier when Helle remembers an ex-lover's horsemanship, her ability to
ride like a centaur, as if she and the horse were one: "What you couldn't see,
watching Maeve ride, was how thoroughly the element of tyranny had informed
this relationship. By fixing on the beauty of the myth ... you missed the operation
of will that made myth possible" (282). The horse is completely subsumed into
Maeve's rule, and becomes part of her myth. In this respect, I think the tyranny
operating here is similar to that described by Barthes and Carter in their critiques
of myth. Stories cause harm when they become ideology, fixed and unmoving;
they become tyrannous when they suppress responses and revisions.

Harold Bloom writes that "Health is stasis" (95). This is a pretty thought,
but those who cope with asthma, epilepsy, depression, sickle-cell anemia, or one
of numerous other chronic illnesses are fully aware of the activity, energy, and
effort required for health. Barthes comments that myth is self-naturalizing, and
Carter argues that it "deals in false universals" (*Sadeian Woman* 5). Thus myth
acknowledges no change, no response in itself to particular areas and histories,
and this is what Carter and Barthes agree is its most dangerous quality. The myth

of stasis, let alone stasis itself, is not health. It is empty, and when prolonged, it is death. Barthes argues that the best way of defanging myth is to mythify it in its turn; I have suggested above that this is exactly what revision does. The tyranny of myth, its inability to acknowledge other versions of its story, can be undone by constant revision. Revision, however, is different from repetition. Revision rings changes on a theme, it both incarnates and reworks its originary story, and it depends as much on difference as it does on connection; repetition is merely another face of unchangingness, another form of naturalization.

Helle connects repetition to patriarchy and female subjugation. In the opera she is writing based on the Andersen story, instead of being condemned to hell for her pride, Inger is instead taken under the wing of the subterranean Bog Queen, who trains her to assist in combating a God whose creation is more like a cancer than a pregnancy: "God is now the enemy, and the Bog Queen, together with her furious daughters, the inevitable worms in the rose of creation. Without them God's mindless replication of his own heart might have gone on forever and ever" (17). That replication is a figure for patriarchal constraint rather than generative creation:

> God engages in endless replication of His form ... but whatever diversity He appears to promote is limited by His overwhelming desire to see Himself wherever He looks, to be everything—this is the world "analogous to man's imaging," as Inger sings, and clearly we're meant to understand that she's making a crucial distinction, that the world as imagined by a woman might be completely different. (387–8)

Indeed, the ending of the novel valorizes revision over replication as well. Helle has died, killed by the habit she shared with the narrator Fran, the habit that killed Angela Carter as well: smoking. She leaves her unfinished opera to Fran to complete, and in an effort to find out what and how Helle would have finished the piece, Fran attempts to piece together the different tales of Helle's life. The novel interweaves this tentative biography with Fran's memories of her relationships with Helle and with Sam, the husband of Helle's niece—but Fran finds herself creatively blocked, in large part because of the awe in which she holds Helle. She is not able to finish the opera until she throws off her commitment to finish it as Helle would have, making the finished piece a revision not only of Andersen's story, but of Helle's inspiring, misanthropic, and violent vision as well. She has to combine her admiration for Helle's work with a respect for her own experiences before she can make art.

Carter's "The Lady of the House of Love" deals with the inhumanity of repetition and its fatality as well. Repetition is the trap in which the vampiress is caught: "She is herself a cave full of echoes, she is a system of repetitions, she is a closed circuit. 'Can a bird sing only the song it knows or can it learn a new song?' She draws her long, sharp fingernail across the bars of the cage in which her pet lark sings ... She likes to hear it announce how it cannot escape" (195, 196). The insular, closed world of the vampire girl is her own cage: the castle is her eternal, unchanging tomb. She cannot create anything anew—all she has is echoes of her undead ancestors. She repeats the same pattern every evening, casting her future in Tarot cards that never vary:

> The Tarot always shows the same configuration: always she turns up La Papesse, La Mort, La Tour Abolie, wisdom, death, dissolution ... She resorts to the magic comfort of the Tarot pack and shuffles the cards, lays them out, reads them, gathers them up with a sigh, shuffles them again, constantly constructing hypotheses about a future which is irreversible. (197)

This future is already decided, it is already the present. Carter's vampiress is caught like a fly in amber in an unchanging present.

And yet, one evening, the Countess turns up Les Amoureux, and wonders "could love free me from the shadows?" Consciously she does not know any form of consummation besides the vampiric. Unconsciously, though, she makes her own break with the past, by forgetting to take off her dark glasses before removing her dress. She drops the glasses and they shatter upon the floor:

> She fumbled the ritual, it is no longer inexorable ... There is no room in her drama for improvisation; and this unexpected, mundane noise of breaking glass breaks the wicked spell in the room, entirely ... What is she to do now? ... How can she bear the pain of becoming human? The end of exile is the end of being. (207)

I have previously discussed how her repetition, her eternal unlife, was exile from humanity. Becoming human is a freedom, but it is also a promise of death, for all change and growth leads toward death. The soldier's kindness toward the Countess allows her to free herself, opening the windows to the sunshine that she knows will kill her but will also allow her pet lark to leave its cage. And yet, is her freedom entirely the result of the soldier's love? The following morning, he finds her once again sitting at her table over the Tarot: "She has dropped off to sleep over the cards of destiny that are so fingered, so soiled, so worn by constant shuffling that you can no longer make the image out on any single one of them" (208). These cards show nothing. They can determine nothing. The repetition, the trap, was made by the Countess herself—and so was the first break with it that led to her freedom, the turning over of a new card. This reading is supported by various comments Carter has made in interviews. In one, she argues that myth is a construct manipulated by human beings in order to curtail freedom, and draws a parallel with her early novel, *The Magic Toyshop*:

> *The Magic Toyshop* has a whole apparatus about Leda and the swan, and it turns out that the swan is just a puppet. I wrote that a very long time ago, when I really didn't know what I was doing, and even so it turns out that the swan is an artificial construct, a puppet, and somebody, a man, is pulling strings on the puppet. (Interview Katsovos 11)

In an essay, she argues that "Reading is just as creative an activity as writing and most intellectual development depends upon new readings of old texts" ("Notes" 37). The Countess's trap is created by her repetitive readings of the illegible Tarot cards, but her freedom is created by a revision of those readings. Like Fran in *The Girl Who Trod on a Loaf*, the Countess does not cast off and destroy all that had come before; she makes one significant change, and all else follows from that— revision does not dismiss the past, but nor does it repeat it. It incorporates the past and uses it to throw a few significant changes into sharp relief.

Kirsty Gunn's second novel, *The Keepsake*, is a beautifully written, disturbing, and poignant meditation on the destructive potential of repetition. It is a re-imagining of the fairy tale of Donkeyskin, in which a princess disguises herself in the skin of a donkey in order to flee her father, who is forcing her to marry him. Gunn examines the story in light of the consequences of incestuous sexual abuse. Part of the novel's beauty is its enigmatic, impressionistic style, and the plot is rarely clear. It is a first-person narrative told by a young woman whose mother fled from her own sexually abusive father to an older, equally destructive man, who impregnated her with the protagonist, wrapped her in the still-warm skin of a flayed horse, and then abandoned her. The mother subsequently became a drug addict and died, and her grown daughter finds herself unable to break free of this pattern of abuse, allowing herself to be imprisoned and abused in turn by an older man who, we grow to suspect, may in fact be the vicious father who abandoned her pregnant mother. None of the characters are ever given names, further encouraging confusion between mother and daughter, father and lover, on the part of the reader.

As the mother descends further into helplessness and addiction, she turns inward, and her constant repetition of the stories of her idealized, romanticized past signify her inability to recover from the damage inflicted on her:

> For my mother, her stories were all her words. Her whole language told her story, of the man who took her and then, after his daughter was born, went to some other place where she could never find him. "Far away… " she said, as if it was the ending of a story but there was never an ending for her. The words continued to turn for her, and turn and turn. (34)

The protagonist's mother is unable to live outside of this one story, and significantly, this is a story in which she is completely passive. Her *language* tells the story, a man takes her, *his* daughter *was born*, he went away, the words turn. The mother's only active role in this story is to fail: she could *never* find him. The protagonist's mother is trapped in objecthood and the passive voice, and so she is killed, just as Carter wrote in *The Sadeian Woman*. This story is as destructive to the mother as her various drugs:

> Whatever she took for her body had made her mind unwell, as if the pills and powder and clear liquids she burned for the needle had given her addiction as remedy for her stories, but in the end addiction only made the stories stay. She would never give them up. The past had become her. She was nothing else. (35)

Again we see not Eliot's and Freud's ability to understand the presentness of the past as well as its passing, but an *inability*, a trap in which there is no present, and no future, only an unchanging past/present/future—a timeless eternity. The narrator associates the mother's stories with her drugs, and both work to keep the mother passive, the drugs making the past trauma permanent and present. The mother even replicates her own abuse by molesting her daughter while bathing her. The mother never experiences herself as an agent in her own life; her story is represented as carrying her along in its inevitability. When contemplating her mother and father's first meeting, the daughter thinks,

> How strange it is, and sad and perfect, that my poor mother, when stepping into the room and catching sight of his dark starving eyes, really does think the other thing is over, all that oldness ... When, really, the old story is only beginning again, the broken wheel turning slowly on its axle, so for seconds, minutes, it's like a perfect circle and everything has changed, then turns again, another fragment of a degree turns past, turns and begins its broken circle again. (104)

The mother never gains consciousness of herself or any sense of her own power, and so is carried around through repeated abuses, again and again, never sensing her own power to intervene. Like the Countess, she is trapped, first by her father, and then by her own passivity. Unlike the Countess, though, she is not able to free either herself or her caged daughter/lark. She dies young, beaten into submission by the abuse she has suffered and the drugs with which she bludgeons her own consciousness.

The daughter too is trapped by her mother's passivity. She can understand no other way to live but by repeating—not revising—her mother's stories. The stories themselves had begun as a kind of abuse, as the mother forces unwanted secrets upon her daughter. As a child, the daughter then experiments with making her own stories, but finds them unsatisfying: "I began to make up stories of my own ... But most times the stories began as my mother told me" (36). Finally, the daughter adopts these stories as her own: "All my mother's stories were like this, deeply known to me by heart. So closely printed that when I found a lover for myself, I had the writing in me already that he would meet me in a European café, talk to me there in queer half American, with a guttural tongue" (10). The daughter too experiences herself as without volition, as having been inscribed by a story, rather than generating it, because her mother's stories never change. They are "deeply known to me by heart," and so impervious to any revision or alteration. They shut down any possibilities for change. When the protagonist meets an older man, perhaps her father, perhaps her mother's father, who will keep her, his "promise was like the beginning of one of my mother's stories" (10), and she allows herself to be carried along by it and trapped by it just like her mother.

The daughter, however, is conscious of what she is doing, even while she feels powerless to change the story. Unlike her mother, she is aware that the man into whose arms her mother fled was not very different from the sexually abusive father she was fleeing, but she still cannot imagine a path different from her mother's:

"Mother. Daughter. They rise, they fall, the same. Repeating is a truth of nature, like one flat cloud forms in the sky after its sister. They are not identical, but in the blue sky they are the same" (149). The daughter understands her own and her mother's repetitions as natural phenomena, something in which no-one has the power to intervene, and so she allows herself to be absorbed into the same self-destructive story: "For so many years my mother's stories were me, they were the only thing I knew, to continue her line, to continue" (185). And continue the daughter does, until her lover tries to wrap her in what she recognizes as the same dead horse's skin that had belonged to her mother, and the daughter, gaining an understanding that her mother was never able to, refuses: "*But it's not the same,*" she thinks, "*it's not the same*" (163).

The mother's stories disguised the horrible events of her life, papering over the unendurable abuse and trauma with a romanticized, idealized lie, and the horse's skin is a symbol of the denial which trapped the mother:

> She let herself be wrapped in the freshly killed skin as if it was a lovely thing, a gift, the keepsake she always said it was, because she could only believe in gifts, only lovely stories … And this is why, I know now, for so long I had no story of my own. Because I thought my mother's life was my life, something to be told over and over again until the words became my own, when all the time she did not really know her own story, she was too afraid to tell it. And I am here, years later, and I have let myself live out her life, told her story so entire so even the ending is in me, and it is why for so long I had no story of my own. Because the ending of my mother's story is the beginning of my own. (204)

In a very literal sense, the ending of the story the mother is continually telling, being wrapped in the horse's skin and then abandoned, is indeed the beginning of the daughter's story, as it marks her own conception. But the daughter also is able to mark the end, the limits of her mother's stories in a way that the mother herself never could. The daughter is able finally to take ownership of her own memory and story:

> For the first time in my own life I felt the weight, the shape and colour and texture of my own memories, details of things I alone knew, the bright pieces to take with me into age. I remembered as something that belonged to me, the room my mother and I shared … For the first time the room was mine. (208–9)

The protagonist's mother was never able to find agency in her own story because she could never articulate the truth of her own life; instead, she trapped herself in "lovely stories." The daughter, however, can recognize the difference between a gift and the skin of a flayed horse, between love and abuse, and in doing so, she is able to revise rather than repeat her mother's story. The details and the memories remain the same, but now she understands them as belonging to her, not as merely being borrowed from her mother. Her new vision permeates her understanding of her life and childhood when she finally walks free out of the mansion in which she had been kept: "I turn the corner and pass the house where

I lived with my mother, years ago when I was a child. It is derelict now, and it seems strange I used to think it was beautiful" (213). It is her understanding that has changed. This change in understanding, this re-vision, restores her identity, and when the daughter makes her way back to the café that had been the only truly lovely memory of her childhood, the proprietor, who had tried to warn her against the man who would become her lover, recognizes her and "calls me by my name, no one else's name, not a father's name or a mother's name" (213). And yet, even this ending is not a complete abandonment of her mother's story—her new understanding and revision has brought her to the same shop that her mother had always loved.

If repetition is dangerous, even fatal, what, then, differentiates a revision from mere repetition, or, in Zipes's language, a duplicate? Revision, as much as it preserves old stories, as I have argued throughout this chapter, also demands strategic change, change that is consciously meaningful in order to be a true revision. But it is change in the context of a familiar cultural tale that produces the greatest meaning: we cannot throw out the old stories that formed us, giving us great pleasure and constraining us in equal measure. Even if we wished to, it is simply not possible. These stories are a part of us, and so they make us part of them. Denying this truth is merely a form of repression, and will give those tales greater power over us than we may wish.

How, then, do we make the changes that turn a duplicate into a revision? In the novel *Witches Abroad*, a pastiche of disrupted fairy tales, Terry Pratchett meditates on the nature and power of stories, the harm they can do, and ways we can change them. The novel is set in Pratchett's fictional Discworld, a flat world in which magic is rampant, and concerns Esme (Granny) Weatherwax, Discworld's most powerful witch. Esme and her coven, consisting of her best friend, Gytha (Nanny) Ogg and the younger Magrat, journey to Genua, a city modeled on New Orleans, in order to free its denizens from an enchantress bent on forcing them to live in an unchanging fairy tale. After a series of adventures that entangles Granny in various fairy tales, she is brought face to face with the enchantress, her estranged sister, Lily or Lilith, as she now calls herself, a fairy godmother intent on using the power of stories to control people's lives and inflict happy endings on others whether they want them or not. The resulting novel is funny, moving, and provocative.

Like many of Pratchett's novels, *Witches Abroad* begins not with an introduction to the characters but with an introduction to the philosophical themes informing the work. Thus within a few paragraphs, the reader is immersed in a theory of stories:

[S]tories are important.

People think that stories are shaped by people. In fact, it's the other way around.

Stories exist independently of their players. If you know that, the knowledge is power.

> Stories, great flapping ribbons of shaped space-time, have been blowing and uncoiling around the universe since the beginning of time. And they have evolved. The weakest have died and the strongest have survived and they have grown fat on the retelling ... stories, twisting and blowing through the darkness.

> And their very existence overlays a faint but insistent pattern on the chaos that is history. Stories etch grooves deep enough for people to follow in the same way that water follows certain paths down a mountainside. And every time fresh actors tread the path of a story, the groove runs deeper.

> This is called the theory of narrative causality and it means that a story, once started, *takes a shape*. It picks up all the vibrations of all the other workings of that story that have ever been.

> This is why history keeps on repeating all the time. (8)

Pratchett envisions stories as independent entities that are nourished by repetition in a cyclical fashion. The story pulls people into the tracks it has laid out, and the action of people following those tracks makes the grooves deeper and thus the power of the story to pull in and control people stronger. Prachett constructs an illuminating way of understanding the power of familiar stories. The daughter in *The Keepsake* follows her mother's story because it is familiar, and as she does so, it becomes more familiar and more natural. In a recent essay lamenting the death of Andrea Dworkin, Katha Pollitt discusses Dworkin's observation that our unconscious sense of "what feels right" is deeply permeated and shaped by ideologies of power. Thus we find ourselves enacting patterns that may not be in our own best interests or in the best interests of those who most need our support: this is the power of strong stories.

Pratchett also acknowledges the power of stories to bend other stories. Thus he writes that stories are constantly incorporating all other workings and versions, being affected by them and affecting them at the same time. Implicitly, then, if a story "picks up all the vibrations of all the other workings of that story that have ever been," once written, no story can ever be unwritten; once known, never fully forgotten.

Lily acknowledges that her power comes from repetition in her penultimate confrontation with Granny, saying, "And the *stories* ... to *ride* on stories ... to borrow the strength of them ... the *comfort* of them ... to be in the hidden centre of them ...Can you understand that? The sheer pleasure of seeing the patterns repeat themselves? I've always loved a pattern" (272). Lily derives her power and pleasure from forcing others to repeat stories while believing that she holds herself separate from them. She refers to herself as *riding* on stories, believing herself dominant over them, and also supported by them (perhaps here we might remember Maeve's skill at riding in *The Girl Who Trod on a Loaf*), while the people *in* the stories, we are told over and over again, are being *fed* to the stories; they are *inside*. Lily does say that she is in the "hidden centre," but previously Granny compared her to the ringmaster at a circus, standing in the center, cracking a whip, but not actually part of any of the acts. Still, the conflict suggests that Lily is confused about her actual relation to the stories, a conflict echoing the one she unwittingly states one page earlier when she tries to lure Granny over to her way of seeing things: "'But *we're* outside the stories,' said Lily. 'Me because I ... am the medium through which they happen, and you because you fight them. We're the ones in the middle. The free ones—'" (271). To Lily, outside becomes the same as the middle; she thinks she is outside the stories, but she is mistaken, and that is one of the reasons that she is defeated.

Lily feeds people to stories, and the stories grow more powerful for being fed. Pratchett emphasizes early the qualities that allow people to be consumed by stories, the pleasure of a contained narrative, a desire to identify with heroes, a desire for *order* (this last seems to be Lily's own motivation): "a thousand heroes have stolen fire from the gods. A thousand wolves have eaten grandmother, a thousand princesses have been kissed. A million unknowing actors have moved, unknowing, through the pathways of story" (8–9). I do not think that the repetition of the word "unknowing" is a mistake; rather, I think it is a deliberate emphatic device. People are consumed by stories because they are *unconscious*, unknowing, unaware, just as we can be unconsciously compelled to absorb and repeat patterns unless and until we force ourselves to become aware of what we are doing and why. On the Discworld, witches have achieved that awareness ("All witches are very conscious of stories. They can *feel* stories, in the same way that a bather in a little pool can feel the unexpected trout" [102]) and Lily has deliberately kept other witches out of Genua, so as to avoid the kind of disruption such awareness would bring.

By the time that Granny Weatherwax and her allies, Nanny Ogg and Magrat Garlick, arrive to try and battle the story Lily has constructed, it has become a juggernaut, combining more than one tale, and it is practically unstoppable. Part of the stories' power is the ability to absorb antagonists, and that is what Genua almost succeeds in doing to Granny, Nanny, and Magrat. Lily watches their approach in her magic mirror, but she is not even slightly worried, telling the Duc, whom she has set on the throne, "They're just ... part of the story. Don't worry about them. The story will just absorb them (64)." An attempt to disrupt the story from the outside would fail: Lily thinks to herself, "here in Genua was one story no-one could stop. It had momentum, this one. Try to stop it and it'd absorb you, make you part of its plot. She didn't have to do a thing. The story would do it for her" (146). An attempt to disrupt the story is actually *necessary* to the smooth progress of the story: "We shall need them for the story. It won't work properly unless they try to stop it" (147). And of course this is true; without antagonists, there is no story at all. Without wicked stepmothers, Cinderella and Snow White would have no plot; without the wolf, the story of Little Red Riding Hood becomes very dull indeed.

It is precisely because stories have this power to seduce and to force people into predetermined roles that they are so dangerous, according to Pratchett. Twice Granny says that Lily is "feeding" people to stories, flattening the depth and variety of humanity into prescribed characters. But stories also abandon people who do not fit their plots, creating injustice that way as well, just as ideologies flatten the complexities of some experiences and completely efface others: "Stories are not, on the whole, interested in swineherds who remain swineherds and poor and humble shoe-makers whose destiny is to die slightly poorer and much humbler" (236). While Granny is fighting Lily on behalf of those who are caged by stories, another witch, Mrs. Gogol, mounts an attack on Lily powered by those whom the stories have abandoned. Lily only notices such people when they fail to play their allotted bit parts acceptably, which she considers "crimes against narrative expectation" (75). So Lily condemns an innkeeper to the dungeons because he is not fat and does not have a big red face and a toymaker because he neither whistles while he works nor does he tell stories to children. Pratchett writes that "Lilith held a mirror up to Life, and chopped all the bits off Life that didn't fit" (75). Thus she limits people, or as Granny Weatherwax puts it, cages people, "You can't go around building a better world for people. Only people can build a better world for people. Otherwise it's just a cage. Besides, you don't build a better world by choppin' heads off and giving decent girls away to frogs" (250). The humor in Granny's final sentence belies the seriousness of the point she is making, which is that happiness and a better world cannot be achieved by forcing people to be other than what they desire to be. Lily is trying to force people to fit an ideal world/ story, rather than helping to make a world/story that accommodates people. Lily turns people into *parts*, and condemns them when they don't fit: "Sometimes she despaired. People just didn't seem to play their parts properly" (146). Essentially, as Granny says in the epigraph to this section, Lily tries to turn people into things: "She [Granny] hated everything that predestined people, that fooled them, that made them slightly less than human" (239). Just as does Carter in "The Lady in the House of Love," Pratchett writes of repetition as ultimately dehumanizing, in that it flattens out the variety of human experience and potential.

Finally, the effects of immersing herself in the repetition of stories redound onto Lily herself. In the first half of the book, Granny says darkly, "That's what happens ... You get too involved with stories, you get confused. You don't know what's really real and what isn't. And they get you in the end. They send you weird in the head" (114). Lily thinks that she is in control of the stories, but we have already discussed how they grow in power with each repetition, and eventually, they turn on her; a story finds a sequence on which to feed that is not under Lily's control, and when Baron Saturday/Samedi appears before her, bent on revenge, her magics do not avail her against him, and all she can do is run away. In her final confrontation with Granny, Lily is similarly paralyzed: "'But ... I ... I ... *I'm* the good one,' Lily murmured, her face pale with shock. 'I'm the good one. I can't lose. I'm the godmother. You're the wicked witch'" (276). But lose Lily does, at least in part because she believes that she can control stories and that she is outside of them. Stories end, but life goes on, and if you cannot think beyond unchanging repetition, like the mother in *The Keepsake*, you will eventually be left without a map:

And so stories end.

> The wicked witch is defeated, the ragged princess comes into her own, the kingdom is restored. Happy days are here again. Happy ever after. Which means that life stops here.

> Stories *want* to end. They don't care what happens next ...

> And stories just want *happy* endings. They don't give a damn who they're *for*. (267, 281)

A rigid understanding of how stories work and the parts people can play paralyzes Lily in the end, as she has been depending on the power of the story to save her, the good one (Lily imagines herself as both *outside* the stories and as the "good one"). But her control over the story is not as absolute as she has imagined, and so she has fallen victim to Granny's revision.

Granny fights Lily's repetition with revision, a revision that begins with consciousness of the stories and her own roles within them. I discussed above the importance of awareness and knowledge of stories to fighting repetition in this novel, and it is in part because of that need for knowledge that I do not believe that this novel is opposed to stories and tales; without an understanding and knowledge of how stories work, and of traditional tales in particular, Granny would not have been able to have successfully changed the story. Unknowingness, ignorance of one's own place in dominant ideologies, merely condemns you to repetition.

Granny becomes involved with the troubles in Genua through the agency of Desiderata Hollow, a neighbor witch and fairy godmother who had been fighting Lilith. Desiderata is dying, and has decided to pass the fight on to Granny. Speaking to Death, who has come to collect her, she says, "And it's [Lilith's plan] all going to happen. Because that's how stories have to work. And then I thought: I knows some people who makes stories work *their* way" (16). Desiderata does not choose Granny because she thinks Granny can destroy or erase Lilith's story, but because Granny can *rework* the story. Granny shapes the story rather than letting it shape her—she revises rather than repeats.

Granny, Nanny, and Magrat are able to overcome one of the minor stories they encounter on their way to Genua, a Sleeping Beauty tale, through sheer disruption:

> It had been like this for ten years. There was no sound in the—
> "Open up there!"
> "Bony fidy travelers seeking sucker!"
> —no sound in the—
> There was a tinkle of broken glass.
> "You've broken their window!"
> —*not a sound* in the—
> "You'll have to offer to pay for it, you know." (113)

The story attempts to reassert itself but is repeatedly disrupted by the witches' direct action, which contradicts the story's description. Closer to Genua, they encounter a Little Red Riding Hood story, and this time they use similarly direct action (escorting the little girl through the forest, smashing the wolf over the head with a frying pan) to end the story. Their verbal assessments of the stories are, in Kevin Paul Smith's words, "similar to that of feminist revisers, in that his revisions highlight the patriarchal assumptions underlying the classical fairytale and change the stories in order to make them more equitable" (133). In their first attempt to defeat Lily in Genua, they try using the same technique (destroying the Cinderella figure's dress, coach, etc.) to stop the story, but those actions are simply incorporated; Granny, Nanny, and Magrat have been absorbed into the story and they must learn to fight it from the inside rather than the outside. After their first interventions, the witches are enjoying a drink at the carnival, but Granny is not sanguine about their success because she is aware of how stories work:

> "It doesn't make a good story," said Granny.
>
> "Oh, bugger stories," said Nanny loftily. "You can always change a story."
>
> "Only at the right places," said Granny. (206)

Granny is unsettled because she knows that for revision or change to work, it cannot just override a story any old way. Revision demands a certain kind of change, a resonant change at a resonant moment; for revision to work in the unconscious, to affect our sense of "what feels right," it must strike similar narrative chords to the ones hit by the story itself. Old stories cannot just be done away with or smashed up; they will remain in our minds and hearts even if nowhere else. As Farah Mendlesohn says in her article on narrative in *The Unofficial Companion to the Novels of Terry Pratchett*, we must "use story to undermine story" itself. Lily can overcome the actions taken by Granny, Nanny, and Magrat, because such obstacles are easily absorbed by stories. They have been behaving as if they were external to the story, as they were to the Sleeping Beauty and Little Red Riding Hood stories they had encountered previously, but in Genua, they are part of the story, and they must change it from the inside out. Granny figures out how to do so during her first confrontation with Lily at the ball:

> Granny Weatherwax leaned against a wall in the shadows. All stories had a turning point, and it had to be close.
>
> She was good at getting into other people's minds, but now she had to get into hers. She concentrated. Down deeper ... past everyday thoughts and minor concerns, *faster, faster* ... through layers of deep cogitation ... deeper ... past things sealed off and crusted over, old guilts and congealed regrets, but there was no time for them now ... down ... and there ... the silver thread of the story. She'd been part of it, was part of it, so it had to be a part of her.
>
> It poured past. She reached out.

> She hated everything that predestined people, that fooled them, that made them slightly less than human.

> The story whipped along like a steel hawser. She gripped it.

> Her eyes opened in shock. Then she stepped forward. (239)

At this point, Granny grabs the glass slipper from the Duc and smashes it, breaking one piece of the story. This action disrupts the story whereas the previous ones had not because Granny has *used* her role in the story to find the story's weak point. She and the story run through each *other*; there is a reciprocal relationship between them created by Granny's consciousness of the story and her awareness of her own part in it. She finds the story in the deepest layers of herself, past what she had repressed—in fact, in her unconscious, and finding the story there allows her to awake and move forward. Instead of trying to keep herself outside of the story and attack it, she uses the fact that she is inside to fight it from the inside. What, after all, predestines us and fools us? All too often, it is our own unconscious and our own history. And once something that has been moving us from the unconscious has been pushed into the conscious mind, it is no longer a compulsion; it becomes a choice. The story, which had been pulling Granny along, is jerked off track when Granny pulls back. Once she has done so, Lily's story is violently disrupted, and never quite comes back under Lily's control; although she takes the witches to the dungeons, the story line that Granny broke finds its way to the Baron and eventually returns to destroy Lily.

Early in the novel, Pratchett suggests that successful challenge to a story must come from someone already part of it, fed to it. In the opening meditation, he writes that "It takes a special kind of person to fight back, to become the bicarbonate of soda of narrative space-time" (8). Later on, Lily wonders what the opposite of a fairy godmother would be and concludes that "she wouldn't be a *bad* fairy godmother, because that's just a good fairy godmother seen from a different viewpoint. The opposite would be someone who was poison to stories, and, thought Lilith, quite the most evil creature in the world" (146). Poison can only work, though, once it has been absorbed. Revision changes stories from the inside out. Freud posits that the repeated, self-defeating patterns that so many of us engage in are compulsions that arise as the unconscious re-creates failed relational and behavioral patterns in an attempt to make the pattern work *this* time. The principle behind talk therapy is that a thorough exploration of the roots of such compulsions and repetitions in a safe atmosphere will allow the unconscious to become conscious, allowing one to understand what it is that drives one's behavior. One can learn to recognize the beginning of such patterns and to intervene in them, to revise them rather than repeat them. This process is what Granny Weatherwax engages in when she wrenches the story out of joint by grasping it in her soul. And while she can't undo Lilith's stories, she can allow them to diverge into pathways that Lilith had never charted.

Chapter 4
Through the Looking Glass:
Mirrors, Fantasy, and Reality

Lily Weatherwax accomplishes her manipulations of stories and via them, of people, by means of mirrors, charged objects in both fairy tales and in feminist thought. Mirrors can alienate and estrange women from themselves, turning them into objects on display—but then who is the subject looking into the mirror? As well as estranging, is a mirror not singular in allowing one to be both subject and object simultaneously? The word "reflection" perfectly captures that dual state, as it means not only "An image or counterpart thus produced [by the action of a mirror or other polished surface]" but also "The action of turning (back) or fixing the thoughts on some subject; meditation, deep or serious consideration"; not only outer appearance but also inner thoughts.

While the mirror is not as prevalent a motif in fairy tales and myth as is the mother-daughter relationship, it makes several memorable appearances. The fairy tales of "Snow White" and Hans Christian Andersen's "The Snow Queen" both revolve around a wicked queen who uses an enchanted looking-glass; the Beast gives Beauty a magic mirror in which she can see what is happening at her father's home while she is in the Beast's castle; and of course Narcissus dies of a broken heart after falling in love with his own, unattainable reflection. Most cultures, including almost all Western European cultures, have long traditions of folk wisdom surrounding mirrors and reflections, usually having to do with the mirror's ability to foretell the future and/or to steal one's soul.

Mirrors are even more important in contemporary revisions of fairy tales, where they turn up in unexpected places, such as in the glass of Snow White's coffin or Cinderella's shoes. They do not appear in all fairy-tale revisions, but when they do, they are often the engine of magical power that drives the entire story. Here, I examine the relationship between mirrors and the element of fantasy in revisions of fairy tales, using a few key fairy-tale revisions to argue that mirrors represent a form of fantastic tale closely identified with female power and creativity.

These revisions take up a trope charged within second-wave feminism, but provide a far more positive valance to that trope. Scholars such as Luce Irigaray, and Sandra Gilbert and Susan Gubar have detailed the ways in which mirrors in literature can stand for entities hostile to women in general and to the female protagonist in particular, but in the revisions under study, the mirror reflects women's fantasies, experiences, and desires under conditions often hostile to their expression. In this way, mirrors not only represent fantasy stories in general, but also specifically stories of female fantasy, desire, and transformation.

There is a long historical association between femininity and the trope of the mirror, so strong that in her comprehensive and fascinating history of the mirror, Sabine Melchior-Bonnet asserts that "[f]emininity is a creation of the mirror" (214). Melchior-Bonnet is referring not merely to the artifice contemporary women are expected to employ in creating a socially acceptable "feminine" appearance, but also to the ways in which a misogynist culture identifies the evils of womankind with the evils of the looking-glass: "From the thirteenth century on, Eve is depicted brandishing a mirror" (187, 200). Eve's connection with mirrors suggests the medieval emblem of *vanitas*, always depicted as a woman gazing at herself in a mirror.[1] This long association tends to be one of derision and scorn for both women and their mirrors; as is so often the case, women are made scapegoats for failings common to both sexes as well as bearing the blame for living up to patriarchal views of their worth, by valuing their own beauty. In turn, then, many feminist critics have justifiably developed analyses that focus on the mirror's role in subjugating women. Writers representing two different schools of second-wave feminist criticism find in mirrors a perfect metaphor for patriarchal subordination of women.

Sandra Gilbert and Susan Gubar use the mirror as a figure for patriarchy, for women's oppression by men's ideals and fears. In their analysis of Snow White, they describe the mirror as "the patriarchal ... judgment that rules the Queen's— and every woman's—self-evaluation ... [H]aving assimilated the meaning of her own sexuality ... the woman has internalized the King's rules: his voice resides now in her own mirror, her own mind" (38). The mirror is "the male-inscribed literary text" in which she finds only "those eternal lineaments fixed on her like a mask to conceal her dreadful and bloody link to nature" (15).[2] Luce Irigaray invokes the mirror throughout her work for a number of purposes, but it is often negative: in "The Looking Glass, from the Other Side," a woman on the other side of the mirror describes herself as stuck, paralyzed, and frozen; in *Speculum of the Other Woman*, Irigaray argues that men have used women as mirrors in order to validate their own worth, each man making "her into a reflection of himself, thereby denying her a subjectivity of her own ... [Women] must liberate themselves from negative definitions and mirror functions and start to assign a positive subjectivity to themselves" (54).[3] But the mirror has the potential to fulfill far more positive functions for women as well. Just as fairy tales, dismissed by certain second-wave feminists as inherently patriarchal,[2] were reclaimed and

---

[1]   My experience concurs with Nancy Mitford's when she writes, "I have often noticed that when women look at themselves in every reflection, and take furtive peeps into their hand looking-glasses, it is hardly ever, as is generally supposed, from vanity, but much more often from a feeling that all is not quite as it should be" (quoted in LaBelle 18).

[2]   For a thorough discussion of very early second-wave analyses of the fairy tale as a genre, please see Chapter 2 of Vanessa Joosen's *Critical and Creative Perspectives on Fairy Tales: An Intertextual Dialogue Between Fairy-Tale Scholarship and Postmodern Retellings*.

retold by writers contemporary to said feminists, so too is the mirror, associated with sinful women, being reclaimed by those same writers as a potential source of power, self-creation, and magic.

Because Angela Carter's *The Bloody Chamber* is in many ways the foundational text for writers of feminist revisions of fairy tales, I will first examine the symbolic use of mirrors in three of her stories and then draw upon that analysis in order to explore texts by Kelly Link, Terry Pratchett, and Tanith Lee, all of whom develop connections suggested in Carter's work.

Angela Carter, the Mirror, and the Fairy Tale

Angela Carter's collection of fairy-tale revisions, *The Bloody Chamber*, is an ideal case study, not only demonstrating the significance of the mirror in her own work, but bringing together the myriad ways mirrors are used in the field of fairy-tale revisions in her time and in the time of her artistic descendants. Carter is a particularly self-aware writer of fairy tales, having translated Charles Perrault's work, edited two collections of fairy tales, and maintained an interest in literary and psychoanalytic theory. Her collection demonstrates both the patriarchal hostility of the mirror to feminine subjectivity and the ways in which the mirror can support the development of that subjectivity. The title story, "The Bloody Chamber," a revision of Bluebeard, is a perfect illustration of the Gilbert and Gubar/Irigarayan model of mirrors. Mirrors in the story are ubiquitous, and they are associated with the Marquis and the financial, sexual, and physical power he wields over the protagonist. The first mention of mirrors in the story comes when the protagonist recounts a night at the opera with the sadistic Marquis who is to become her husband, and the mirror turns her into an object or an animal, trapping her: "I saw him watching me in the gilded mirrors with the assessing eye of a connoisseur inspecting horseflesh, or even of a housewife in the market, inspecting cuts on the slab" (115). The mirror turns the narrator from a shy musician into a tame animal or a piece of meat by revealing the Marquis's perception of her. Furthermore, the mirrors' "gilding" suggests the gilded cage of song, a connection strengthened by the protagonist's statement later on that she had been "bought with a handful of coloured stones and the pelts of dead beasts" (122). In the mirror, opulence has turned her into flesh on display, just as the corpses of the Marquis's dead wives have been put on display in his secret chamber. In this story, the mirrors are extensions of the Marquis, watching the young woman when he is away, as she finds after her discovery of the dead wives: "I could not take refuge in my bedroom, for that retained the memory of his presence trapped in the fathomless silvering of his mirrors" (132–3). The bedroom may be hers, but the mirrors are his.

Mirrors not only turn the narrator into a caged animal, but they also estrange her from herself. Upon reaching her bedroom in her husband's odd, sea-surrounded castle for the first time, she is surprised to see

> Our bed. And surrounded by so many mirrors! Mirrors on the walls, in stately
> frames of contorted gold, that reflected more white lilies than I'd ever seen in my
> life before. He'd filled the room with them, to greet the bride, the young bride.
> The young bride, who had become that multitude of girls I saw in the mirrors ...
> "See," he said, gesturing towards those elegant girls. "I have acquired a whole
> harem for myself!" (118)

The young woman finds herself multiplied, one of a cavalcade of
indistinguishable wives, adumbrating her later discovery of her future in the room
of murdered brides.[4] Her husband's language underlines the ownership he had
contemplated in the earlier mirror. Whereas before he had been contemplating a
purchase, he has now "acquired" the goods. The juxtaposition of the Marquis's
mirrors and the marital bed underline the protagonist's status as sexual object, as
one whose experience of sex will be as something that is done *to* her, rather than
as something she does.

Using the mirrors, the narrator distances herself from what is happening to her
during her first sexual encounter with her husband: "I could not meet his eye and
turned my head away, out of pride, out of shyness, and watched a dozen husbands
approach me in a dozen mirrors and slowly, methodically, teasingly, unfasten the
buttons of my jacket and slip it from my shoulders" (118). The mirrors provide the
young woman with a mechanism of dissociation; made profoundly uncomfortable
by her husband's sexual manipulation even as she is aroused by it, she takes refuge
in becoming an observer, in distancing herself from the events she is witnessing
in the mirror. She is not feeling; she is watching. The mirror has estranged
her as a subject, watching, from herself as an object, being watched—and not
just any object, either. As Mary Kaiser points out, "the bride perceives herself
as a pornographic object," noting the protagonist's comparison of herself to an
engraving shown to her by her then-fiancé (33). This estrangement is made even
clearer when the heroine has sex for the first time. She remains completely passive,
describing the encounter as a series of things her husband is doing *to* her, until the
moment of consummation, when she breaks from first-person narration into third-,
saying that "A dozen husbands impaled a dozen brides while the mewing gulls
swung on invisible trapezes in the empty air outside" (121). Here, the narrator
not only distances herself from her own experiences by using the mirrors, but she
also underlines this distance by the sudden switch into third-person narration, as
though what is happening is happening to someone else, to the 12 girls she sees in
the mirror, rather than to her. Unlike Lacan's formulation, in which the (implicitly
male) subject's sense of self is formed by the coherent image of himself that he
sees in the mirror, here the female subject's sense of self is undermined by the
reducing effect of that image, a comment perhaps on how often women have been
reduced to objects of the gaze, rather than subjects in their own right. In this way,
Carter suggests that the mirror is not an indifferent reflector; it is more akin to the
cinematic gaze described by second-wave critic Laura Mulvey.

The mirrors are integral to the sexual play between the heroine and her husband
from the very beginning, but that play is always on his terms and in his eyes.

Even when attempting to save her own life, the protagonist offers up her masochism using the bedroom mirrors: "I forced myself to be seductive, I saw myself, pale, pliant as a plant that begs to be trampled underfoot, a dozen vulnerable appealing girls reflected in as many mirrors, and I saw how he almost failed to resist me. If he had come to me in bed, I would have strangled him, then" (137). The mirrors never reflect the protagonist as an active being, or allow the self that is seen to unite with the self that is seeing, and here, her dissembling attempt to use the masochistic role the Marquis and the mirrors have assigned her to save herself fails: the Marquis does not see what she wants him to; he does insist on seeing the fatal key; he attempts to murder his wife.

Mirrors are destructive to the young heroine of "The Bloody Chamber," estranging her from herself and her experiences as well as emphasizing her sexual passivity and economic vulnerability, illustrating Carter's assertion in *The Sadeian Woman* that "sexual relations between men and women always render explicit the nature of social relations in the society in which they take place and, if described explicitly, will form a critique of those relations" (20). Carter was intent on highlighting the social construction of female masochism and sexual passivity by bringing to the fore the material and economic conditions that have prevented women from interacting with men on equal footing, forcing them to sublimate their own sexuality into a male fantasy simply in order to survive. But what about the cultural and psychological fall-out from such a history? The protagonist of this story is genuinely sexually aroused by her husband's behavior and her own status as an object; indeed it is the very seduction of the reader and the protagonist to which Avis Lewallen objects, claiming that Carter's story merely replicates the structures of patriarchal pornography (151).[3] The mirrors reveal her own potential enjoyment of the kind of destructive sexuality offered by her husband: "for the first time in my innocent and confined life, I sensed in myself a potentiality for corruption that took my breath away." Kathleen Manley argues that the "mirrors, by providing opportunities to see herself as others see her, allow the protagonist to begin to a have a more complete sense of herself as a subject" (85). While I disagree, and think instead that the mirrors awaken the protagonist to a sense of herself as an *object*, it is my belief that Manley is picking up on an important function of the mirrors: for women under patriarchy, sexual maturation is intertwined with consciousness of oneself as an object. The protagonist is awakened to her own sexual pleasure by the mirrors, but they reveal early on the heroine's potential fate if she loses herself completely in their proffered passivity: she would become a cut of meat on the slab, a corpse like her literal predecessors. The mirrors in "The Bloody Chamber" illuminate Carter's observation: "To be the *object* of desire is to be defined in the passive case. To exist in the passive case is to die in the passive case—that is, to be killed" (*Sadeian Woman* 76).

---

[3]   For a summary of feminist critical responses to Carter's fairy-tale revisions, please see Chapter 3 of Jessica Tiffin's *Marvelous Geometry: Narrative and Metafiction in Modern Fairy Tale.*

If "The Bloody Chamber" stood alone in Carter's collection in dealing with mirrors, the story would be an indictment of the part mirrors play in objectifying women, even to themselves. But Carter's project is a multi-faceted one. The very multiplicity of her perspective is what troubles Patricia Duncker, who sees Carter's divergent meditations as inconsistency, but Mary Kaiser understands that multiplicity as part of the point. For her, Carter's various approaches to gender relations in her tales are "a reflection of [her] project … to portray sexuality as a culturally relative phenomenon" (33). The collection ends with "Wolf-Alice," a tale in which the ability to see and recognize one's reflection marks one's entrance into knowledge, self-awareness, and humanity.[4] "Wolf-Alice" opens with a girl raised by wolves living in the castle of an undead Duke who lives on corpses. Neither the ghastly Duke nor the girl, Alice (clearly an allusion to Lewis Carroll's *Through the Looking-glass and What Alice Found There*), is fully human. Like a vampire, the Duke casts no reflection, and while the girl has one, she does not understand what she is seeing when she looks in the mirror, and so for all practical intents and purposes neither one truly has a reflection. The mirror catalyzes and signifies Alice's emergence into human consciousness after which she is able to bring the Duke into humanity as well, an achievement signified by his reflection finally appearing in the mirror on his bedroom wall, a point made by Sarah Sceats when she writes that "As a result of Alice's caring attention the Duke is brought into focus, literally, in the mirror. He thus achieves an identity" (145).

In Carter's story, it is the man and not the girl who finds himself on the wrong side of the looking-glass: "[His] eyes open to devour the world in which he sees, nowhere, a reflection of himself; he passed through the mirror and now, henceforward, lives as if upon the other side of things" (222). What does it mean to live on the other side of things? In Carter's story, it means to eat corpses, gaining life from death, to have everything familiar reversed, and not to see evidence of oneself anywhere. Carter alludes to the meditations of Lewis Carroll's Alice about living on the other side of things when she immediately follows the above-quoted passage with the words "Spilt, glistering milk of moonlight" (222). In *Through the Looking-Glass*, Alice wonders aloud "Perhaps Looking-glass milk isn't good to drink" (142) leaving open the question whether or not things that are food on this side of glass would be edible on the other, or whether a visitor would have to eat what is forbidden to us—to reverse our order of being so that he transforms our corpses, our death, into his life. To live on the wrong side of the mirror is to become a monster.

Like Carroll's Alice, Wolf-Alice is fascinated by the mirror, and in the beginning of their stories, neither girl seems to have quite grasped the imitative, two-dimensional nature of the glass. Wolf-Alice's realization of the meaning of reflection is connected to her menarche and maturation. Wolf-Alice initially understands her reflection as a playmate: "She rubbed her head against her reflected

---

[4]   Such a test is commonly used to measure whether or not animals have a sense of self; chimpanzees and dolphins regularly recognize themselves in the mirror (Keenan xi).

face, to show that she felt friendly towards it, and felt a cold, solid, immovable surface between herself and she" (225). Carter's confused syntax reflects Wolf-Alice's own confusion about the nature of her reflection and thus about her own identity. Wolf-Alice looks outward, thinking she is exploring her surroundings, only to find that she is looking inward as the reflection's "fidelity to her very movement finally woke her up to the regretful possibility that her companion was, in fact, no more than a particularly ingenious variety of the shadow she cast on sunlit grass" (226).

When Wolf-Alice finds that her playmate is only a reflection, "A little moisture leaked from the corners of her eyes, yet her relation with the mirror was now far more intimate since she knew she saw herself within it" (226). She then puts on a wedding dress that "the Duke had tucked away behind the mirror" and knows that she has "put on the visible sign of her difference from them [the wolves]" (226). Becoming human requires Alice to understand the mystery of the mirror, and to find out what is hidden behind it, for behind the mirror is not the other room with the companion that the mirror appears to frame, but a dusty wall against which is hidden clothing, the symbol of knowledge (Adam and Eve fashion clothing for themselves after eating fruit from the Tree of Knowledge of Good and Evil) as well as the human separation from animals. Wolf-Alice becomes human, or at least unbeastly, when she understands the nature of mirrors and finds what is hidden behind them.

Wolf-Alice's power to bring both herself and her beastly landlord into the human compass is marked by the mirror. The evening after she becomes human, the Duke is shot and comes home injured:

> The lucidity of the moonlight lit the mirror propped against the red wall; the rational glass, the master of the visible, impartially recorded the crooning girl. As she continued her ministrations, this glass, with infinite slowness, yielded to the reflexive strength of its own material construction. Little by little, there appeared within it, like the image on photographic paper that emerges, first, a formless web of tracery ... , then a firmer yet still shadowed outline until at last as vivid as real life itself, as if brought into being by her soft, moist, gentle tongue, finally, the face of the Duke. (227–8)

The connection between the mirror and moonlight is an ongoing motif in this story, and in this passage the moon and the red wall underscore the importance of Wolf-Alice's menstruation in bringing her to human consciousness, and in her bringing the Duke to humanity as well (a preceding sentence tells us that Wolf-Alice is distressed by "his wound that does not smell like her wound"). Alice and the Duke travel similar paths: she becomes human when she learns that the figure in the mirror is none other than herself, and his entrance into humanity occurs when he, too, appears in the mirror. Further, "the rational glass, master of the visible" must reflect the visible but can only reflect what is there, that which exists; far from being the bearer of mysticism or irrationality, Alice's empirical experiments in coming to consciousness are the most rational actions possible in the Gothic world of her story. Rationality (reasoning, thinking), femininity, and humanity are all inextricably linked at the tale's conclusion.

In Carter's lush and allusive prose, we have almost all the elements of the significance of mirror-as-fantasy. The mirror is essential to an understanding of femininity, humanity, and the self; it is closely tied to magic; and it troubles the boundaries between reality and fantasy, self and other by creating Alice's illusion of a playmate, which is nonetheless real enough to comfort her, and the illusory "harem" into which the protagonist of "The Bloody Chamber" finds herself refracted.

These two stories, which bookend the collection, seem to be reflections of each other, so that the stories themselves become mirrors, an observation made by Elizabeth Wanning Harries in *Twice Upon a Time: Women Writers and the History of the Fairy* Tale, when she notes that

> "Wolf-Alice" is in many ways a reversed, wavering mirror image of the first story, "The Bloody Chamber." ... The life-giving, transforming mirror of "Wolf-Alice" redeems, or at least gives us an alternative for, the dozens of mirrors in "The Bloody Chamber" that cruelly reflect and multiply the desires of the monstrous husband and his supposedly innocent bride. Carter suggests that it is the site or position of the mirror that matters. (159)

The central situation of each story is that of a young girl who leaves the home of her mother and finds herself living in the castle of a monstrous nobleman. Both stories have mirrors, white dresses, and blood-stained sheets among their central symbolic elements. Yet, despite these common elements, the stories themselves are very different, not only in their outcomes, but in what they suggest about relations between the sexes and about how it is possible for a woman to come to terms with her own sexuality under patriarchy. It is this simultaneous similarity and difference that I would argue identifies the stories as mirrors. What one sees in even the most perfect mirror is not a perfect replica but a re-arrangement: a reflection is the *converse* of the original image, in which every element is present, but reversed. In the most perfect mirror, one sees one's converse; in any other mirror, one sees a distorted converse. Therefore, the two stories' differences— even the ways in which they are opposites—are *essential* to understanding them as mirror-images of each other. Each story is the other's converse, and thus its reflection; "Wolf-Alice" is "The Bloody Chamber" in the looking-glass, and vice versa, and the stories themselves are mirrors.

Carter presents the mirror as fantastic tale itself in the story "The Tiger's Bride." This story is a revision of "Beauty and the Beast" in which the heroine's father gambles her away to a Beast who is also lord of the Italian village they are visiting. The Beast promises her untold riches and immediate return to her father if she allows him to see her naked, but the protagonist refuses, scorning the pretense that in a society where women are chattel, she is any different from a prostitute. She watches most of her story unfold in mirrors and relates it to us. Her father loses her during a game of cards, and while she is present at the game, her opinion is not sought; she has no agency in this situation, and all she can do is watch:

... the mirror above the table gave me back his [her father's] frenzy, my impassivity, the withering candles, the emptying bottles, the coloured tide of the cards as they rose and fell, the still mask that concealed all the features of The Beast but for the yellowed eyes that strayed, now and then, from his unfurled hand towards myself. (154–5)

The scene is set and the players, of whom the daughter is not one, described through a mirror, and as we read the story printed on the page, so the daughter reads her fate in the mirror: "My father said he loved me yet he staked his daughter on a hand of cards. He fanned them out; in the mirror, I saw wild hope light up his eyes ... A queen, a king, an ace. I saw them in the mirror" (156). This game of cards is a central event; it opens the story and is the excuse for all that follows, and we, like the daughter, know it only through a mirror. The daughter, the narrator of the story, is a reader for most of the tale, but rather than reading her story from books, she reads it from the mirror. The girl does not see herself in the mirror, but rather than allowing her to escape the mirror-trap of the "The Bloody Chamber," in which the protagonist learns to see herself as an object and to dissociate from her immediate experiences, being confined to the role of watcher places her in a similarly detached and passive position, as she is excluded and distanced from the actions that determine her fate. Once she arrives at the Beast's palace, she continues to read her story in the magic mirror held by the automaton-maid provided for her: "I saw within it [the mirror] not my own face but that of my father, as if I had put on his face when I arrived at The Beast's palace as the discharge of his debt. What, you self-deluding fool, are you crying still?" (162). This mirror reveals not only events which she would otherwise be unable to see, but also her status in this world: whenever the girl looks into this magic mirror, she sees her father's face before she sees her own. In the patriarchal world she inhabits, she exists only as an extension of her father; she has no self to see that can rival that status.

Poignantly, even through the mirror, she is denied any recognition of her own personhood by her father, any genuine emotional interchange. After being told that she may return to her father, she looks in the mirror "but it was in the midst of one of its magic fits again and I did not see my own face in it but that of my father; at first I thought he smiled at me. Then I saw he was smiling with pure gratification" (167). The Beast has recompensed her father for the vast wealth he lost at cards; her father is not smiling at her, but instead with happiness at his renewed socio-economic status. Indeed, his daughter's status as but another commodity is indicated by a note reading "The young lady will arrive immediately," which she at first misinterprets to refer to a prostitute (167). This alienation from her father—his smile is not an emotional connection but merely a response to a re-accumulation of wealth—is followed by the girl noting that "When I looked in the mirror again ... all I saw was a pale, hollow-eyed girl whom I scarcely recognized ... my maid, whose face was no longer the spit of my own, continued bonnily to beam" (167). Here, the mirror finally reveals to the young woman the person she has become, a person quite distinct from the literally heartless, cosmetics-wielding clockwork girl who holds the mirror out for her. Her story had taken place in the mirror, and now she is leaving that story behind. "The Tiger's Bride" ends shortly thereafter, with the transformation of the girl into a jungle cat. In this story, one of the mirror's many functions is to tell the story, and to identify the woman watching events unfold in the mirror with the woman reading the story; the mirror is her book.

The Book as Mirror in the Field of Fairy-Tale Revisions

> The robber girl's boots cover the scars on your feet. When you look at these scars, you can see the outline of the journey you made. Sometimes mirrors are maps, and sometimes maps are mirrors. Sometimes scars tell a story, and maybe someday you will tell this story to a lover. The soles of your feet are stories—hidden in the black boots, they shine like mirrors.
>
> — "Travels with the Snow Queen," Kelly Link (119)

Subsequent writers of fairy-tale revisions have picked up on the role the mirror plays in "The Tiger's Bride," expanding it so that the mirror comes to represent women's fantasy stories in many revisions of fairy tales. Among the many recurrences of the motif, Kelly Link's "Travels with the Snow Queen," Terry Pratchett's *Witches Abroad*, and Tanith Lee's *White as Snow* in particular show how strongly Carter's work has affected our thinking about fantasy, femininity, and mirrors. The passage opening this section occurs close to the end of Kelly Link's short story, a revision of the Hans Christian Andersen tale in which a young girl searches for her kidnapped friend; in Link's version, Gerda searches for a vanished, unkind lover. As Gerda travels, she reflects on her journey, her unhappy relationship with Kay, and her decision to leave him where he is and go into business with the Snow Queen. Gerda's feet have been scarred because, in searching for Kay,

> The map that you [Gerda] are using is a mirror. You are always pulling the bits out of your bare feet, the pieces of the map that broke off and fell on the ground as the Snow Queen flew overhead in her sleigh ...
>
> ... When you are pulling the shards of the Snow Queen's looking-glass out of your feet ... you tell yourself to imagine how it felt when Kay's eyes, Kay's heart were pierced by shards of the same mirror. Sometimes it's safer to read maps with your feet. (100)

While for Link's Gerda the mirror is a map which she follows to find Kay, that same map is a story to the reader, as he or she follows Gerda's travels not with a mirror-map, but via the story itself. Most of the story is told in the second person, and the person being addressed is Gerda, so Gerda and the reader are closely identified. This identification results in Gerda's mirror-as-map becoming the reader's mirror-as-story—"Travels with the Snow Queen" itself. That mirror becomes a part of Gerda. At the end of the story, the scars left by the shattered mirror turn Gerda's own feet into a simultaneous mirror-map-story: "When you look at these scars, you can see the outline of the journey you made ... The soles of your feet are stories—hidden in the black boots, they shine like mirrors ... You tell the geese that your feet are maps *and* your feet are mirrors" (120). Gerda's feet are maps, mirrors, and stories. She incarnates the story through the medium of the mirror, and tells her story to the reader and the geese. The mirror reflects her shifting consciousness with respect to her own story, as she comes to realize that she does not want to free Kay after all, but chooses to make a new life by partnering with the Snow Queen.

Terry Pratchett's *Witches Abroad*, a pastiche of fairy tales, also represents the mirror as a story itself. The action of the story proper, our first glimpse of the main characters, is introduced by the following:

Look into the mirror ...

... further ...

... to an orange light on a cold mountaintop, thousands of miles away from the vegetable warmth of that swamp. (11)

Thus the novel itself becomes a mirror to "show" us the events of the story. Though we are actually reading a book, we are told that we are looking into a mirror—reading a story and looking into a magic mirror become the same thing. The parallels between the reader and/or the writer, and a woman looking into a mirror are further suggested when Lilith, the aforementioned witch-queen, uses mirrors to spy on the rest of the world:

Lilith sat in her tower, using a mirror, sending her own image out to scan the world ... Wherever there was a sparkle on a wave crest, wherever there was a sheet of ice, wherever there was a mirror or a reflection then Lilith knew she could see out. You didn't need a magic mirror. Any mirror would do, if you knew how to use it. (27)

Mirrors allow Lilith to see any place at any given moment, just as fantasy as a genre frees the reader and the writer from the constraints of the realist story. If the book is a mirror, and the earlier quotation suggests that it is, then the writer must be Lilith. Thus the book and the mirror are not only conflated into one, but the mirror becomes expressive of Lilith's plans and fantasies, as she uses mirror-magic to inflict her will on a captive populace.

Just as Terry Pratchett turns his novel into a mirror, so too does Tanith Lee in *White as Snow*, a novel-length revision of "Snow White" set in a patriarchal, violent world. The novel opens with the statement that "Once upon a time, in winter, there was a mirror." The Grimm Brothers' version of the tale of Snow White opens with "Once upon a time in the middle of winter, when snowflakes were falling like feathers from the sky, a queen was sitting and sewing" (196). For Lee, the mirror takes the place of the queen as the primary mover in the tale (in the earliest version of Snow White collected by the Brothers Grimm, this first queen who bears the princess is the very same queen who persecutes her later on). The indication is that this story is the mirror's story. Like Pratchett, Lee then turns the novel into a mirror. The reader "sees" the pivotal events of one evening through the mirror; in this extended passage, the mirror becomes the story: "The mirror saw the Hunter King invoke the night, and the spirits of the dead who were, that night, there to dance with them" (121). The reader reads what the mirror sees. The phrase "The mirror saw" is repeated four times in two pages, underlining the reader's dependence on the mirror for the story—rather than allowing text to be the medium through which we experience the story, the novel repeatedly tells us that we are watching the events in a mirror. As in Pratchett's novel, text becomes mirror and mirror, text.

The connections among Lilith's chamber of mirrors, Arpazia's magic mirror, and the art of writing are not only to be found in Pratchett's Discworld or Lee's Belgra Demitu; they are also historical fact. *Les contes des fées* (literally, fairy tales), baroque, glittering tales written and read by seventeenth-century French noblewomen, are the sources for some of our best-loved tales. Marina Warner has argued persuasively that these writers often figured themselves in the tales they wrote as fairy godmothers (215–7, 233–5)—and indeed, Pratchett's Lilith, who, I have argued above, is a figure for the writer/reader, is an official fairy godmother with the wand to prove it. *Les contes des fées* often feature magic mirrors, perhaps unsurprising in tales written during the century when the large mirror was an opulent, novel object of status, wonder, and beauty that no noble or bourgeois family would be without—making crystal-clear sheet glass was difficult, expensive, and a closely guarded secret. Indeed, according to Sabine Melchior-Bonnet in her history of the mirror, "Each era chooses a particular social venue in accordance with its tastes and ways of thinking and feeling. In the seventeenth century, the *cabinet lambrisse*, or paneled study, was the new standard, and the crystal mirror its crowning adornment" (140). These studies were paneled with mirrors on every wall, not unlike Lilith's chamber of mirrors in *Witches Abroad*. Lilith is a fairy godmother who obtains her power through mirrors—a powerful figure for the writer of fairy tales, working in a mirrored chamber that symbolizes her social and economic power.

To Lilith, stories and mirrors are the very same thing. Contemplating the differences between herself and her sister, Lilith thinks "Esme Weatherwax had never understood stories. She'd never understood how *real* reflections were." (63). Much of the novel concerns the difference between reality and fantasy: both stories and reflections are representations of real life, representations that ultimately lack physical substance, but can be used to control people. This is especially true of mirrors, the secret of Lilith's magic powers. The novel explains: "You can use two mirrors like this, if you know the way of it: you set them so that they reflect each other. For if images *can* steal a bit of you, then images of images can amplify you, feeding you back on yourself, giving you power" (47); This trick has intensified Lilith's considerable magical talents into an amazing amount of power, like a concave mirror focusing the sun's rays. When Esme's friend Nanny Ogg realizes that Lilith has the power to transform animals into human beings, she is amazed and says that she herself could not do that. Granny replies "She didn't used to be able to either, for more'n a few seconds. That's what using mirrors does for you" (193). Controlling reflections allows Lilith to control real creatures, just as controlling stories allows her to control real lives. Mirrors and stories are two sides of the same coin—in the Discworld, they are practically the same thing.

In *Herself Beheld: The Literature of the Looking Glass*, Jenijoy La Belle examines the history of the literary connection between books and mirrors. She finds that books and mirrors have long been linked—and gendered as well. She argues that rather than being simply in opposition, the book and the mirror are also in apposition, that in literature, women search in the mirror for what men seek in books. Furthermore, she finds that when women turn to books, they acquire similar kinds of knowledge as they do when consulting a mirror. Despite the similarities between books and mirrors, however, La Belle concludes that ultimately the mirror is a far more restrictive, narrow way of knowing in the literature she has studied. I would suggest that such a conclusion is due to La Belle's own focus on realist literature. While her book is comprehensive within that field, the potential for the mirror to show more than one sign has already been deliberately excluded. Within the genre of fantasy literature, the mirror can hold power and knowledge on a par with any book, and so the correspondence between book and mirror becomes much more powerful.

And yet ... Mrs. Gogol, a voodoo witch who fights Lilith, is scornful of her powers. She says that "All anyone gets in a mirror is themselves" (79). How, then, can mirrors function as stories? Perhaps because, like mirrors, stories need to reflect in order to communicate. Consider Freud's essay "Creative Writers and Day-Dreaming," in which he argues that creative writing is a form of fantasy/ daydreaming made enjoyable by artistic disguise of the essential egoism of the fantasy. Nonetheless, he insists, the egoism is there, not only in the writer's identification with one or several characters, but in the godlike powers the writer wields over the characters, setting, and narrative itself. Thus a piece of writing is *both* a communication with a larger world *and* a reflection of the mind that created it. A similar dynamic is in play for the reader. The significance of the novel to the reader is dependent on the reader finding him or herself in the text—that is, in order for a piece of writing to open up new vistas for a reader, or even to give the reader pleasure, it must reflect some of what already exists inside the reader. Thus the communicating function of the mirror/story is only effective if the reflection in the mirror/story is recognizable, even if only to the subconscious. Warren Motte argues that

> reading can be conceived as a kind of mirror-gazing ... among the many things we "see" in literature, one of the salient things is *ourselves*, writ large ... In doing so, we construct a version of ourselves, one whom we may sometimes recognize immediately, sometimes by dint of effort, and sometimes not at all. (785–6)

The corollary is that mirror needs to reflect in order to allow communication.

Mirrors and reflections are stories and/or tell stories (often these two aspects run together)—but what happens when a "real" character becomes a reflection? I would argue that she becomes a character in *someone else's story*—she loses her agency and control over her own story, and is absorbed into someone else's. This absorption into another's story is exactly what has happened to women in patriarchal culture (consider the alienating and objectifying effects of mirrors on the protagonist of Carter's "The Bloody Chamber"). Women are pressed into service as vamps, innocents, whores, sexless mothers, and denied the ability to write their own stories; worse, their stories are ignored. The connections between loss of self, reflection, and control over stories is made clear in Neil Gaiman's "Snow, Glass, Apples," a dark retelling of Snow White in which the queen is a benevolent witch and her stepdaughter is a murderous vampire. Ultimately the witch loses her life and kingdom to Snow White, and just before she is roasted alive, she tells us that her stepdaughter "looked at me … ; and for a moment I saw myself reflected in her eyes" (339). What she has been reflected into, of course, is the evil stepmother that most versions of the tale make her out to be—she has been overcome by the stories put about her by her stepdaughter, and transformed into a reflection of herself in her stepdaughter's eyes. Reflections tell stories; reflections are stories. And losing oneself in reflections puts one at the mercy of somebody else's stories. It is a fate from which Lilith, like Gaiman's protagonist but unlike Esme, is unable to escape.

Mirrors can be stories only if the one looking into them brings with him or her the dimension of time. Otherwise they are merely fleeting snapshots. Scars such as Gerda's are one way to mark the passage of time, but memory is another. Tanith Lee highlights the connection between memory and the story-function of the mirror in *White as Snow*. Arpazia, the mad witch-queen, finds that her memory is actually in the magic mirror. When Arpazia re-encounters the soldier who had captured her during the invasion of her father's castle, she is not sure who he is. She turns to the mirror for guidance:

> She lit one thin wax taper, and saw the flame litter across the mirror's lid. When she had undone the lid, looking in the glass, she could see a black forest of pines and, there inside, something shining, which was the candle-flame, but then it became a bulbous golden tent. Draco's tent, far in the past, to which a Cirpoz, almost two decades younger, had conducted her …
>
> Cirpoz had raped her maid, Lilca, but not Arpazia. All he had done with *her* was give her to Draco.
>
> She remembered very vividly now. (160)

Arpazia's memory is stored in the mirror, and that memory provides the element of time that mirrors require in order to tell stories. When Arpazia gives away her mirror, she disposes of her last thread of sanity, and thenceforth her mind is cast adrift in time. She becomes unable to distinguish among events that have occurred in the distant past, those that have occurred in the recent past, those that she has dreamt, and those that are actually occurring around her. She is lost in time, thinking of herself as a little girl in a crone's body (245). By giving up the mirror, she gives up her memory as well, and renders herself unable to understand the story of her own life. La Belle describes a similar dynamic, and genders the temporal aspect of mirror-gazing feminine:

> Repeated acts of mirroring give the glass a temporal dimension. When a woman looks at her reflected image, it is often difficult for her to avoid two other faces besides the one existing in the present tense: what she has seen before in the mirror, and what she hopes or fears she will see in the future. (76)

The temporality of the mirror is based in the remembered past, a fantasy insofar as it continues to exist only in the mind, and the fantasy of the future. And this aspect of fantasy, La Belle argues, is an aspect of feminine subjectivity: "Women, when they look in mirrors, apprehend things that are not literally present. They can see a future … or a past" (81). Of course, in literature of the fantastic, there is a name for women who see the future or the past in a mirror: we call them witches. What La Belle describes as women's everyday experiences with the mirror are quite easily mappable onto the magic that makes fantasy. The necessary element of time that makes mirrors into stories also makes mirrors into fantastic stories— and *feminine* fantasy at that.[8] Like a text, the mirror changes and the reflection is re-arranged with every new looker. Indeed, as noted earlier, a reflection is always a re-arrangement. The visual elements that compose the real object are all shown; they are simply inverted, or converted, into a new image. For this reason, the mirror is an ideal symbol for the writer of fairy-tale revisions to use for her/his brand of literary magic; such writers rewrite, invert, and convert a continually changing but ultimately recognizable story.

Mirrors are not merely stories; they are specifically fantasy stories. Reflections are insubstantial creations of light or thought—and the dual meaning of "reflection" is related to the mirror's status as fantasy. Reflections, like fantasy, are contained only in the mind, are nothing more than a trick of the light. And yet without reflections, without either kind of reflections, how on earth would we know how we are in the world, or what the world was, or how we wish to relate to it? Similarly, fantasy is utterly necessary to our understanding of reality. Without the capacity to fantasize, without fantasy literature, we would not be able to conceive of the world other than it is, and our desires, hopes, and fears would be the poorer.

Mirrors, Women, and Fantasy

In *Through the Looking-glass and What Alice Found There*, Alice embarks upon her journey to queen-hood by fantasizing. Before she has begun her second adventure, the narrator tells us that fantasy is Alice's favorite pastime: "I wish I could tell you half the things Alice used to say, beginning with her favorite phrase, 'Let's pretend'." Alice herself describes her fantasies:

> "Oh, Kitty, how nice it would be if we could only get through into Looking-glass House! I'm sure it's got, oh! such beautiful things in it. Let's pretend there's a way of getting through into it, somehow, Kitty. Let's pretend the glass has got all soft like gauze, so that we can get through. Why, it's turning into a sort of mist now, I declare! It'll be easy enough to get through—"
>
> ... And certainly the glass *was* beginning to melt away, just like a bright silvery mist. (155–6)

Once inside the mirror, Alice achieves her desire to become a queen and thus have "all feasting and fun" (180). The mirror not only reflects Alice's physical environment, but also reflects and responds to her inner landscape, the fantasies, experiences, and desires in her mind. This segment of *Through the Looking-glass* is a fine precursor of the roles mirrors play in fairy-tale revisions: the mirror reflects girls' and women's fantasies, experiences, and desires under conditions often hostile to their expression. In this way, mirrors are not *only* stories. They are specifically stories of female fantasy, desire, and transformation.

In many original fairy tales written by women, mirrors are *not* the agents of patriarchy we may expect them to be based only on "Snow White." Jeannine Blackwell writes in her introduction to *The Queen's Mirror: Fairy Tales by German Women, 1780–1900*:

> Queens and mirrors ... form a deadly combination for women, according to contemporary feminist critics. What we have found, on the contrary, is that mirrors are indeed truth machines for German women writers. They show girls their future so that they can act autonomously ... , mirrorlike surfaces reveal subterfuge, slavishness, and bad character in one's mate ... They tell bitter truths about one's own worst emotions. (7)

In this alternative fairy-tale tradition, mirrors offer women knowledge and power. La Belle also finds many positive valances to mirrors: "In the works of a few acute novelists in the nineteenth century ... we begin to see the psychological processes that come into play when a woman looks in the glass" (14). She argues that examining women writers' and characters' responses to and uses of the mirror leads to

> plac[ing] the mirror at a historical focus of female identity and question[ing] dichotomies between self and reflected image, between spirit and flesh, between psychological presence and physical body ... [,] the very oppositions basic to representations of masculine selfhood which underlie a great deal of Western thought. (2)

The mirror, condemned by moralists for its incitement to vanity and lust, associated with equally sinful women, and often a vehicle for the oppression of women, has nonetheless been pressed into service by women writers as a potential source of power, self-creation, and magic.

As discussed earlier, La Belle's study is inherently limited by her focus on mainstream realist literature. In that literary context, what the mirror has the potential to show is innately limited; Elizabeth Bennett cannot look into a mirror in order to see how Mr. Darcy is faring. Mimetic fiction is bound by conventions of mimesis.

In the field of texts under study here, however, the mirror often fulfills a function similar to the psychological fantasy, and fantasy is deeply related to stories—fantasy is the raw material that writing fashions. The mirror offers a place of exploration, representation, and display for women's inner landscapes, their experiences, understandings, and desires. As masculine subjectivity has laid claim to being objective truth, the possibility of a world in which female desire and power matter becomes marginalized into a fantasy, a fantasy reflected in the feminine trope of the mirror. And these fantasies are specifically women's fantasies. I have yet to read a revision in which a male character owns or even uses a magic mirror.[5] La Belle argues that mirrors are far more important for women than for men, and that women's experiences of looking in the mirror are far more complex and conflicted than men's:

> In European culture for at least the past two centuries a female self as a social, psychological, and literary phenomenon is defined, to a considerable degree, as a visual image ... Many women have accepted such definitions, and as a result their self-identities have an exteriority—and hence a vulnerability— greater than masculine egos. What women do with mirrors is clearly distinct from and psychically more important than what men do with mirrors in pursuit of generally utilitarian goals. I think it is significant that in my search for mirrors scenes I have found precious few in which men use the mirror for acts of self-scrutiny. Men look at their faces and their bodies, but what they *are* is another matter entirely—ultimately, a transcendental concept of self ... women explore the reaches of the mirror for what they really are. (9)

The mirror is an ideal medium for conducting women's fantasies—and here I think it is important to understand that fantasy, like metaphor, is a way of understanding and representing the truth of one's own experience—because it attaches meaning to external identity even while illuminating inner considerations. Because the thinking subject doing the looking is also the object of the gaze, the mirror undoes a simplistic dichotomy between external appearance and internal

---

5   Harry Potter, in *Harry Potter and the Sorcerer's Stone*, stumbles across a magic mirror that shows one's heart's desire. This is a rare exception to the feminine gendering of the magic mirror, and does not occur in a fairy-tale revision.

identity, and thus is more genuinely reflective of women's lived experiences in maintaining a dual consciousness of the self as object/other and as subject.

Far from imprisoning women in a superficial appearance-based identity determined by patriarchal values, mirrors are major sites in which women explore and express their inner selves and experiences, sexual and otherwise. *The Magic Toyshop* begins with the adolescent Melanie adopting different poses and personas in front of her bedroom mirror; while other critics have justly understood Melanie to be using the mirror in order to enter into patriarchal fantasies (Melanie fantasizes about being various male artists' models, rather than an artist or agent in her own right), and linked her seduction by such glamorous passivity with her later, more brutal experiences, it is nonetheless important that these fantasies are *Melanie's*, and that she is using the mirror to explore potential roles for herself as well as to develop sexually. The mirror is a vehicle for Melanie's own desires and pleasure, and in fact, the first time the mirror is explicitly named is when she is distracted from her patriarchal fantasies by her own physical capabilities: "She revealed a long, marbly white leg up to the thigh (forgetting the fantasy in sudden absorption in the mirrored play of muscle as she flexed her leg again and again)" (2). Here, the mirror shows Melanie her muscle, her strength. Further, in arranging herself in various costumes and poses in imitation of male artists, Melanie is taking on the role of both artist and model—she is the one creating a given image. The open-ended play with mirrors is abruptly cut off, however, when Melanie's parents die, and she is forced to live with her working-class uncle in a house too poor for mirrors. Later, she discovers that in the room belonging to her uncle's wife's brothers, Finn and Francie, "A square of mirror [was] propped against a pink-washed wall. Beside the mirror hung a painting" (108). Again, mirrors are associated with art, suggesting that the use of a mirror is a creative act similar to painting, writing, or even reading.

Melanie enacts her fantasies in front of a mirror—the mirror enables her to become, however momentarily, her fantasy—and in "Wolf-Alice," the mirror is far more responsive to Alice's experience of reality than it is to any punitive objective reality. At first Alice understands her reflection to be a friend, and the reflection has meaning for her only in that context. Because she is the only character using the mirror, the reflection has meaning only in that context. The reader "knows" that the mirror is merely reflecting Alice herself—but how sure can the reader be? In the context of *The Bloody Chamber*, magical events occur regularly, and the reader knows that the Duke does not have a reflection; already the reliability of the mirror is in question. The glass responds not to physics, but to Alice. Only when she determines that the Duke is human, is real and worthy of care, does the mirror finally reflect him, "as if brought into being by her soft, moist, gentle tongue" (228).

While both Melanie and Wolf-Alice use the mirror to mature, the mirror's power as a place of solace and sanctuary is most evident in *White as Snow*, in part because the world portrayed in that novel is so unremittingly and brutally misogynist. Arpazia's mirror is perhaps the only place—or perhaps one of two places, the other being her lover's cottage—in which she can even acknowledge that she has desires or a perspective that differs from that of the men who control her. The mirror displays Arpazia's understandings of the world around her, even when she is too damaged and dissociated to be conscious of those experiences. When Draco, the king who first rapes and then marries her, returns the mirror, which had been similarly pillaged from her father's castle,

> She undid the clasp of the lid, and opened it out, and when she looked in the glass, she did not see herself, gazed straight past herself, at the room beyond, its painted walls and long narrow windows, her bed, the carved chair with King Draco in it.
>
> She saw Draco, the dragon-bull, as if for the first time, in the mirror. He was almost faceless, a suit of flesh with hot appetites. (53)

Arpazia does not see herself because she is not, at this moment, *aware* of herself—she is in what the novel calls the long "trance" of her pregnancy, the state of mindless dissociation she has been in ever since the rape. Instead, she sees Draco—but not as he sees himself, or as his subjects see him. She sees him in the mirror through the lens of her own experience, a lens that has been heretofore denied her. In the mirror, which Draco calls "frippery," "women's nonsense," and a "witch's glass," Arpazia's experiences can be safely seen and stored without endangering her. Arpazia is not the only one who sees her experiences in the mirror. After she has given birth, Draco visits Arpazia and rapes her again. Halfway through,

> Still raised over her, still inside her, he caught sight of *himself*, across the room, in the edge of the mirror.
>
> Quite how he did so, he was afterward unsure, for the mirror did not seem to be a the right angle to picture him. Was that some of her sorcery?
>
> What he saw was distorted. The man-creature in the glass was swarthy with hearty meat and drink, panting and piglike. While she—she was simply a mound of velvet that might only have been one more cover on the bed. As if she were not there at all. (73–4)

Draco believes that what he sees in the mirror is distorted because it does not correlate with his experience of reality, but the mirror is indeed presenting reality—Arpazia's reality. The mirror is showing Draco what Arpazia is experiencing: Draco is barely human, a monster, and she herself is "not there," completely dissociated and turned into an object. The mirror presents her experience as reality whereas Draco forces her to live in his experience of reality. This expression of Arpazia's inner landscape, her experiences, does her a service, as the sight causes Draco to lose his erection.

The mirror shows Arpazia's inner self not only psychically but physically as well, and this too is knowledge and reality often denied to women. La Belle notes:

> For a man, to explore his "interior space" or "look within" himself means just what it meant for Socrates. It has nothing to do with mirrors or physical examinations of his anatomy. But for these women—I am tempted to say "for most women"—it does. To construct an interior sense of selfhood, women need to explore their bodies in this way. Male concepts of human identity are founded on a radical division between mind and brain, soul and body, spiritualized self and physical container. For women, there is a continual two-way flowing back and forth of a very complex sort between their corporeal existence (how they look as physical objects to themselves and to others) and how they conceive of themselves as female human beings in a psychological or spiritual sense. (178–9)

She is alluding to the way women often use mirrors to learn what their vulva, often derided within misogynous cultures as disgusting, looks like, and suggesting that this aspect of becoming familiar with one's physical self is essential to a feminism that accepts and celebrates the female body. Arpazia too uses the mirror to gain inner knowledge—physically *inward* knowledge, even when this knowledge bypasses her consciousness: "A child darted along the colonnade ... Arpazia was aware the almost-child, rushing through the mirror, must not reach her. So she clapped the lid shut" (53). As the mirror remains shut, so Arpazia's pregnancy extends for an unnaturally long time, until she undoes the mirror and

> stared at her belly through the thin shift. As she saw in through the linen, she saw in next through her own body—
>
> Inside her belly was a black bowl, and in the bowl a red apple, but the heart of the apple was white. The flesh of the apple was a white serpent lying coiled there. Like herself, though taking sustenance and sometimes moving, it had been asleep. Now Arpazia saw it had woken. (56)

With this knowledge, this *in*sight provided by the mirror, Arpazia goes into labor. When she again finds herself pregnant, she again gains that knowledge through the mirror:

> Arpazia moved abruptly back to the mirror.
>
> "What is it? *Show* me what it is."
>
> The surface of the mirror dappled like water. That was all. Arpazia turned. She regarded the profile of her body. Was there some change? Could it be—
>
> She stared deeply in at the glass and now, now—her gown became transparent, in one place, across her belly. She saw, a second time, her snow of flesh, and the black wood which flourished below, whose center was a rose. But then, straight through her belly she saw, straight through the crimson rose of her womb ...
>
> The glass went black. In blackness, she heard a woman in labor screaming and screaming.

But Arpazia leaned in to the mirror. She glared down at the tiny little seed.

"You shall be killed." And her breath formed on the glass like mist. (112)

The mirror allows Arpazia insight into her own body; it allows her to see inside herself and to learn what is happening inside herself, and thus to take control of what is happening to her. The book is profoundly ambivalent about Arpazia's abortion; on the one hand sympathetic characters proclaim her right to have one, on the other, the abortion ends her idyll with her lover, the only happiness in her short and miserable life. Nonetheless Arpazia is able to avoid the potential horror of childbirth and its consequences due to her mirror. The need for this kind of knowledge, provided metaphorically in the novel by a mirror, is sex-specific; a man may need to know what is happening within his body due to illness, but pregnancy is simply not a concern. Again, the mirror provides access to a female reality through mythic fantasy (the rose).

The mirror becomes Arpazia's only sanctuary. In it she finds a "friend," herself, her own reflection ("she only talked to the woman she saw in her mirror, who would always answer" [76]), and it is specifically a realm of myth and fantasy:

At twilight, looking in the mirror, conversing with her reflection, the lamp or candle sinking, she beheld a crow which sat above the window, blinking orichalc eyes. Later, a white owl. Or two shadows stood behind her, one of whom held a spindle with white wool on it. Or a tree grew in a corner, laden with rosy fruits, while a serpent twined the trunk. (77)

The mirror that expresses Arpazia's inner state provides her with a mythic sanctuary; in it she becomes Eve, Odin, Athena, and one of the three fates. The mirror intertwines women's experiences and fantasy/myth—in patriarchal culture, women's experiences are deliberately excluded from dominant conceptions of reality, and so become fantasy.[6] Such a reading dovetails nicely with Rosemary Jackson's definition of fantasy as the genre of subversion precisely because it "attempts to compensate for a lack resulting from cultural constraints: it is a literature of desire, which seeks that which is experienced as absence and loss" (3).

This mythic world becomes, for Arpazia, the real world, because it reflects her experience of reality—Draco has raped her, Draco is a monster, she is an object. The "real world" denies her reality, proclaiming instead that Draco has done the honorable thing by marrying her, he is king, the match is a lucky one for her, she should be honored to sit by his side. In a world in which women are subjugated and men's subjective interpretations of reality are accepted as "objective," women's experiences become part of the world of fantasy. For Arpazia, the mirror is the real world, and reality the reversed distortion. When she falls in love, she thinks of

---

6   In "The Language of Sisterhood," Angela Carter writes that "we feel a compulsive need to rewrite ... myths, since myth is more malleable than history, in order to accommodate ourselves in the past." In other words, since women have been written out of history, our presence in myth becomes of great importance.

her lover as existing with her in the mirror: "None of these people—no people at all—were real for Arpazia. Only one other was alive in Arpazia's world. She lived with him, inside the mirror. Indeed, now and then, she glimpsed him in the mirror, as before she had seen the raven and the owl, and the mythical hags of fate" (111). When Arpazia gives away her mirror, she loses all sense of reality, especially her own; she depends on another, inferior mirror, to understand her fate: "Peering into its hazy depths, Arpazia could not see clearly what had become of her" (237). What she remembers seeing in her own mirror remains her touchstone for reality, so that when she finally does see herself, aged, frostbitten, and haggard, she does not accept the truth of that reflection:

> For a second she saw herself, an old beggar-woman with a basket—
>
> She had caught in her vision a long glass crack showing in the covered mirror on the shack's wall.
>
> *Mirror, mirror on the wall,*
>
> *Am I the fairest of them all?*
>
> She was not.
>
> But now—now the actuality replaced the lie. (269)

"The actuality" is Coira, Arpazia's daughter, and physically, her double. "The lie" is the reflection of Arpazia as an old woman. Arpazia accepts only what she remembers from her mirror as being true, as the mirror was the only thing she could trust to show her own experiences. But now it has passed out of her hands, and no longer shows Arpazia what she knows to be true, that she is a young girl, damaged and insane, who needs a mirror in order to know what truth is.

Eventually, Arpazia is hanged, and she is unable to believe in her own afterlife until it is confirmed in a natural mirror: "They looked down into the mirror of the collected water, and Arpazia saw herself as she had been at fourteen, at twenty, in the beauty of her flesh. And Klymeno, handsome and a god, standing by her" (315). The mirror makes Arpazia's final respite real to her, and the novel releases her into a world that simply could not have existed in the reality of the novel, a world in which she can be at peace with her beloved, without the danger of rape or any other kind of violence. Far from being the medium through which misogyny controls Arpazia, the mirror is perhaps the one item in her world that allows her to escape it.

Even in novels which do not take place in overtly patriarchal settings, such as Pratchett's *Witches Abroad*, mirrors specifically represent *women's* powers and fantasies.[7] The book could be read superficially as an indictment of mirrors and

---

[7]   Of course, such novels are still being written and read in a more or less patriarchal context, but there is nonetheless a significant difference between Lee's novel, in which

their power, as Lilith, the powerful villain and evil despot, holds an entire city-state in thrall with her mirror-magic, a magic in which she forces real life to take the shape of the fantasies she develops in her mirrors, and cannot understand the difference between fantasy and reality:

> "He's a frog, and you killed the old Baron," said Granny.
>
> "You'd have done the same," said Lily.
>
> "No," said Granny. "I'd have *thought* the same, but I wouldn't have done it."
>
> "What difference does that make, deep down?"
>
> "You mean you don't *know*?" said Nanny Ogg. (247)

But while the mirrors are vehicles for Lilith's massively destructive and dehumanizing fantasies, they are also the medium of Esme's victory. Esme defeats Lilith *not* by rejecting mirrors outright, but by acknowledging their power and using them. Indeed, the novel opens by positioning Granny as Lily's reflection. Mrs. Gogol, a swamp witch working against Lilith,

> took up a fragment of mirror and tied it to the top of the post ... The piece of mirror gleamed between the darkness of the hat and the coat.
>
> "Will it work?" he said.
>
> "Yes," she said. "Even mirrors have their reflection. We got to fight mirrors with mirrors ... We've got to find *her* reflection." (10)

Of course, the reflection called to fight Lilith is Esme, Lilith's opposite number—and indeed Esme and Lilith are identical, but opposite. They look the same; they are the most powerful witches in the Discworld; but they use their powers for completely opposed goals and in very different ways. Esme is able to defeat Lilith only once she accepts the role of mirror and reflection, and this climax is implied throughout the novel. Granny first becomes aware that Lilith is behind the turmoil she encounters in her travels when she glances into a mirror at a late colleague's house and sees not herself, but Lilith. She sharply rejects the association the reflection indicates by smashing the glass with her bare hand, but about 30 pages later, Mrs. Gogol tells a friend that "All anyone gets in a mirror is themselves" (79). Lilith's ambition, violence, and desire for control over other people's lives reflect Esme's own firmly controlled desires, which she never allows to dominate her actions, and so when she looks into the mirror and sees her sister, she is also seeing herself as she might have been had her self-control been

---

women literally struggle to survive against male-perpetrated violence in a world run by and for men, and Pratchett's, in which all the major characters are female, and they all wield varying degrees power for various reasons of their own.

less rigid. Later, in an enchanted castle on the way to Genua, Magrat witnesses Granny's reaction to a mirror and thinks, "It wasn't like Granny Weatherwax to be frightened of her own reflection" (117). On the one hand, of course, Granny is not frightened of her own reflection; she is disturbed by seeing Lilith where her own reflection should be. But as the trio leaves the castle, Granny is repeatedly "recognized" by people who are mistaking her for Lilith; in a purely visual sense, then, Granny's reflection is Lilith.

As readers, we are being encouraged to associate Granny with Lilith's reflection, and vice versa. The implication of such an association is made overt in Granny's conversation with Mrs. Gogol when she finally arrives in Genua. In an effort to find out exactly how much the other woman knows about Lilith, she asks Mrs. Gogol what kind of power is protecting the figurehead-ruler of the city, the Duc. In reply, Mrs. Gogol says "You look in mirrors a lot these days, Mistress Weatherwax?" (184). The answer is triple-barreled. Of course, it refers to the mirror-magic Lily uses to control the city, and to the close kinship and resemblance between Granny and her sister, but it also harkens back to the opening of the novel, in which Mrs. Gogol is searching for Lily's reflection in order to defeat her; Granny is that reflection, and in order to win, she has to accept that aspect of her identity. Later, Granny tells Mrs. Gogol, "It occurs to me … that you ain't everything you seem." Mrs. Gogol responds by saying "Oh yes I is, Mistress Weatherwax. I never bin nothing else, just like you" (186). Again Mrs. Gogol pushes Granny to accept what she *seems* to be—the mirror image of Lily. The first time Esme confronts Lily, she doesn't use mirrors at all, and she is soundly defeated. At the climax of the novel, however, Lily

> glided into the place between the mirrors.

> Her myriad selves looked back at her approvingly. She relaxed.

> Then her foot struck something. She looked down and saw on the flagstones, black in the moonlight, a broomstick lying in shards of broken glass.

> Her horrified gaze rose to meet a reflection.

> It glared back at her. (275)

Believing she has finally disposed of Esme, Lily assumes her accustomed place within the room of mirrors, and even relaxes under the comforting gazes of her infinite reflections—but one of these reflections is Esme herself. Esme finally takes on the role of Lily's reflection by smashing one of the mirrors and taking its place. This confrontation leads to Lily's downfall. By breaking the mirror, Esme has released the reflections to seize Lily. While she avoided and rejected mirrors, Esme was unable to defeat her sister, but by accepting the reflection as an aspect of her own personality, she triumphs. It is, of course, a bittersweet victory, and Granny tries to save her sister from the ravening reflections, but Lily's defeat is unavoidable due to her own inability to distinguish between reality and fantasy, substance and reflection—it is the logical end to her reign of mirror-terror.

Lily is defeated, but mirrors persist. The final scene of the novel gives us the three witches, Granny Weatherwax, Nanny Ogg, and Magrat Garlick, travelling home on their broomsticks. Granny Weatherwax has lost her hat during the trip, and there is no greater loss to a witch than her hat, the mark of her profession, status, and identity. Mrs. Gogol has given her a replacement ... but it is not entirely what Granny expects of a witch's hat; it is more like Carmen Miranda's hat of fruit, and Granny is not entirely comfortable with it. She tries it on:

> "Would you like to have a look?" said Magrat. "I have a mirror somewhere ..."
>
> The silence descended like an axe. Magrat went red. Nanny Ogg glared at her.
>
> They watched Granny carefully.
>
> "Ye-ess," she said, after what seemed like a long time, "I think I should look in a mirror."
>
> Magrat unfroze, fumbled in her pockets and produced a small, wooden-framed hand-mirror. She passed it across.
>
> Granny Weatherwax looked at her reflection ...
>
> "Well," said Granny, grudgingly, "maybe its fine for foreign parts. Where I ain't going to be seen by anyone as knows me. No-one important, anyway."...
>
> They relaxed. (284)

Granny's selfhood is not created by the mirror—the novel emphasizes throughout that Granny has an almost unbelievably strong, unified sense of self— but it is *confirmed* by the mirror. A few pages earlier, Nanny was concerned that Lily might have "puled a farst one in the mirror," and presumably replaced Granny during their final confrontation (282), but Granny's use of the mirror confirms that she remains herself, despite her sojourn as a reflection and her unusual hat.

Granny's relationship with the mirror is different from Lily's, and even from Magrat's (Magrat resorts to the mirror in times of confusion, and has a very weak sense of self and little confidence). While she must accept the role of reflection in order to be effective, she accepts it as one of a number of powers, and so she is not trapped in the mirror after her showdown with Lily. She remains able to recognize the difference between reality and fantasy even after having temporarily become the mirror and used fantasy for her own ends. After the mirrors shatter, Granny finds herself trapped in the mirror, conversing with Death.

> Granny Weatherwax looked out at the multi-layered, silvery world.
>
> "Where am I?"
>
> INSIDE THE MIRROR.

"Am I dead?"

THE ANSWER TO THAT said Death, IS SOMEWHERE BETWEEN NO AND YES.

Esme turned, and a billion figures turned with her.

"When can I get out?"

WHEN YOU FIND THE ONE THAT'S REAL.

"Is this a trick question?"

NO.

Granny looked down at herself.

"This one," she said. (281)

Granny uses the mirror without losing herself in the process; her sister is trapped forever in the mirror, searching in her reflections for that which inheres in herself. The relationship between fantasy and reality is thus represented via the relationship between mirrors and the real world of the novel. Lily inflicts her fantasies about how the world "should" operate—according to fairy tales—on the people and animals around her, forbidding alternate interpretations or fantasies; Granny has worked to deny herself such fantasies in favor of helping people with "real things," as Nanny tells Magrat. Ultimately Granny defeats Lily only after accepting her own mirroring, her own fantasies of control.[8] These political power-plays are entirely female. The men in the novel are puppets: the murdered ruler of Genua is present as a zombie, given life and power by Mrs. Gogol, and Genua's current Duc is a frog transformed into a human by Lily. The role of the mirror in this novel specifically pertains to female power and female fantasy.

Cristina Bacchilega uses the mirror as the guiding metaphor in her 1997 book *Postmodern Fairy Tales: Gender and Narrative Strategies*, which is of particular interest in the context of this research. While she continues to use reflection as a metaphor for mimesis, she includes two other important aspects of mirroring: refraction, which she uses as a symbol for varying desires, and framing, which she uses to denote artifice. She argues that postmodern fairy tale revisions "reproduce those mirror images while at the same time they make the mirroring visible to the point of transforming its effects" (10). She argues that the mimesis of the fairy tale (our emotional experience of life) changes with varying desires (within a culture, within a person) and that their representation is finally determined by the

---

[8]   The potential for Granny, an enormously powerful witch, to give in to her darker fantasies and become evil is a constant theme in those of Pratchett's books that deal with her.

artifice of the frame: "If we see more of the mirror rather than its images, questions rather than answers emerge. Who is holding the mirror and whose desires does it represent and contain? Or, more pointedly, how is the fairy tale's magic produced narratively?" (28).

Language is full of puns regarding mirrors: "psyche" in French is also a word for a free-standing mirror of the sort found in a lady's boudoir; "reflection" refers to both one's outer appearance and one's inner meditations and *pensées*. Mirrors don't lie, proverbial wisdom tells us, but an illusion is "smoke and mirrors." Mirrors combine truth and illusion, and such a combination is fruitful rather than deadly if we recognize and understand what we are seeing/reading. They show us simultaneous, fully integrated similarity and difference; they show us the confluence of thought and seeming. It is precisely in that sense that fantasy can be an accurate, feminist reflection as reality: it can provide a mutually interacting, exquisitely responsive understanding of the world around us and, as I will explore in the next and final chapter, the mirror and the doubles it generates provide one way to understand the potential that the genre of fantasy holds for women and for feminist writers. For Bacchilega, the main point of interest in the technique of tale-telling is the frame, which she identifies with artifice. I argue, however, that it is the reflection, the mirror-surface itself, which produces the fantastic effects. The mirror creates an uncanny double, one that is simultaneously familiar and strange—it reverses the viewer's image, and that doubling, as I will explore in the next chapter, is what makes the fantastic such an appealing genre for writers grappling with feminist concerns of the 1970s and 1990s.

Chapter 5
Double Vision:
Women and Fantasy

Genre
exploration

The first section of this book examined the importance and construction of revision in the 1970s and 1990s; I found that the mother-daughter relationships considered essential to the construction of feminine selves by the theorist/clinicians of that time and its understanding of feminine subjectivity are closely associated with the act of literary revision itself, and that therefore we can think of revision as a mode of writing that is closely tied to women's experiences of themselves and the world around them. In the previous chapter, I examined various fantastic revisions of fairy tales, finding that over and over again, mirrors are figured as women's fantasies. In this chapter I address the mode of the fantastic and the genre of fantasy.[1] What does fantasy hold for women and feminist writers? Why turn to this particular genre?

Gayle Greene once claimed that "[a]ccessibility is a sine qua non for any writing concerned with social change, which is why realism is the mode of feminist writers—as it has been the mode of women writers in the past" (3–4). Greene seems to have been deliberately overlooking the massive popularity of non-realist literature, as well as the history women writers have of success with the Gothic and the romance, for example. Suzette Haden Elgin, a science fiction writer devoted to feminism, has said that she chose the genre specifically for its ability to reach a wide audience (18). Certainly it is possible to write feminist revisions of fairy tales and classical myth in a realist mode: Margaret Atwood's "Bluebeard's Egg" and Gregory Maguire's *Confessions of an Ugly Stepsister* are two examples. But the great majority of revisions of these tales partake of the fantastic one way or another; whether they are high fantasy, such as Robin McKinley's *Deerskin*, or comic fantasy, such as Elizabeth Ann Scarborough's *The Godmother*, or employ the mode of the fantastic, as does Toni Morrison's *Beloved*, or use such elliptical stylistics as to confound the reader of straightforward realism, such as Kirsty Gunn's *The Keepsake*, or invoke magic realism, such as Kathryn Davis's *The Girl Who Trod on a Loaf*, or involve science fiction, as does Sheri S. Tepper's *Beauty*, revisions of fairy tales and classical myth come to their fullest flower when they depart from mainstream realism. What does this mode of writing offer to the feminist writer? Why do so many adopt it?

Having argued in the previous chapter that the trope of the mirror represents feminine magic and fantasy itself, I will now examine the importance of one

---

[1]   For an explanation of the difference in literary criticism between the mode of the fantastic and the genre of fantasy, see the Introduction.

particular element of fantasy that the mirror invokes, the double. Fantasy, like revision, lays bare a particular correspondence between feminine subjectivity as described by theorists contemporary with the texts and these writers' chosen mode. I will begin by discussing the recurring motif in fantastic literature of the double, or *doppelganger*, its appearances in the texts under study, and its special relationship to feminine subjectivity. I will then go on to examine the dichotomy between seeming and being, highlighted by the mirror, and corresponding to what Joan Rivière called the masquerade of femininity and Judith Butler conceived of as the performative construction of sex and gender. Ultimately, I will argue that the mirror's—and fantasy's—illusion of another world, identical and yet opposite to ours, creates a space for expressing the lived experiences of women and envisioning the feminist change necessary to improve those experiences.

Double, Double, Toil and Trouble: The Double in Fairy-Tale Revisions

The trope of the double, or doppelganger, is very closely related to that of the mirror for obvious reasons. In his influential and early study on the subject, Otto Rank uses a double who emerges from a mirror as the first example of the breed. He goes on to analyze the significance of the double by discussing the superstitions surrounding mirrors in various cultures. If, as argued above, the mirror is a symbol for fantasy itself, the doppelganger is the quintessential figure of that fantasy.

Rank notes that in culture after culture, the myth of the double signifies both a defense against and a harbinger of death. The appearance of a doppelganger signifies the imminent death of the one so doubled in English folklore, a connection that Rank associates with the concept's origin in the idea of an eternal soul that can separate from a body necessarily doomed to death and destruction. Thus, the appearance of that soul-self separated from the still-living body can mean nothing but disaster. Rank also notes that in his contemporary literature, the double appeared as a symbol of both narcissism and the desire to avoid responsibility for one's darker wishes or acts (69, 64–79). Such themes are obvious in texts such as Oscar Wilde's *Picture of Dorian Gray* and Robert Louis Stevenson's *The Strange Case of Dr Jekyll and Mr Hyde*. But is there a gendered component to such an unremittingly negative reading of this motif? Certainly the folklore Rank studied to arrive at his conclusion is common to both men and women of its given culture, but the valence of the doubled characters in the texts by the writers under review in this study seems to be considerably more ambivalent than the valence of the doubled characters by the male writers Rank considers. Of course there are evil or wicked doubles who must be done away with (though usually not before an attempt has been made to redeem them), but, in contrast to texts so centered around masculine experience as are *Dorian Gray* and *Dr Jekyll and Mr Hyde*, there are also positive valances attached to having a multiplicity of possible selves.

Building on Rank's work, Freud cites the doppelganger as being one of the quintessential examples of the uncanny, which he defines as "everything that was intended to remain secret, hidden away, and has come into the open" ("Uncanny" 132). The distinction he highlights as essential to understanding the uncanny in life and literature is between public and private, a distinction very meaningful to discussions of gender. Women who have left their assigned role or sphere in Western culture are women who have stepped out of the private world, have refused to remain hidden away, who have brought themselves and the abuses heaped upon them that depended upon secrecy, such as incest and other forms of sexual abuse, out into the open. Might not, then, feminist writers feel a particular affinity to the uncanny itself? Moreover, the particular motif of the doppelganger mimics the experiences of women emerging from this particular form of oppression. Freud describes the uncanniness of the double as being intensified by the spontaneous transmission of mental processes from one of these persons to the other—what we would call telepathy—so that the other becomes co-owner of the other's knowledge, emotions, and experience. Moreover, a person may identify himself with another and so become unsure of his true self; or he may substitute the other's self for his own. The self may thus be duplicated, divided, and interchanged (141–2).

Freud attributes the uncanny quality of this concept to "the fact that the double is a creation that belongs to a primitive phase in our mental development"—but if we reject a teleological understanding of human history, how do we understand this uncanniness? I would suggest that for women, and for writers following on in the work of second-wave feminism, the uncanny quality of the double has to do with very real social and psychological circumstances. It is telling that David McLintock, Freud's translator, used the word "co-owner" to describe the sharing of another's knowledge, emotions, and experience, because for a very long time, women's ability to own property, even her own intellectual property, was curtailed; a married woman's earnings were the property of her husband (women's rights to control her own body rather than to see it become the property of another are still in dispute). Similarly, the question of who owns, or gets to determine, women's knowledge, emotions, and experience has been a central one for psychology, as the patriarchal abuses perpetrated by male "experts" on women diagnosed as mentally ill not only prevented women who were truly suffering from getting the treatment they needed, but also provided ideology that justified male control of women's inner lives and determined what was "normal" and what was pathological without interrogating the misogynist sex roles into which women were expected to fit themselves.

What if we were to examine Freud's claims regarding the double's uncanny nature while bearing in mind the models of feminine subjectivity described in earlier chapters, including Chodorow's, Irigaray's, and the Stone Center Theorists' descriptions of the psychological interplay between mother and daughter, as well as the relational self whose strength lies in empathy outlined by the Stone Center Theorists? The reason for the double's uncanniness might look very different indeed. Male social and physical control of women may be one cause for anxiety over a loss of self or of identity (until very recently, women in Western cultures were expect to change their names at marriage, for example), but the figure of the double also suggests the distress caused by an inability to determine the difference between self and (m)other or self and daughter in a society that valorizes such sharp divisions as markers of maturity. Such issues, as discussed earlier, informed the very heart of second-wave feminism. Furthermore, the "duplicated, divided, and interchanged" self seems like it would have particular resonance to a self predicated on relations with others as well as to members of a group who have traditionally been cast as the "other," as opposed to the masculine norm, or subject. In *The Second Sex*, Simone de Beauvoir astutely observes that sexual maturity for the girl involves "becoming prey in order to gain her ends. She becomes an object, and she sees herself as object; … it seems to her that she has now been doubled; instead of coinciding exactly with herself, she now begins to exist *outside*" (355). As examples of this phenomenon, de Beauvoir discusses literary examples of women contemplating themselves in the mirror. Unlike men, who take on the role of sexual subject, women are forced to understand themselves as *objects*, and to internalize exactly the division of self that the mirror, origin of the double, encourages: the division between self as subject and self as object.

From one division to several: for women, the double is uncanny in its familiarity, in that it makes manifest and literal what patriarchy demands of them, that they split off their own active selves in order to send forward simulacra that fulfill men's desires. But the literalization of that experience exposes the artificiality of what is supposed to be women's "natural" role, underscoring that which is elided by a coherent discourse that pretends to be objective reality, as Rosemary Jackson argues the function of fantasy genre is.

Angela Carter highlights this splitting of the female self into the private subject and the public object that conforms to patriarchal desires in "The Tiger's Bride." When the protagonist of this story arrives at the castle of the Beast, she is escorted to a small room. She is given an automaton as an attendant, one with "a looking glass in one hand and a powder puff in the other and … a musical box where her heart should be" (162). The protagonist suddenly realizes that this pretty doll is in fact a replica of herself. While the girl is angry about her radically disempowered status, however, the replica "tinkles as she rolls," and her face always "continue[s] bonnily to beam" (162, 167). The automaton carries with her the implements of patriarchally approved femininity: make-up with which to "improve" one's looks for the benefit of male watchers, and a mirror with which to inspect the results. She is also heartless, with a mechanism that repeats a pre-set tune in the place of the metaphorical seat of human emotion. The maid then attacks the protagonist with her accoutrements: "She raises her arm and busily dusts my cheeks with pink, powdered chalk that makes me cough, then thrusts towards me her little mirror" (162). The aggressive nature of the maid's attentions suggest the pressure on the daughter to conform to patriarchal desires, a pressure that she resists, rejecting the beast's request to see her naked, and rejecting any illusion that her relationship to him is anything other than one of property to its owner. Thus, while the automaton is "the spit" of the protagonist, she is significantly different as well; it is this difference that marks the double as the signifier of fantasy rather than being purely mimetic of the protagonist's "real" self and "real" world. As with the reflections with which doppelgangers are so closely identified, doubles are simultaneously identical and opposite to their originals.

Fantasy is the literary technique best suited to making literal that which is so often considered to be only metaphor. In fact, according to Rosemary Jackson in her landmark study, *Fantasy: The Literature of Subversion*, this function is essential to fantasy as she understands it:

> Part of its subversive power lies in this resistance to allegory and metaphor. For it takes metaphorical constructions literally … [T]he movement of fantastic narrative is one of *metonymical* rather than of *metaphorical* process: one object does not *stand for* another, but literally becomes that other, slides into it, metamorphosing from one shape to another in a permanent flux and instability. (41–2)

The internal divisions required of women find literal shape in the fantastic rendering of the double. Jackson finds that, indeed, the double is of utmost importance to the genre of fantasy, as the quintessential example of the "themes of the self" that she identifies as being one of the two primary concerns of fantasy, in which "the source of otherness, of threat, is in the *self*" (58). She notes that the mirror, with its ever-present double, is the major signifier of these themes, noting that "the reflection in the glass is the subject's other … suggesting the inseparability of these devices and mirror images from fantastic themes of duplicity and multiplicity of selves" (45). Jackson also uses the mirror as a metaphor for the genre of fantasy itself, though from a different perspective than I have done in the previous chapter. She suggests that "The notion of 'paraxis' [the area that appears to exist "behind" the mirror, in between the self and the image, but which is really illusory] is useful … in considering topography, for many of the strange worlds of modern fantasy are located in, or through, or beyond, the mirror. They are spaces behind the visible, behind the image, introducing dark areas from which anything can emerge." When fantasy grapples with themes of the self, as it does in so many revisions of fairy tales, these "dark areas" are often in the protagonist herself; when fantasy grapples with themes of the other, these dark areas occur outside the protagonist and give rise to creatures that attempt to turn her into one of them (i.e. vampires); when the self *is* the other, which is the position de Beauvoir and Irigaray argue that women have been put into, I argue that these themes collapse together and coalesce in the figure of the double.

Rosemary Jackson's work on fantasy was published in the early 1980s, contemporaneously with the second-wave feminist scholarship under discussion in this project. But as helpful as Jackson's formulation may be to my analysis, it contains a significant problem: in her definition of fantasy, she includes almost no texts that contemporary genre readers would recognize as fantasy. She specifically excludes such canonical texts as J.R.R. Tolkien's *Lord of the Rings* series, L. Frank Baum's Oz books, and the work of Ursula Le Guin, and uses as the majority of her examples texts that most readers would classify as the foundations of horror, such as Bram Stoker's *Dracula*, the works of H.P. Lovecraft, and *The Strange Case of Dr Jekyll and Mr Hyde*. Indeed, she argues that the texts she excludes "belong to that realm of fantasy which is more properly defined as faery, or romance literature," and that such works "fill up a lack, making up for an apprehension of actuality as disordered and insufficient" and serving to "stabilize social order by minimizing the need for human intervention" (9, 174). She contrasts these works with what she considers to be the "true" fantasy that "traces the unsaid and the unseen of culture ... tells of the impossible attempt to realize desire" and "attempts to compensate for a lack resulting from cultural constraints ... which seeks that which is experienced as absence and loss" (4, 3).

I accept Brian Attebery's characterization of genres as "fuzzy sets" orbiting a center, and I reject the distinction that Jackson attempts to make. Even in Jackson's own words, the books that "fill up a lack" and those that attempt "to compensate for a lack" begin to blur together. I would suggest that the books Jackson dismisses as "faery" are indeed as subversive as the ones she chooses to celebrate, though they may be subverting different ideologies. The resistance found in Tolkien's *Lord of the Rings* to industrialization is well known; while that resistance or subversion may encompass distressingly conservative notions of class and racist ideologies, it is inarguable that the Industrial Revolution holds sway, that we live in an age of mass production, and that the ideology of industrial capitalism, along with providing working people with cheap and accessible consumer goods, and thus making a higher standard of living accessible to more people, has also enabled the ravaging the environment and destroyed the lives of many workers. Tolkien's protest against this dominant ideology is indeed subversive, and while Jackson may claim that "[m]ovement into a *marvelous* realm transports the reader or viewer into an absolutely different, alternative world" and that this "secondary, duplicated cosmos is relatively autonomous, relating to the 'real' only through metaphorical reflection and never, or rarely, intruding into or interrogating it," to do so is to overlook the very real critique of industrial capitalism encoded in the novels (42). Because the reader of books of "faery" is always living his or her life in the real world, the sharp differences between that world and the world of the novel create a tension that cannot help but be an interrogation into the values of the real world. Further, this literature *is* literature of desire—it is literature that stimulates the desire of its readership for that which is experienced as missing or devalued in the contemporary world: magic, wonder, respect for nature, meaningful human action.

If the faery or marvelous is indeed fantasy, contrary to what Jackson believes, is it possible to invoke her analyses of what I would term the genre of horror and still find them to be applicable? I would say yes; the themes of self and other, and the trope of the double which I am arguing are so integral to the genre of fantasy appear even in Tolkien's novels. The poisonous, titular ring of the series is a vampiric object, an external object that invades its wearer's mind and turns him into an evil being (a theme of the other). But it does so by arousing the wearer's own jealousy, pride, ambition, lust for power, and other such socially unacceptable attributes: the evil comes from the dark places of the wearer himself (a theme of the self). There is even a double for the heroic Frodo, the hobbit charged with bearing the ring to the only site at which it can be properly destroyed: the pathetic Gollum is a repulsive husk who had once owned and borne the ring himself and had then fallen victim to its power. He dogs Frodo's steps, serving as a warning and a figure of fear: Gollum was once a hobbit like Frodo, and Frodo, if he fails, could find himself turning into the wretched Gollum.

Thus, while Jackson herself rejects those texts of fantasy that she considers unworthy, her observations about the genre hold true for those very texts, emphasizing the incisiveness of Jackson's theories even when she herself was unaware of their power. The power of Jackson's work to shed light upon fantasy texts she rejects is of vital importance to this project, as her remarks upon the subversive function of fantasy help to explain why it has been of such importance to feminist writers. Fantasy, she argues, points to or suggests the basis upon which cultural order rests, for it opens up, for a brief moment, on to disorder, on to illegality, on to that which lies outside the law, that which is outside dominant value systems. The fantastic traces the unsaid and unseen of culture: that which has been silenced, made invisible, covered over and made "absent" (4).

Patriarchy is an almost overwhelming example of a "basis on which cultural order rests," of a "dominant value system." Women's voices, interpretations, and desires have been "silenced, made invisible, covered over and made 'absent'" in a variety of ways over the past several hundred years, and such radically misogynist ideology has come to seem "natural," so that the protagonist of Charlotte Perkins Gilman's "The Yellow Wallpaper" has no tools with which to fight the combination of patriarchal and medical discourses that immobilizes her; her only mode of protest is to turn to what is considered "irrational," or beyond the civilized pale of acceptable belief and discourse—to symbolically free the trapped woman who is her double. Fantasy is not just *any* subversive discourse; it is one in which the figure of the double is of vital importance, and it is for this reason, I would argue, that feminist writers have been drawn to these texts.

But what is the double? Is the doppelganger the perfect replica of the self? Obviously not. In "The Tiger's Bride," the protagonist differs from her automatic maid most significantly by having a heart, or access to her own subjectivity, even if she is prevented from expressing it. She ceases to resemble the automaton even slightly after she enters into a *mutual* pact with her wild host, as they both disrobe and examine each other's bodies, beast and woman, free from the objectifying ownership of men. Upon her return, she looks into the maid's mirror and "all I saw was a pale, hollow-eyed girl whom I scarcely recognized ... my maid['s] ... face was no longer the spit of my own" (167). The girl has changed significantly in her understanding of her status and potential freedom. That change is reflected physically in the mirror, and the resulting difference in looks between herself and her maid. On discovering that she is now free to return to her father, if she so chooses, the protagonist fantasizes: "I will dress her [the maid] in my own clothes, wind her up, send her back to perform the part of my father's daughter" (167).

Patriarchy requires nothing of the girl that an automaton could not perform as easily, and her father, it is implied, would not be able to tell the difference.

The double is not a perfect replica; it is a simulacrum, or a replica with a significant difference that makes it opposite. It is the reflection discussed in the previous chapter—not mimetic, but reversed, distorted, and perhaps shattered. It is that difference that makes it so threatening and at the same time potentially alluring: the protagonist of "The Tiger's Bride" *could* easily have gone home and resumed the mechanical life she had been leading before. She could have taken on the implements of objecthood, make-up and mirror, and cast aside her emotions and experiences in favor of a music-box that played pleasantly. This double, its threat and its potential, makes literal the internal divides demanded of women under patriarchy, and enables writers to embody the quotidian compromises expected of women in a way that demonstrates their horror and their potential for transcendence.

The double's relationship to feminine subjectivity is addressed directly in Kathryn Davis's *The Girl Who Trod on a Loaf*, when Helle, the older composer enamored of Fran, tells the younger woman:

> We were the same, all right. It was only men who found this idea frightening, only a man who couldn't tolerate the idea that somewhere in this world there might be another man identical to himself. When you got right down to it, wasn't that why they kept plying the doppelganger, that tired old theme, in their art? Whereas women weren't afraid of similarity. (21)

Helle suggests that double-hood, doubleness comes naturally to women, that for women, the doubled or multiplied self is normative, rather than frightening. Frightening or not (and of course, this distinction depends on the double in question), the double is an intrinsic part of fantasy fiction, and emblematizes what I argue is the particular draw of the genre for writers working with second-wave feminist themes.

As discussed previously, Nancy Chodorow's theories of feminine subjectivity and personality development state that due to the gendered division of labor that allocates almost all childcare to women, many women develop a significantly more diffuse sense of self than men, that girls' "internalized and external object relations become and remain more complex, and at the same time more defining of her than do those of [boys]," leading to the development of more flexible ego boundaries (252). Does it not seem, then, that the figure of the double, the self spread out over more than one subject, is a particularly apt way of figuring the same concept? The relational self posited by the Wellesley Stone Center theorists suggests that the capacity for empathy depends on being able to imaginatively take in the affective cues of another and then to resolve oneself again as a separate being. Judith Jordan writes:

> In order to empathize, one must have a well-differentiated sense of self in addition to an appreciation of and sensitivity to the differentness as well as the

sameness of another person. Empathy always involves affective surrender and cognitive structuring, and, in order for empathy to occur, ego boundaries must be flexible ... If either relaxation or restructuring of ego boundaries is impaired, empathy will suffer. (69)

Empathy

As the Stone Center theorist/clinicians note, women tend to be, and are expected to be, more empathic than men, with the result that this process of relaxing and then restrengthening ego boundaries is more essential to feminine subjectivity than to masculine, and the potential risks as well as the rewards are ever-present in women's daily lives. For Western women from the 1970s to the 1990s, "[p]roblems with empathy ... typically involve difficulty reinstating a sense of self and cognitively structuring the experience" (30). Thus, empathy, an important measure of psychic health for women and for men, and a "complex, developmentally advanced, and interactive process, involves a temporary surrender of self followed by a regaining of self and separate perspective; for many women, this important process often entails a risk, or a difficulty in regaining that sense of self" (30).

Thus the double or doppelganger can simultaneously represent the demands of dual consciousness that patriarchy makes on women, the actual lived experience of women with flexible ego boundaries and a shared sense of self, and the fear of a loss of self that is more immediate and real for women than for men.[2]

Mothers and Daughters in the Mirror

Mothers and daughters often serve as doubles of each other, reflecting the dissolution of distinction that such pairs often experience psychologically, and the medium of their doubling is often a mirror. Thus the two guiding tropes of this survey are intertwined; in this section, I will examine the ways in which mothers and daughters are doubled, and the relation of that doubling to mirrors.

Psychoanalysts have placed mother-daughter relationships at the center of the relational paradigm described in earlier chapters, but how can we fit the mirror, with its long but mistaken association with narcissism, into such a system? In other words, how can we conceive of the mirror as not only creative and narrative, but also relational? Mother-daughter relationships and mirrors are absolutely central to these tales. I have discussed those themes in separate chapters, but I do not think that they occur together merely by coincidence. Rather, I would argue that the joined motifs suggest that a sufficiently sophisticated understanding of mirroring provides a complex vision of the mother-daughter relationship *as* a form of mirroring.

Both mother-daughter relationships and mirrors represent a certain fluidity with respect to identity, and I use the word "fluidity" advisedly, as both mothers and mirrors are associated with water (the sea as maternal symbol/origin, and water

---

[2]   For a more detailed discussion of the work of Nancy Chodorow and Judith Jordan, see Chapter 1.

as the earliest mirror). Indeed, one of the French words for mirror, "glace," can also mean "ice." In "And the One Does Not Stir Without the Other," Luce Irigaray argues that when the fluidity suggested by one's mirror image is reified/frozen into ice by the lack of any other kinds of interactions or non-visual communications, so too does the relationship between mother and daughter freeze, and what held the potential for transformation and mutuality becomes a sheer, icy impasse (*passim*).

One of the great tragedies of Tanith Lee's *White as Snow* is that the two main characters, Arpazia and her daughter Coira, almost *never* interact. Coira, the result of rape, is born when Arpazia is still very young and deeply traumatized by the violence in her life. Arpazia immediately rejects Coira, and interacts with her only four times over the course of her life. Thus all mother and daughter have of each other are isolated images. In the absence of other sense cues common to mother-daughter relationships, such as conversation and touch, Arpazia and Coira freeze their notions of each other into massively oversimplified visions of each other as "the same. Like looking in a mirror" (245). Thus both women are frozen not only into their external appearances, but into their external appearances as they were at one given moment. The all-important temporal element is missing.

Also missing, as the frozen image assumes all significance, is a more nuanced understanding of mirroring, of what a reflection is. Arpazia and Coira cannot afford to unsettle their images of each other by considering what the mirror shows critically, because those images are all they have; those images may well be all they are. But such a simplistic perception of each other precludes a more fruitful consideration of what it means for a mother and daughter to function as each other's mirrors. A reflection displays the most faithful similarity simultaneously with the most exact reversal. An understanding of mirroring that admits this complexity can allow mothers and daughters to be reflections in the fullest sense: to encompass similarity and difference, to be and experience the most complex meditations and sequences of thoughts.

Historically, psychoanalytic theorists have not allowed for such flexibility or mutuality in their consideration of the role of mirrors or mirroring within the mother-child relationship. D.W. Winnicott and Heinz Kohut agree that mirroring is the necessary role of the mother (the mirror in Jacques Lacan's mirror stage seems to be largely gender neutral, though at least one critic assumes that his "mirror" is in fact the infant's "mother"[3]), and that unless she is a sufficiently good mirror, the infant will never understand himself as a unified being, or "the infant's creative capacity begins to atrophy" and prevents "that which might have been the beginning of a significant exchange with the world" (Winnicott 19), or

---

[3]   Lacan's essay suggests to me that he is literally writing about physical mirrors, but John P. Muller and William J. Richardson, in *Lacan and Language: A Reader's Guide to Écrits*, comment that "the essential here apparently is that a human form be the external image in which the infant discovers himself and the 'reality' around him, but presumably that human form could also be—and in concrete is more likely to be—the mothering figure" (30).

the infant will develop a narcissistic personality disorder. Of these three theorists, Winnicott's concept of mirroring is most interesting from a relational point of view; he writes:

> What does the baby see when he or she looks at the mother's face? I am suggesting that, ordinarily, what the baby sees is himself or herself. In other words, the mother is looking at the baby and *what she looks like is related to what she sees there* ... I am asking that this which is done naturally well by mothers who are caring for their infants shall not be taken for granted. (19)

Here, when the baby looks at her mother, she is participating in a reciprocal interaction: she responds to her mother's response/view of her. This mirroring is not capped and finite on the mother's part, unlike Kohut's, who refers to good mirroring as "the gleam in the mother's eye which says it is good you are here and I acknowledge your being here and I am uplifted by your presence" (226).[4] The mirroring described by Winnicott is far more fluid than the frozen response granted to Kohut's ideal mother, and of greater and more flexible duration than the mirror stage described by Lacan. Winnicott also directly connects the *interaction* of mirroring with the development of the child's creative capacities, implying, as I have argued, that mirroring is deeply related to creative acts such as reading and writing. Yet all three theorists make the classic mistake of writers considering infant and child development prior to Nancy Chodorow's work: none of the three considers the mother's internal life and its impact on her childcare. In that sense, all three flatten and freeze the mother into a mirroring screen, and none consider how her own experience of self affects her ability to mirror and to be mirrored.

Luce Irigaray takes up exactly this problem in "And the One Doesn't Stir Without the Other," in which she examines the consequences of a lack of attention to mothers' internal selves on their capacity to mirror. Such self-less mothers, she writes, produce self-less daughters, a set of empty mirrors reflecting infinite absence. The first sentence of the essay is usually translated as "With your milk, Mother, I swallowed ice" (60), but Laurie Corbin, in her study of the mother-daughter relationships in the works of Colette, Simone de Beauvoir, and Marguerite Duras, notes that

> the word "glace" can be read as meaning either ice or mirror but in this context I would suggest that the emphasis is on the mirror that the mother gives to her child so that the child can reflect an image back to her mother. This is again an inversion of Lacan's theorization of the mirror phase as Irigaray makes the mother dependent on her daughter for a coherent self-view ... The mother in these texts can only reflect the daughter's imposition of her own view ... if a

---

4   I am not suggesting that this kind of response is somehow inferior to the interaction described by Winnicott; of course it is not and it is necessary for babies and children (to say nothing of adults) to have that sort of positive response from their mothers/caretakers. I am merely noting that Kohut's conception of mirroring requires nothing in return from the child.

mother's face appears in the mirror, it is the daughter's vision of herself which put it there. The concept of mother as mirror will always relegate the mother to the position of object, rather than subject. (99, 144)

And a subject-less mother, a self-less mother, will pass on to her daughter the empty mirror, the lack of self that informs both daughter and mother in Irigaray's essay:

By pouring your ice [mirror] into me, didn't you quench my thirst with your paralysis? And never having known your own face, didn't you nourish me with lifelessness? ... Of necessity I became the uninhabitable region of your reflections ... Each of us lacks her own image; her own face, the animation of her own body is missing. (64)

The mother's mirror is empty—she cannot see her own face—and when she gives that emptiness of self to her daughter, the daughter too becomes paralyzed.

Irigaray's daughter has a wistful fantasy of the kind of mirroring relationship she and her mother might have had if the mother hadn't been without a sense of self:

I would like us to play together at being the same and different. You/I exchanging selves endlessly and each staying herself. Living mirrors. We would play catch, you and I. But who would see that what bounces between us are images? That you give them to me, and I to you without end. And that we don't need an object to throw back and forth at each other for this game to take place. I throw an image of you to you, you throw it back, catch it again. (61–2)

The daughter's fantasy is not one in which the mirrors are shattered, but one in which they are full of selves and infinite images. This is a playful, mutual, reciprocal interchange, based on the mother's subjectivity rather than objecthood, a fluid exchange rather than a frozen surface. This concept of mirroring requires two selves to be present; it is Lacan's, Winnicott's, and Kohut's mirroring, and it is more as well.

Tanith Lee's *White as Snow* can be read as a case study of the damage caused by selflessness described by Irigaray, or as a cautionary tale about flattening out and freezing the significance of the mirror and its reflections into simple replication, or about the insufficiency of mirroring alone. As described before, Arpazia and Coira, mother and daughter, know each other almost entirely through their mirror images. They have no other relationship, no other interaction, nothing on which to build a sense of each other except these fleeting visions. Without any more complex relationship, they are trapped in the most simplistic understanding of the mirror and of each other: a forced choice between fusion and the absolute separation that Adrienne Rich calls "radical surgery" (236).

Arpazia, who has dissociated radically in response to the various traumas of her life, understands both the mirror and her daughter Coira as aspects of herself, and disposes of them both in a kind of attempt at suicide, by giving them both into the hands of the soldier who brought her to Draco: the mirror is the man's payment for abducting and killing the girl: "*She is me. Take her away. Take her away from me. Take her away and take the mirror away,*" Arpazia thinks as she contracts out her daughter's death (170). Coira, too, cannot tell herself from her mother, and is horrified to find her mother's reflection lurking in the mirror when she looks into it:

> Coira looked down and down into the mirror's glass …
>
> Is that me? Is that Coira? Or—
>
> Is it she—my mother—as I saw her that day I said, "You're so beautiful— more beautiful than anyone in the whole world."
>
> Coira felt she would soon fall into the mirror-pool, whirl down for ever and be lost. (199)

Coira later tells the mirror that "I still won't look at you. I may see her there. Her reflection, caught there" (200). Towards the end of novel, Coira is believed dead and put into a coffin made of the glass of her mother's mirror; in a dream, she is horrified to realize that "I'm shut inside in the mirror" (287). The mirror traps Coira just as it trapped Arpazia's reflection—inner and outer, for once Arpazia gives up the mirror, as described earlier in this chapter, she loses the last vestige of her fragile connection to reality. Except for one climactic rapprochement, which ends tragically, these trapped images are all Coira and Arpazia have of each other. Neither is capable of being fully present for the other, and thus until Coira falls in love and then experiences that moment of reconciliation with her mother, neither is fully real: both mother and daughter are trapped in the endless selflessness Irigaray describes. Indeed, earlier in the novel, when each, unbeknownst to the other, is attending a pagan ceremony, Lee writes that "If the sorcerous looking glass looked out to find the first Full Moon of winter, did it also see, that night, an image and that image's reflection, curiously moving—not toward each other—but one following the other, with the spaces of dark between?" (142). Both mother and daughter are two-dimensional, an image and a reflection, and we are never told which woman is the image and which the reflection. Irigaray warns against this absence of depth when she writes, "Don't remain caught up between the mirror and this endless loss of yourself. A self separated from another self. A self missing some other self. Two dead selves distanced from each other, with no ties binding them. The self that you see in the mirror severed from the self that nurtures" (64). At the end of the novel, Arpazia attempts to reunite these two selves, with disastrous consequences; for her, it is too late.

Robin McKinley's *Deerskin* tells the story of another daughter who must struggle to escape her fate as her mother's double. Resetting the tale of Donkeyskin to a fantasy world, McKinley's protagonist is Lissar, a princess, who, without knowing it, matures into a physical double of her mother, widely known as "the most beautiful woman in seven kingdoms" (3, 4, 5, etc.). With this doubling comes immense suffering, however, as her deranged, widowed father forces Lissar to become his fiancée, and when she refuses to wed him, rapes her. Lissar is her mother's double in more than looks, however, as there is more than one allusion to her mother's sexual abuse at the hands of her own father. When Lissar's nurse tells her the tale of her mother and father's engagement (here is another novel in which the mother-daughter relationship is mediated entirely through story-telling), she explains:

> Such a joy was the daily presence of your lovely mother that her father was not eager to part with her. And so he looked to drive her suitors away ... But who could blame him? For she is the most beautiful woman in seven kingdoms, and he died of a broken heart eight months after she married your father and left him. (4–5)

Lissar's mother's father attempted to drive off her suitors, his rivals for her mother's attention; his affection for her is described not in paternal terms but as a result of her beauty, and when she does marry, he "dies of a broken heart." It seems not unlikely that we are meant to understand Lissar's mother as another victim of incestuous abuse; such a reading would explain the horrific dread Lissar feels whenever anyone tells her that she is the image of her late mother. Lissar's mother's portrait occupies as intimidating a role in Lissar's life as does her deranged father, and at the climactic scene of the novel, when Lissar finally publicly confronts her father with what he has done to her, two identical women appear, and only the man who loves her is able to tell the difference between them. Exorcising both the abuse of her father and the internalized image of her mother, Lissar is only then able to contemplate a life in which she is self-aware and can pursue happiness for herself.

Sister My Sister: The Doubling of Equals

Having discussed the doubling of mothers and daughters, I would like now to consider those texts in which women are doubled outside of the mother-daughter relationship. There are few characters in literature with as unified and solid a sense of self as Granny Weatherwax. Indeed, Terry Pratchett's *Witches Abroad* depends on Granny's sense of self for its denouement. Throughout the novel, we are assured that Granny has never entertained a moment's self-doubt; when Magrat, her junior colleague, wakes Granny up, we read:

> Most people, on waking up, accelerate through a quick panicky pre-consciousness check-up: who am I, where am I, who is he/she ... And this is because people are riddled by Doubt. It is the engine that drives them through their lives ... Early morning is the worst time—there's that little moment of panic in case You have drifted away in the night and something else has moved in. This never happened

to Granny Weatherwax … She never needed to find herself because she always knew who was doing the looking. (81–2)

Granny is different from most people because she is entirely unified; this unity prevents her from fully understanding Magrat's own identity crisis, or desire to "find herself." When confronted with the anxious Magrat's worries, Granny tells her "Simplicity Garlick was your mother, Araminta Garlick was your granny, Yolande Garlick is your aunt and you're your … you're your *me*," and then relaxes "with the satisfied look of someone who has solved everything anyone could ever want to know about a personal identity crisis" (22). Of course, as I argued in the previous chapter, Granny is able to emerge victorious over her wicked sister only after she accepts her role as Lily's reflection.

But more than reflections, Granny and Lily are aspects of each other: they are each other's doubles. Physically, we are told that they are almost identical, save for the odd wrinkle (Lily, despite being significantly older, looks younger), and Magrat is almost deceived by her looks: "As she passed the mirror she saw a movement in it. It wasn't her face. It looked a lot like Granny Weatherwax. It smiled at her—a much nicer and friendlier smile than she'd ever got from Granny, Magrat recalled—and then vanished" (80–1). Lily looks like Granny—only nicer, embodying a kindness that Granny cannot afford. They are doubles in more than looks, however, as Lily echoes Granny's own mantra. More than once, Granny justifies her rigid, demanding persona to Magrat by telling her, "If you ain't got respect, you ain't got a thing" (159). When the three witches first confront Lily Weatherwax, she justifies her murder of the Baron of Genua and usurpation of his land by saying that "he didn't show me any respect. If you've got no respect, you've got nothing," and Nanny and Magrat "found themselves looking at Granny." Lily represents the turn to evil that Granny has consciously fought against for her entire life; a particularly telling exchange, also discussed in the previous chapter, comes when Granny catalogues Lily's misdeeds ("The girl doesn't want to marry a frog," she says of one character whose life is being manipulated by Lily to fit a story):

"You'd have done the same," said Lily.

"No," said Granny. "I'd have *thought* the same, but I would have done it."

"What difference does that make, deep down?"

"You mean you don't *know?*" said Nanny Ogg. (247)

Here Lily asserts that she and Granny are exactly alike, that there is no difference between thought and action; Granny and Nanny know differently. Granny has consciously rejected Lily's way of being, not because she cannot see its allure, but because she considers it immoral. This difference is what makes Lily a double, and it is the same difference that makes a mirror reflection not a duplicate: Lily is Granny's opposite, her reverse, *at the same time* as she is similar to Granny. Further, Lily, unlike Granny, does not maintain a unified self. Her power comes from a multiplication of herself. When Lily stands in the center of her maze of mirrors,

> She could feel *herself* pouring into *herself*, multiplying itself via the endless reflections ... When Lilith sighed and strode out from the Space between the mirrors the effect was startling. Images of Lilith hung in the air behind her for a moment, like three-dimensional shadows, before fading. (18)

Lilith uses mirrors to multiply herself—that multiplied self is the source of her magic, or even synonymous with her magic, for when she finds herself engaged in magical battle, "the ghost images suddenly focused on her, so that she became more iridescent" (258). Lily believes that multiplying or splintering herself for power is the safest route, saying that "with mirrors, you're beholden to no-one but your own soul" (63). It is precisely this desire for a soul—or a self—that puts Lily in danger from her own powers, as we are told that with mirror magic, "there's a million billion images and only one soul to go around," and later that if a witch does try to use mirror magic, she would be "spread out among the images, [her] whole soul was pulled out thin, and somewhere in the distant images a dark part of you would get out and come looking for you, if you weren't very careful" (47, 217). The simultaneous allure and danger of double or multiplied selves becomes clear. The source of magic and power, they are not so biddable as Lilith would like to think, and the threat comes from one's own self: "a dark part of *you* would get out" (emphasis added). The double is magical, seductive, and ultimately deadly. Lily loses herself when Granny, the double she had not planned for, smashes the mirror in front of her, upsetting the balance, and in the intact mirror behind her, "the image of Lily Weatherwax turned around, smiled beatifically, and reached out of the frame to take Lily Weatherwax into its arms" (277). The image pulls Lily into the mirror, and she is unable to escape. By relying on mirror magic and a multiplied self, she leaves herself vulnerable to an indirect attack: Granny never touches Lily, but by smashing a mirror, the repository of part of her soul, she undoes her. Lily is vulnerable to the darkness in her own soul, and she is ultimately destroyed not by Granny, but by one of her own selves, her own doubles.

Lee's *White as Snow* makes extensive use of the mirror and language of reflection in order to construct a mother and daughter who are virtually identical, not only in appearance, but in upbringing and trauma as well. While explicitly Arpazia occupies the role of both Demeter and Snow White's wicked mother and Coira, as her name suggests, plays the part of both Persephone and Snow White, Arpazia too is a figure for Persephone, a Persephone without a mother to save her. Like her daughter, she is abducted as a teenager and raped by a king identified with death; when Coira's nurse explains the myth of Demetra and Persepheh (as it is known in the world of the novel) to her, she describes the Hades figure as driving a "chariot drawn by seven black horses, each snorting fire—or they might have been seven black bulls, like the king's banner." The king is, of course, Draco, Coira's father, who abducted and raped her mother. Like Coira, Arpazia grows up motherless, with attendants who are her own father's illegitimate daughters. Arpazia and Coira are doubled in experience, in myth, and in physicality.

But Arpazia is haunted by another double as well, her childhood maid and half-sister Lilca, who dies early in the novel. Lilca was "the bastard daughter of the lord, but had a look not of Arpazia, or her father, but of her own mother, a narrow-boned woman with coppery hair" (36). Lilca, then, physically doubles her own mother, but is the shadow of what Arpazia might have been, had she been born out of wedlock to a non-noble mother, and she initially presents herself as an ally to Arpazia, helping her to avoid the fate their father had planned for her should the castle be taken by Draco's army, an "honorable" death. Lilca and Arpazia sneak out of the castle together, and the juxtaposition of the sisters, one white as snow with black hair, and the other with red hair, recalls the doubled, loving sisters of the fairy tale "Snow White and Rose Red," a story from the Grimms' collection without cognates in most other cultures. While the Snow White in "Snow White and Rose Red" is a very different character from the Snow White in "Little Snow White," or, as it is better known, "Snow White and the Seven Dwarfs," the association between the two tales is inescapable. "Snow White and Rose Red" concerns the adventures of two sisters who love each other so as to be inseparable, and always venture forth into the forest arm in arm.

In *White as Snow*, the sisters are quickly separated. Lilca shows Arpazia a secret way out of the castle, but it is no escape; it is instead a betrayal. Lilca has struck a bargain: in exchange for letting the invaders into the castle and delivering up the legitimate princess, she hopes to escape with her life. She is mistaken, however, as she is first raped by four soldiers and then hanged for her treachery, because Draco "did not like faithlessness, and ... sought always to make vivid examples of his moral stance" (38). Arpazia misses Lilca's execution, but the figure of her sister returns to haunt her, and ultimately she re-enacts her fate, enduring rape, and ultimately being hanged as "punishment" for her "crimes" by a misogynist king.

The seemingly minor character of Lilca is introduced and disposed of in three pages; Arpazia does not think of her sister again until Cirpoz, the soldier who had first raped Lilca, re-appears. She looks into her mirror in order to gain access to her memory and her past returns to her—she quickly disposes of both the mirror and her daughter, but that past clings to her still. After fleeing the castle and enduring a harsh winter in the woods, Arpazia begins to lose the little that is left of her mind and is prematurely aged by frostbite. When found by a local woodsman, she remembers that she should not reveal her true name (she has been accused of witchcraft): "She remembered another name. 'Lilca'" (231). She then thinks, "He would rape her, inevitably, the price for shelter or assistance. That had been Lilca's fate. And something else had happened to Lilca" (231). Arpazia takes on Lilca's identity and her understanding of her place in this brutal world, but she cannot remember Lilca's final end; she has repressed the memory of what will be her own fate. She continues to call herself Lilca during her stay at an inn, though she then becomes "Mistress Lilca," as the innkeeper's wife recognizes her attitude of aristocracy; thus she intertwines her own status with the identity of her illegitimate half-sister and seals her fate, a fate she does not remember until she is at the end of her life: "Lilca had been hanged. In Draco's war-camp, they had told the fourteen-year-old Arpazia, making sure she was given the details. She had forgotten them, had named herself Lilca. Now, she recollected" (312). From rape to hanging, Arpazia's life patterns itself on that of the half-sister who shadows her, whom she doubles.

Without an understanding of the significance of the double to the fantastic in general and to feminine subjectivity in particular, the recurrence of the figure of Lilca might seem inexplicable, or gratuitous. But given the 1970s and 1990s understanding of women as having more diffuse identities, as discussed earlier, the use of Lilca as a double for Arpazia highlights not only the misogyny and class-based cruelty of Arpazia's world, but also the contingency of her identity on her relational status: her status as "legitimate" daughter, which prevents Draco's soldiers from raping her and motivates his decision to marry her, as well as her status as sister. Arpazia has left pieces of herself in her mirror, in her daughter, and in her sister: she herself exists at the relational nexus of these three, and she is destroyed by a confluence of all of them.

Melanie, the daughter who believes that she has caused her mother's death by attempting to take her place in her mother's wedding dress in Angela Carter's *The Magic Toyshop*, is doubled not only by her mother, but also, ominously, by an ill-fated marionette. After her parents' deaths, she goes to live with her abusive Uncle Philip, her mute Irish Aunt Maggie, and Finn and Francie, Maggie's younger brothers. In an attempt to cheer her up, Finn takes her on a tour of Uncle Philip's workshop, and there she sees "[l]ying face-downwards in a tangle of strings ... a puppet fully five feet high, a *sylphide* in a fountain of white tulle, fallen flat down as if someone had got tired of her in the middle of playing with her ... She had long, black hair down to the waist of her tight satin bodice" (67). The doll is unmistakably a double for Melanie on that fateful night when she unbound her hair, put on her mother's wedding dress, and walked into the garden. The doll has collapsed and been abandoned, but just as it invokes Melanie's earlier ill-starred adventure, it presages a future ordeal, Uncle Philip's decision to use Melanie as a puppet in his marionette theater. When Melanie is forced to watch the puppet enact a sequence called "Morte d'une Sylphe, or, Death of a Wood Nymph," the puppet's demise and collapse prefigures the trauma Melanie will endure when, as Leda, she is performatively raped by the swan-puppet. In that role, she is once again draped in diaphanous white fabric; she "would be a nymph crowned with daisies again; he saw her as once she had seen herself" (141). Her trauma is reinscribed in part through the process of returning her to the person she had been at the beginning of the novel, when she explored her identity by taking on various styles of feminine objecthood, posing in the manner of famous paintings of women as sexual objects. She is no longer in that state: note that Uncle Philip saw her "as *once* she had seen herself" (emphasis added). At the cusp of sexual maturity, Melanie had adopted a male gaze—perhaps a visual version of what Carter found about her writing when she noted that she found herself "using the turns of phrase which contain within them the idea that I am male, and the person I'm addressing is male." The puppet, constructed and controlled by Uncle Philip, is Melanie's double, frozen at that earlier moment; it occupies a similar status to the automatic maid in "The Tiger's Bride," but rather than being able to shed the implicit patriarchal role, Melanie is forced back into it, re-clothed in the costume of daughterly loss, and forced to endure a faux-rape. Unlike her double, though, Melanie is flesh and blood, and can move beyond her prescribed identity. When Uncle Philip sets the toyshop on fire in rage, she and Finn escape. She imagines all the puppets burning, and she and Finn "face each other in a wild surmise" (199), a reference to Keats's "On First Looking into Chapman's Homer," when he compares his delight in discovering Ancient Greece through Chapman's translations with the moment when Cortez "stared at the Pacific—and all his men / Look'd at each other with a wild surmise— / Silent, upon a peak in Darien." Cortez, in a settlement in what is now Panama, first sees the Pacific Ocean, and the implications and possibilities of this ocean beyond the world known to him elicit wonder and "wildness." The invocation of the European exploration of the New World takes us back to the beginning of the novel, which opens with the following:

> The summer she was fifteen, Melanie discovered she was made of flesh and blood. O, my America, my new found land. She embarked on a tranced voyage, exploring the whole of herself, clambering her own mountain ranges, penetrating the moist richness of her secret valleys, a physiological Cortez, da Gama or Mungo Park. (1)

Melanie here is both Cortez and America, both explorer and New World, both masculine subject (the quotation "O, my America, my new found land" is from John Donne's "To his mistress going to bed") and feminine object; she has divided herself, but for her, this division is joyful, as she herself explores the recent changes in her body, which, unlike that of Donne's mistress, is not "manned" at all. Like the protagonist of "The Tiger's Bride," Melanie's body changes: throughout the novel we read of her hair growing and her legs growing too long for her pajamas, and on this first page she does "cartwheels and handstands out of sheer exhilaration at the supple surprise of herself now she was no longer a little girl" (1). The puppet, like the automatic maid of the "The Tiger's Bride," is a static double, one who cannot grow or change in herself, and represents entrapment in a patriarchal vision. The novel ends, then, with Finn and Melanie having found the space, or ocean, beyond this vision.

The multiplied self is not necessarily negative, as we saw above in Melanie's joyful division of self. For McKinley's Lissar in *Deerskin*, the divided self is a necessary stage of healing. After miscarrying the result of her father's rape, Lissar is visited by the Moonwoman, a local goddess who heals her physically and brings her emotional peace by temporarily blocking her memory. She also changes Lissar's coloring and transforms her loyal dog. When Lissar realizes that these transformations have taken place, she has the following conversation with herself:

Good, said a voice in her head. They will never recognize either of you. Recognize me? she answered the voice. If no one recognizes me, how will I learn who I am? But her heart quailed even as she asked the question, and she was relieved when the voice had an answer to this. Be glad of your curly dog and your white hair and black eyes. Be glad, and go boldly into human lands, and find a new self to be. (157)

Lissar's ability to rejoin humanity after suffering great trauma is predicated on her ability to take on a new persona, to divide herself and become her own double. She takes on a new name, "Deerskin," after the enchanted dress the Moonwoman bestows upon her, and finds a new identity in a new country. She does not decide to tap into her earlier memories until she encounters a picture of her double—a portrait of the princess she used to be in the storeroom of the castle she works at in her new country. When she sees this portrait, she recognizes her dog in it, and is forced to understand both her selves: "It was only because she could not refuse to acknowledge Ash [her dog] that she had to look into her own flat, painted eyes and aloof expression and say Yes, that was I" (266). Lissar has trouble containing and integrating her two selves, but finally is able to do so in order to prevent her father from marrying the princess of her new country; she confronts him publicly with his crimes against her, again using the magic of the Moonwoman, and in that moment becomes both Lissar and Deerskin. The re-integration is the climactic scene of the novel, but it is predicated upon the importance of doubling, of dividing her self, to Lissar's sanity and survival.

As well as being necessary, multiple selves can be cause for celebration. In Kelly Link's "The Girl Detective," the 12 tap-dancing bankrobbers who are also figures for the 12 dancing princesses of the Grimms' "The Worn-out Dancing Shoes," are completely indistinguishable. They are almost always described as a collective ("They wore tiny black dominos," "They spun," "They were carrying purses" [243]), and there is even some indication that the Girl Detective might be one of them, or might be related to them, or might be another version of them, as they wear the same underpants and all have long, long legs. When the Girl Detective and the princesses end up at the same nightclub, the narrator begins to refer to the group of women as "the girl detectives," saying that "in the mossy glow, they all look like the girl detective. Or maybe the girl detective looks like all of them. They all look so happy" (264). This proliferation of girl detectives occurs at perhaps the most joyful, climactic moment in the story, when the girl detective is reunited with her long-missing mother, and the princesses, the girl detective, her mother, and the waiters in a Chinese restaurant that leads to the underworld celebrate in a whirling, dizzying, extravagant dance.

Even when she is separate from the 12 tap-dancing bankrobbers, the Girl Detective's identity encompasses a great many potential selves; the narrator tells us that "[s]ome people say that she is not one girl but many—that is, she's actually a secret society of Girl Scouts. Or possibly a sub-branch of the FBI." Even the narrator is implicated in the Girl Detective's multiplicity: "At least I don't think that I am the girl detective. If I were the girl detective," he/she writes,

"I would surely know." Self and other are ineluctably intertwined in this story—in one passage, entitled "Why we love the girl detective," the narrator speaks in the first-person plural, constructing her- or himself as a multiplicity as well. Identities remain merging, multiplied, and conjectural.

In fact, the chameleon-esque nature of the Girl Detective means that she can be anybody's double. At the end of the story, the narrator tells us:

> I thought I saw the girl detective in the bar in Terminal B ... disguised as a fat old man ... someone sat down next to her. It was a kid about twelve years old. She had red hair. She was wearing overalls ... I realized that [the old man] wasn't the girl detective at all ... It was the kid in the overalls—what a great disguise! Then the waitress came over to take their order ... Maybe *she* was the girl detective. (265)

The girl detective's multiplied identity allows her to be anywhere, anyone, at any time, which is of course a great help in her line of work. In "The Girl Detective," multiplied selves signal happiness, celebration, and mastery.

It is only in a fantasy text that such self-multiplication can reach its ultimate height. Brian Attebery notes that fantasy, unlike other genres or modes, can use magic to call "into question the continuity of traits by which the reader is accustomed to identify characters ... Virtually any character trait can be altered magically: appearance, age, voice, emotional state, memory ... When, then, might the character be said to change identity?" (73–4). The doubling between Arpazia and Lilca could, perhaps, occur in a work of realism, but Lissar's physical and emotional transformations could not; nor could the bewildering mosaic of constantly interchanging identities found in "The Girl Detective." Fantasy's unique ability to question the nature of character allows feminist writers to make full use of the double.

At Least Two Sides to Every Story: Narrative Doubling

Characters are not the only elements of a text that can be doubled; often, especially in fantasies, the story itself is doubled or multiplied. Margaret Atwood's *Penelopiad*, a retelling of the story of *The Odyssey* from the point of view of those who stayed in Ithaca, in fact contains several retellings and alludes to even more. The dominant story in this novel is a first-person narrative by Penelope, emphasizing her anger and resentment of her husband, the suitors, her cousin Helen, and almost anyone else who exists in the realm of the myth. But even within its own boundaries, that story cannot drown out its own doubles; within the first few pages Penelope tells us that "I realized how many people were laughing at me behind my back—how they were ... making jokes about me ... ; how they were turning me into a story, or into several stories, though not the kind of stories I'd prefer to hear about myself" (3). She is, of course, referring to the multiplicity of legends about Penelope—the multiplicity of Penelopes, if you will. There is the Penelope of Homer's *Odyssey*, the faithful stay-at-home, of course, but there is also the legend about how Penelope had sex with all of the suitors, and gave birth to Pan. And the legend about how Penelope had sex with only one suitor, the one she liked best. At the very beginning, this novel acknowledges its variants, the impossibility of containing or identifying one story, because of the doubling and multiplying of legends. The novel goes on to oscillate among many different versions of the tale, interspersing Penelope's narrative with poetry recited by the 12 maids hanged for treachery by Telemachus upon Odysseus's return, with satyr plays showing Penelope in bed with one or more suitors (the prologue acknowledges the doubled story, reading "As we approach the climax, grim and gory, / Let us just say: There is another story. / Or several, as befits the goddess Rumour" [147]), with a faux anthropology lecture by the maids, suggesting yet another interpretation of the myth ("possibly our rape and subsequent hanging represent the overthrow of a matrilineal moon-cult by an incoming group of usurping patriarchal father-god-worshipping barbarians" [165]), with a show trial of Odysseus for murdering the maids.

As discussed above, Lily Weatherwax is a double for Esme not merely because she resembles her physically, but also because she represents a potential path that Esme rejected. These doubles of the story of Penelope resemble the tale we know, and resemble the tale that Atwood's Penelope is telling. Their versions are recognizable, and much of what they portray echoes the concerns of the novel's main tale. During the trial sequence, the maids call upon the Furies to avenge their deaths, crying out, "He hanged us in cold blood! Twelve of us! Twelve young girls! For nothing!" echoing not only the anthropology lecture's suggestion that the number of maids is significant in its connection to the months and subsequent comment, "You don't have to think of us as real girls, real flesh and blood, real pain, real injustice. That might be too upsetting. Just discard the sordid part," but also Penelope's own anger and grief as she mourns, "My helpers during the long nights of the shroud. My snow-white geese. My thrushes, my doves … I would need time in order to fully disguise my true feelings about the unfortunate hanging of my twelve young maids" (177, 168, 160). The emphasis on the number of dead girls and the insistence on their significance tie these disparate multiplied stories together as surely as Lily's insistence on respect ties her to her sister. But these stories are not all the same story—they are doubles, and they represent paths *not* taken. In the main tale told by Penelope, she does *not* publicly try Odysseus for his murder of her maids, nor does she dramatize her bond with them by invoking a matriarchal religion. These story-doubles represent aspects of the same tale, potential ways its concerns can be expressed, just as character-doubles represent aspects of the same self, potential roles it might play.

Catherynne M. Valente's startlingly beautiful *The Ice Puzzle* is a serialized novel that revisits the fairy tale of "The Snow Queen" by shattering it into 25 chapters, termed "shards."[5] Each shard recounts a tale about the figure we know

---

5   *The Ice Puzzle* was originally published on-line. A print edition is forthcoming from Prime Books, but as it has not yet been published, I am unable to provide page-citations.

as the Snow Queen in a variety of cultures, ranging from a tale of the Japanese Yuki-Onna, to the Greek Demeter and Persephone, to *The Nutcracker*'s Sugar Plum Fairy, to Queen Frostine in contemporary versions of the board game Candy Land. The final chapter is an illustration of a mirror with blank spaces for words that are scattered throughout the text, recognizable by the design that surrounds them. By piecing together this final message (the ice puzzle), the reader becomes a double for the little girl abducted by the Snow Queen and chained to a chair unless she can solve the puzzle of the shattered mirror before she freezes to death. We find out that the current Snow Queen herself endured the same test, and when the girl successfully completes the puzzle, she becomes a double of the Snow Queen: "Suddenly there was two of everything: two women, two gazes knotting themselves across the half-mist, and two Mirrors." Ultimately, the girl takes over the Snow Queen's role, extending that identity to yet another self.

The Snow Queen refers to the previous Snow Queen, the one who forced *her* to complete the puzzle, as her "surrogate mother," and Valente describes the doubled relationship between the Snow Queen and the Summer Queen, who tries to hold Andersen's Gerda as she seeks her companion Kay, kidnapped by an earlier Snow Queen: "And who is to say her [the Summer Queen's] daughter is not the Queen of Winter, and who is to say her daughter is not herself, turned inside out and frozen … glowering at the injustice of her separation, self from self." (Step)mother and daughter are similarly doubled in the shard that recounts Valente's version of "Snow White," in which Snow White and her stepmother see only each other when they look into mirrors, and Snow White accompanies her rescuing prince to his castle only to find that he has a daughter from a previous marriage, a daughter with black hair, pale skin, and red lips.

Even our current Snow Queen, the one who has abducted the little girl who becomes her successor, is shattered into a multitude of selves. The giant Mirror in her palace of ice, the centerpiece of the story, has been shattered into pieces, and "the glass ruptured her face, inverted it, caused schisms and rifts in her cheekbones, her eyelashes, her earlobes. She was broken like a Picasso." Ruptured, inverted, schismed, the many aspects and parts of the Snow Queen come together not only to make a whole, but also to create a thing of beauty, a work of art. The Snow Queen's experience of seeing herself as an object while remaining the subject doing the seeing is positive. In fact, to the Snow Queen, it is the idea of a unified self that is monstrous. While out and about, "In a great sheet of window she caught the unfamiliar image of herself, unrefracted by the snow-mirror, the myth-mirror … but this was not the Snow Queen, this was not her own shattered face … This was a monster." The first Snow Queen, the one who shattered the mirror, drew power from her multiple reflections: "How like a puzzle it was, the Mirror still whole, yet utterly destroyed. The other woman [the reflection] was cleft into dozens, a prism of schismatic snowflakes spiraling in at each other … she felt herself flare."

In this context, however, I am less concerned with the doubling between the Snow Queen and her youthful protégée, which seems deeply tied to topics I have explored in previous sections, and more interested in the doubling of the *story itself*. Hans Christian Andersen's "The Snow Queen" is refracted and transmuted into a variety of settings; none of these shards re-creates the original plot of the fairy tale, but each one suggests a tale that, by overlaying "The Snow Queen," suggests not only kinship, but a path not taken by the various tales. The story itself is doubled and multiplied, often in the most elliptical, poetic ways. Just as "The Girl Detective" implicates its narrator in its multiplying selves, so too does *The Ice Puzzle* implicate the reader. The final chapter is an illustration of a mirror with blank spaces for words that are scattered throughout the text, recognizable by the design that surrounds them. The reader's doubling with the young girl, and therefore with the Snow Queen herself, and even further, with Valente, comes as the reader seeks out the proper words with which to compose the puzzle that ends the novel. Here the reader takes on aspects of the murderous Snow Queen as well as the creating writer, suggesting that these figures are also doubles of each other (a reading that is borne out by the fact that for several years, until mid-2012, Valente used "Yuki-Onna" as her screen name on her blog). The very acts of reading and writing fantasy create multiple selves in this beautiful, complex text.

The novel is conceived of as a puzzle itself, and with each chapter termed a "shard," the implication is that something—Andersen's original story?—has been shattered. The shards are, however, associated with the shards that make up the Snow Queen's shattered mirror of ice, part of which is the ice puzzle that the little girl is trying to solve. Consider a shattered mirror and its refractions, how each shard shows its own reflection, creating a kaleidoscopic effect. As mentioned above, in each chapter/shard, certain words are surrounded by a pattern of broken glass. The reader pieces them together into a whole at the end in a puzzle in the shape of a broken mirror, putting the reader in the position of the child, and thus of the Snow Queen herself. Thus it is *us* that the shattered mirror is reflecting, various versions of ourselves as the selves of the Snow Queen, suggesting that we are our various cultures' tales, and that as all these shards/chapters come together to make up one novel, so too do all these tales and various selves come together to make up one identity. Valente refers to the shattered mirror as the "myth-mirror"; it is a mirror used to reflect the self into different shapes, and that is precisely what the novel does. It uses different myths as mirrors of one another and of one female character. If myth is a way to make meaning out of our lives, and I believe that all narrative is, then it is a way of creating ourselves as multiplied selves.

Of course, to a certain extent, all revisionary work embodies doubles, as a revision itself requires a doubling or multiplying of possibilities, of stories. The revision is always a double of the earlier tales. But it is only in the genre of fantasy that this theme can be explored most vividly, as the limitations of reality are suspended, characters can meet literal doubles of themselves, and mutually exclusive stories can co-exist. Earlier I discussed the significance of the divided or multiplied self in the context of psychoanalytic theories of female subjectivity. But what about the "other"-ness of the self-as-other? Does fantasy provide a special avenue into understanding how the other functions in literature, and if so, how does that understanding relate to feminist concerns of self and other?

As alluded to above, Rosemary Jackson considers "themes of the other," fantastic tales that

> deal with problems generated by desire, by the *unconscious*. The relation of self to other is mediated through desire, and fantastic narratives in this category tell of various versions of that desire, usually in transgressive forms ... In [themes of the other], fear originates in a source external to the subject: the self suffers an attack of some sort which makes it part of the other. (51, 58)

Jackson's separation of fantasy into "themes of the self," stories in which consciousness and identity is problematized and the threat comes from within, and "themes of the other," stories in which desire and the unconscious is problematized and the threat comes from without, presupposes a sharp distinction between self and other—a distinction whose blurring constitutes a threat or distress. But this division, between subject and object, self and other, is exactly the division that mirrors and the figure of the doppelganger undo, for the mirror is an external object that transforms the internal subjectivity, while the reflection is an emanation from the subject itself—"themes of self" and "themes of the other" are bound up in this one object, suggesting that the distinction between them is not so clear-cut as Jackson might wish. Martin Horstkotte acknowledges the intertwining of self and other in his work on the other in postmodern British fantasy. He writes of the special significance the other has to fantasy literature, that "it enters the world of everyday reality and provokes a clash of two sign systems, of two realities and of two worlds, the world of the self and the world of the other" ("Worlds" 319). But, he goes on to specify,

> the world of the self and of the other may be more or less entangled with each other ... the borders between self and other are shifting and fuzzy, so that the other may cross the border into the world of the self and vice versa ... the other always carries a certain amount of the self [but] it is not identical with the self ... the collision of two existentially different modes of being that so often governs the fantastic is a collision of two worlds: the world of the self and that of the other. (321)

For Horstkotte, the blurring of the distinction between self and other, rather than being the ultimate threat that Jackson implies that is, is essential to the very categories of self and other.

The Wellesley Stone Center theorists reject that distinction as well, sometimes terming their work the study of "subject relations," as opposed to "object relations," because theorizing the essence of the self as existing only in relation to other selves, entering into empathy and mutual exchange, implicitly requires the recognition that more than one subject can exist at a time, and that a given self can and does operate with this awareness. Such a recognition and the refusal to recognize a hard and fast line between subject and object speaks to the heart of the concerns about gender and the subject-object divide that Luce Irigaray expresses in "Any Theory of the 'Subject' Has Always Been Appropriated by the

'Masculine.'" In this essay, she posits that the subject-object divide is inherently misogynist, as it is always primarily based in the rejection of the mother by the subject as "not-I." In other words, Irigaray argues that the construction of the ego as subject is always predicated on the existence of an object, a background that is rejected or excluded from the realm of subject-hood, and that the most essential rejection or exclusion to that ego-formation, the first rejection or exclusion, is the subject's rejection or exclusion of his/her mother, who is associated with the "stable earth" on which the phallic "tower" of I-ness, of subjecthood is erected. Mothers come to symbolize femininity in general and in essence for that subject, as his or her mother is, in the normative Western family structure described by Nancy Chodorow, the primary representative of womanhood in his or her lived experience. Therefore, Irigaray argues, every understanding of subject-hood has been based not only on the distinction between "I" and "not-I," but also on the assumption that "not-I" is equivalent to "not-subject," and so femininity and subjecthood become incompatible concepts (*Speculum* 133–6).

In this framework, the act of doubling, of bridging the gap between "I" and "not-I," of bringing into full subjectivity a divided or multiplied self or story, as does Valente's *Ice Puzzle* and Atwood's *Penelopiad*, is a feminist literary technique, and one that reaches its zenith in fantastic modes of writing. Doubling, then, is not a threat—the Girl Detective celebrates her multiplicity, and multiple selves add depth to the Snow Queen and to Penelope—but rather a resurrection, a reunion. When the other takes on subjectivity and becomes a self, women, who have been forced to occupy a position of self-as-other, are able to achieve the wholeness of self-as-self, without sacrificing vital aspects of their lived experience in a society that takes masculinity to be normative. We might argue that by enacting "subject relations" within its texts, fantasy allows the literalization and legitimation of the double vision that women have had to develop over the course of their socialization into a culture that regards them as other or as objects. It is no wonder, then, that the reunion and re-collection of these multiple subjects is cause for celebration in "The Girl Detective."

Image and Object: Seeming and Being

One of Rosemary Jackson's most oft-cited observations is that fantasy is a genre based around subversion of dominant ideologies. "Fantastic literature," she writes,

> points to or suggests the basis upon which cultural order rests, for it opens up, for a brief moment, on to disorder, on to illegality, on to that which lies outside the law, that which is outside dominant value systems. The fantastic traces the unsaid and the unseen of culture: that which has been silenced, made invisible, covered over and made "absent." (4)

In its exposure of these elements that have been written out of dominant ideologies, then, fantasy would seem to offer a perfect form for feminist writing, concerned as it so often is with making visible women's experiences and perspectives, which have so often been written out of reality as it has been defined by patriarchy. Both fantasy and feminism, then, are concerned with what has been left out of dominant, normative ways of understanding the world: what has been the cost of a certain kind of coherence, the cost of assuming that realism is an adequate representation of reality, and that male experiences of the world adequately define it? In this sense, fantasy and feminism are concerned with the disjuncture between *seeming* and *being*, between the illusion created by mimesis and patriarchy, respectively, and the experiences that reveal the flimsiness of those ideologies.

Is fantasy, then, the accurate representation of feminine lived experience? This assertion is a risky one. Similar arguments have been advanced about the relationship between postcolonial cultures and magic realism, in which it is argued that magic realism simply reflects accurately the postcolonial worldview. Such an argument is of course deeply problematic, as it assumes a static worldview within a given postcolonial culture, and ignores the long-standing connections between magic realism and works by writers such as Kafka, as well as the use of colonial language to create these supposedly accurate representations of postcolonial life.

I do not, then, wish to suggest that fantasy is merely the mimesis of femininity. I would suggest that fantasy, in exposing the dichotomy between ideology and experience, between seeming and being, speaks to a particularly significant aspect of femininity under patriarchy. As theorists from Joan Rivière to Susan Brownmiller to Judith Butler have discussed, femininity is a masquerade or performance, one that entails costuming, make-up, and a disciplining of the body, mind, and affect. Fantasy's ability to expose the constructed-ness of mimesis, the artificiality of the conventions for representation that have been agreed upon by our arbiters of culture, suggests the ways in which feminism itself exposes the artificiality of the gendered roles and restrictions claimed for so long to be natural by their proponents. It is no accident that feminist writers are attracted to the genre of fantasy; similarly it is no accident that the field of feminist revisions of fairy tales and classical myth continues to grow at a seemingly exponential rate. Revisions of fairy tales and myth allow feminist writers to reaffirm a connection with their foremothers, and to advocate an understanding of self that does not turn those who are non-self into objects; both aspects of the field, revision and fantasy, deny the legitimacy of a zero-sum understanding of relation, be it literary or psychological, and so counter the rhetoric of objectification that has confined women in the past.

Epilogue

> Storytelling is perhaps humanity's primary tool for *changing* reality.
> — Karl Kroeber, *Retelling/Rereading: The Fate of Storytelling*
> *in Modern Times*, 13

To a certain extent, whether or not Karl Kroeber's assertion about the reality-changing power of storytelling is true does not matter; what matters is that enough of us believe it to be true that we continue to use stories to make sense of the world around us and in order to make interventions in that world. Certainly feminist psychoanalysts, feminist writers, and feminist artists of all sorts have believed in the power of stories enough to consider the creation of new stories and the revision of old ones to be essential to their political projects. In this book, I have attempted to trace out the connections and correspondences between the stories told by second-wave feminist psychoanalytic theorists about what it means to be a woman and those told by their fairy-tale rewriting contemporaries.

Psychoanalytic theory and creative (re)writing may be two different ways of telling stories, but both do no more and no less than telling stories. Sometimes these stories resonate with the reader and she adopts them as truths, or as approximations close enough to truths to do until something more resonant comes along. Sometimes they resonate strongly enough with enough influential people that they become adopted as cultural truths; such is what happened, for example, with various Freudian theories such as the Oedipal complex. But without empirical research to support them, they remain stories, though no less meaningful for that.

In *Critical and Creative Perspectives on Fairy Tales: An Intertextual Dialogue Between Fairy-Tale Scholarship and Postmodern Retellings*, a thorough, thoughtful, and illuminating book, Vanessa Joosen opened up the interchange between fairy-tale revisions and their associated scholarship for analysis. Noting that critics and creative writers were often engaged in similar projects and shared similar perspectives, she explores how these texts extended one another's ideas and rang changes on one another. In her conclusion, she notes in particular that, as many revisions take up perspectives or concerns that had been key in academic discourse long previously,

> it can be argued that fairy-tale retelling is also a site where outmoded critical views of the traditional fairy tale live on. Some of these fictional texts recapitulate the development of certain lines of thought with regard to the fairy tale, expressing views of the fairy tale that have long been problematized in academic circles ... Especially in retellings for young children, early feminist and Marxist views still find equivalents today, as if new readers are expected to run through the evolution of these critical paradigms beginning with the most basic views and gradually evolving to more complex ones. (300)

This idea that the new reader might want to recapitulate the phylogeny of a critical point of view in her personal intellectual ontogeny is one with which I actually have a great deal of sympathy. In my experience, nothing creates so thorough an understanding of a critical moment than knowledge of its historical context and philosophical lineage. Indeed, the absence of historical context makes it all too easy to overlook a theorist's or a movement's most important strides, so that "second-wave" with respect to feminist movements comes to connote the worst traits of the movement rather than its best ones. Further, the historical development of readings and ideas is essential to understanding that idea; this is why we as scholars review the literature on a given topic as well as classic essays pertaining to it when developing our own ideas and understandings. The idea that this process is of benefit to scholars, but not to the general public seeking to make sense of the world through literature, seems strange.

But by using the term "outmoded" to describe the critical perspectives adopted by the revisions she examines, Joosen, perhaps unconsciously, implies that if these perspectives or interpretations of the traditional fairy tale are no longer *au courant* among academics, they have outlived their usefulness.

But is that accurate? By suggesting that the critical perspectives adopted by writers of creative texts revising fairy tales are often "outmoded," Joosen implies that an idea or perspective can be thoroughly investigated through the genre of criticism alone, and that the revisions add nothing new to the conversation. Where, in that formulation, is value of artistic, rather than academic, analysis and exploration? Is there no form of understanding or insight better conveyed through fiction or poetry than through academic articles or books? My exploration of the relationship between theories of feminine subjectivity and the explorations of that subjectivity in contemporary feminist revisions of fairy tales and myths suggests the opposite; fiction and poetry are absolutely necessary companions to theoretical explorations, as each genre offers differing kinds of precision and insight, as well as different areas of focus, even while maintaining the same themes and concerns. The fact that poets and novelists continue to work with ideas long after they have passed out of fashion in academia suggests that the ideas are in fact not outmoded, that criticism does not exhaust their potential or interest, but that criticism is a precondition, not the final word, but an early word.

Second-wave feminism saw an immense amount of thought put into the question of identity and what it meant/means to be a woman; indeed, feminism has yet to meet the standard of providing support and advocacy for all women, as too many feminists continue to reject transsexual and transgender people, for example. Both the concepts of mother-daughter relationships and mirrors challenge traditional boundaries understood or assumed to exist between self and other, subject and object, and the valorization of such boundaries had been used over and over again to justify views of women and their subjectivities as deficient or immature.

By focusing on mother-daughter relationships and on mirrors, theorists and fiction writers were able to challenge such assumptions of deficiency regarding women and map out "normalcy" based on women's psyches and experiences.

Theorists did so by openly challenging supposedly "universal" theories and revealing the masculine, misogynist biases encoded in them. In many ways, the project embarked upon by fairy-tale and mythic revisionists was not so different; they rewrote stories that had been supposed to be already universal, highlighting the ways in which those stories had not been universal, had overlooked or violently distorted women's experiences. In doing so, they challenged the borders not only of the self, but of story itself, refiguring the relationships among traditional stories and their revisions, as well as the function of the fantastic.

(reveal or replace)

Bibliography

Fairy Tale and Myth Revisions

Atwood, Margaret. *The Penelopiad*. Edinburgh: Canongate, 2005.
Broumas, Olga. *Beginning with O*. New Haven: Yale University Press, 1977.
Carter, Angela. *The Magic Toyshop*. 1967. New York: Penguin Books, 1996.
———. *The Bloody Chamber and Other Stories*. 1979.
———. *Burning Your Boats: The Collected Short Stories*. New York: Henry Holt, 1995.
———. "Ashputtle or The Mother's Ghost: Three Versions of One Story." *American Ghosts and Old World Wonders*. 1993. *Burning Your Boats: The Collected Short Stories*. New York: Henry Holt , 1995. 390–6.
Davis, Kathryn. *The Girl Who Trod on a Loaf*. New York: Alfred A. Knopf, 1993.
Donoghue, Emma. *Kissing the Witch*. London: Hamish Hamilton, 1997.
Dove, Rita. *Mother Love*. New York: W.W. Norton, 1995.
Frost, Gregory. "The Root of the Matter." *Snow White, Blood Red*. Eds. Ellen Datlow and Terri Windling. New York: Avon Books, 1993.
Gaiman, Neil. "Snow, Glass, Apples." 1994. *Smoke and Mirrors: Short Fictions and Illustrations*. New York: Avon Books, 1998. 325–39.
Glück, Louise. *Meadowlands*. Hopewell, NJ: Ecco Press, 1996.
Gunn, Kirsty. *The Keepsake*. New York: Grove Press, 1997.
Joyce, James. *Ulysses*. Eds. Hans Walter Gabler et al. New York: Vintage Books, 1986.
Lee, Tanith. *White as Snow*. New York: Tor Books, 2000.
Link, Kelly. *Stranger Things Happen*. New York: Small Beer Press, 2001.
McKinley, Robin. *Deerskin*. New York: Ace Books, 1994.
Morrison, Toni. *Beloved*. New York: Penguin Putnam, 1987.
Pratchett, Terry. *Witches Abroad*. 1991. London: Corgi Books, 1992.
Sexton, Anne. *Transformations*. Boston: Houghton Mifflin, 1971.
Valente, Catherynne M. *The Ice Puzzle. A Novel in Pieces*. N.p. 2004. *Web*. 21 July 2012. http://anovelinpieces.catherynnemvalente.com/

Theories of Feminine Subjectivity

Arcana, Judith. *Our Mother's Daughters*. London: Women's Press, 1979.
Caplan, Paula J. *The New Don't Blame Mother: Mending the Mother-Daughter Relationship*. New York: Routledge, 2000.
Chodorow, Nancy. "Family Structure and Feminine Personality." 1974. *The Homeric* Hymn to Demeter: *Translation, Commentary, and Interpretive Essays*. Ed. Helene P. Foley. Princeton, NJ: Princeton University Press, 1994. 243–65.

————. *The Reproduction of Mothering: Psychoanalysis and the Sociology of Gender*. 1978. Berkeley: University of California Press, 1999.

Collins, Patricia Hill. *Black Feminist Thought: Knowledge, Consciousness, and the Politics of Empowerment*. New York: Routledge, 1991.

De Beauvoir, Simone. *The Second Sex*. 1949. Trans. Constance Borde and Sheila Malovany-Chevallier. New York: Knopf, 2010.

De Lauretis, Teresa. *The Practice of Love: Lesbian Sexuality and Perverse Desire*. Bloomington: Indiana University Press, 1994.

Firestone, Shulamith. *The Dialectic of Sex*. London: Women's Press, 1970.

Friday, Nancy. *My Mother, My Self: The Daughter's Search for Identity*. 1977. London: HarperCollins Publishers, 1994.

Friedan, Betty. *The Feminine Mystique*. 1963. London: Victor Gollancz, 1971.

Gilbert, Sandra, and Susan Gubar. *The Madwoman in the Attic*. 1979. New Haven, CT: Yale University Press, 2000.

Irigaray, Luce. "The Looking Glass, From the Other Side." 1973. *This Sex Which Is Not One*. 1977. Trans. Catherine Porter. Ithaca, NY: Cornell University Press, 1985. 9–22.

————. *Speculum of the Other Woman*. 1974. Trans. Gillian C. Gill. Ithaca, NY: Cornell University Press, 1985.

————. "And the One Doesn't Stir without the Other." Trans. Hélène Vivienne Wenzel. *Signs: Journal of Women in Culture and Society* 7.1 (1981): 60–67.

————. "Divine Women." 1984. *Sexes and Genealogies*. 1987. Trans. Gillian C. Gill. New York: Columbia University Press, 1993. 55–72.

Jordan, Judith V. "Empathy and Self Boundaries." *Women's Growth in Connection: Writings from the Stone Center*. Eds. Judith V. Jordan et al. New York: Guilford Press, 1991. 67–80.

————. "Women and Empathy: Implications for Psychological Development and Psychotherapy." *Women's Growth in Connection: Writings from the Stone Center*. Ed. Judith V. Jordan et al. New York: Guilford Press, 1991. 27–50.

————. "The Relational Self: A Model of Women's Development." *Daughtering and Mothering: Female Subjectivity Reanalysed*. Eds. Janneke van Mens-Verhulst et al. New York: Routledge, 1993. 135–44.

————. "A Relational Perspective for Understanding Women's Development." *Women's Growth in Diversity: More Writings from the Stone Center*. Ed. Judith V. Jordan. New York: Guilford Press, 1997. 9–24.

Lampl-de Groot, Jeanne. "The Evolution of the Oedipus Complex in Women." 1927. *The Psychoanalytic Reader: An Anthology of Essential Papers with Critical Introductions*. Vol. 1. Ed. Robert Fliess. New York: International Universities Press, 1948. 207–22.

Lykke, Nina. "Questing Daughters: Little Red Riding Hood, Antigone, and the Oedipus Complex." *Daughtering and Mothering: Female Subjectivity Reanalysed*. Eds. Janneke van Mens-Verhulst et al. New York: Routledge, 1993. 15–25.

Miller, Jean Baker. *Toward a New Psychology of Women*. 1967. Boston: Beacon Press, 1987.

Rich, Adrienne. *Of Woman Born: Motherhood as Experience and Institution.* New York: W.W. Norton, 1976.

Surrey, Janet. "The Self-in-Relation: A Theory of Women's Development." *Women's Growth in Connection: Writings from the Stone Center.* Eds. Judith V. Jordan et al. New York: Guilford Press, 1991. 51–66.

———. "The Mother-Daughter Relationship: Themes in Psychotherapy." *Daughtering and Mothering: Female Subjectivity Reanalysed.* Eds. Janneke van Mens-Verhulst et al. New York: Routledge, 1993. 114–24.

Walker, Alice. "In Search of Our Mothers' Gardens: The Creativity of Black Women in the South." 1973. *In Search of Our Mothers' Gardens.* 1983. New York: Mariner Books, 2003. 231–43.

Winnicott, D.W. "Mirror-role of Mother and Family in Child Development." 1967. *Parent-Infant Psychodynamics: Wild Things, Mirrors and Ghosts.* Ed. Joan Raphael-Leff. London: Whurr Publishers, 2003. 18–24.

Wolf, Naomi. *The Beauty Myth: How Images of Beauty Are Used Against Women.* New York: William Morrow, 1991.

Other Sources

Akoma, Chiji. *Folklore in New World Black Fiction: Writing and the Oral Traditional Aesthetics.* Columbus: Ohio State University Press, 2007.

Attebery, Brian. *Strategies of Fantasy.* Bloomington: Indiana University Press, 1992.

Awkward, Michael. *Inspiriting Influences: Tradition, Revision, and Afro-American Women's Novels.* New York: Columbia University Press, 1989.

Bacchilega, Cristina. *Postmodern Fairy Tales.* Philadelphia: University of Pennsylvania Press, 1997.

Barthes, Roland. *Mythologies.* Trans. Annette Lavers. 1972. London: Vintage, 1993.

Benson, Stephen, ed. *Contemporary Fiction and the Fairy Tale.* Detroit: Wayne State University Press, 2008.

Bettelheim, Bruno. *The Uses of Enchantment: The Meaning and Importance of Fairy Tales.* 1975. New York: Penguin Books, 1978.

Blackwell, Jeannine. "Introduction: The Historical Context of German Women's Fairy Tales." *The Queen's Mirror: Fairy Tales by German Women, 1780–1900.* Ed. Shawn C. Jarvis and Jeannine Blackwell. Lincoln: University of Nebraska Press, 2001. 1–9.

Bloom, Harold. *The Anxiety of Influence: A Theory of Poetry.* 2nd ed. New York: Oxford University Press, 1997.

Carroll, Lewis. *Through the Looking-glass and What Alice Found There.* 1871. *Alice in Wonderland.* Ed. Donald J. Gray. New York: W.W. Norton, 1992.

Carter, Angela. *The Sadeian Woman: An Exercise in Cultural History.* London: Virago, 1979.

———. "The Language of Sisterhood." *The State of the Language.* Eds. Leonard Michaels and Christopher Ricks. Berkeley: University of California Press, 1980. 226–34.

————. "Notes from the Frontline." 1983. *Shaking a Leg: Journalism and Writings*. Ed. Jenna Uglow. London: Chatto & Windus, 1997. 36–43.

————. Interviewed by Anna Katsavos. "A Conversation with Angela Carter." *The Review of Contemporary Fiction*. Fall 1994, Vol. 14.3. Web. https://www.dalkeyarchive.com/a-conversation-with-angela-carter-by-anna-katsavos/

Corbin, Laurie. *The Mother Mirror: Self-Representation and the Mother-Daughter Relation in Colette, Simone De Beauvoir, and Marguerite Duras*. New York: Peter Lang, 1996.

DuBois, W.E.B. *The Souls of Black Folk*. 1903. Eds. Henry Louis Gates Jr. and Terri Hume Oliver. New York: W.W. Norton, 1999.

Duncker, Patricia. "Re-Imagining the Fairy Tale: Angela Carter's Bloody Chambers." *Literature and History* 10 (1984): 3–14.

DuPlessis, Rachel Blau. *Writing Beyond the Ending: Narrative Strategies of Twentieth-Century Women Writers*. Bloomington: Indiana University Press, 1985.

Elgin, Suzette Hayden. "The Feminist Pragmatics of Applied Fantasy." *The Fantastic Other: An Interface of Perspectives*. Eds. Bret Cooke et al. Amsterdam: Rodopi, 1998. 111–20.

Eliot, T.S. "Tradition and the Individual Talent." 1919. *Selected Essays*. London: Faber and Faber Limited, 1951. 13–22.

Freud, Sigmund. "Creative Writers and Day-Dreaming." 1908. Trans. James Strachey. *On Freud's "Creative Writers and Day-Dreaming."* Eds. Ethel Spector Person and Peter Fonagy. New Haven, CT: Yale University Press, 1995. 3–13.

————. "A Child is Being Beaten." 1919. Trans. James Strachey. *On Freud's "A Child is Being Beaten."* Ed. Ethel Spector Person. New Haven, CT: Yale University Press, 1997. 3–28.

————. "The Uncanny." *The Uncanny*. 1919. Trans. David McLintock. New York: Penguin Books, 2003. 121–62.

Gallop, Jane. *The Daughter's Seduction: Feminism and Psychoanalysis*. Ithaca, NY: Cornell University Press, 1984.

Greene, Gayle. *Changing the Story: Feminist Fiction and the Tradition*. Bloomington: Indiana University Press, 1991.

Haase, Donald. "Is Seeing Believing? Proverbs and the Film Adaptation of a Fairy Tale." *Proverbium: Yearbook of International Proverb Scholarship* 7 (1990): 89–104.

Harries, Elizabeth Wanning. *Twice Upon a Time: Women Writers and the History of the Fairy Tale*. Princeton, NJ: Princeton University Press, 2001.

Horstkotte, Martin. *The Postmodern Fantastic in Contemporary British Fiction*. Trier: Wissenschaftlicher Verlag Trier, 2004.

————. "The Worlds of the Fantastic Other in Postmodern English Fiction." *Journal of the Fantastic in the Arts*, 14:3 (2003 Fall), 318–32

Höttges, Bärbel. "Written Sounds and Spoken Letters: Orality and Literacy in Toni Morrison's Beloved." *Connotations: A Journal for Critical Debate* 19.1–3 (2009–2010): 147–60.

Jackson, Rosemary. *Fantasy: The Literature of Subversion*. New York: Routledge, 1981.

Joosen, Vanessa. *Critical and Creative Perspectives on Fairy Tales: An Intertextual Dialogue Between Fairy-Tale Scholarship and Postmodern Retellings*. Detroit: Wayne State University Press, 2011.

Kaiser, Mary. "Fairy Tale as Sexual Allegory: Intertextuality in Angela Carter's *The Bloody Chamber*." *Review of Contemporary Fiction* 14.3 (1994): 30–36.

Kaveney, Roz. "Revisionist Fantasy." *The Encyclopedia of Fantasy*. Ed. by John Clute and John Grant. New York: St. Martin's Press, 1997. 810.

Keenan, Julian Paul et al. *The Face in the Mirror: The Search for the Origins of Consciousness*. New York: HarperCollins Publishers, 2003.

Kohut, Heinz. *Self Psychology and the Humanities: Reflections on a New Psychoanalytic Approach*. Ed. Charles B. Strozier. New York: W.W. Norton, 1985.

Kroeber, Karl. *Retelling/Rereading: The Fate of Storytelling in Modern Times*. New Brunswick, NJ: Rutgers University Press, 1992.

La Belle, Jenijoy. *Herself Beheld: The Literature of the Looking Glass*. Ithaca, NY: Cornell University Press, 1988.

Lacan, Jacques. *Écrits: A Selection*. 1966. Trans. Bruce Fink et al. New York: W.W. Norton, 2002.

Lau, Kimberly J. "Erotic Infidelities: Angela Carter's Wolf Trilogy." *Marvels and Tales* 22.1(2008): 77–94.

Lewallen, Avis. "Wayward Girls but Wicked Women? Female Sexuality in Angela Carter's *The Bloody Chamber*." *Perspectives on Pornography: Sexuality in Film and Literature*. Eds. Gary Day and Clive Bloom. New York: St. Martin's, 1988. 144–57.

Loudon, Irvine. *Death in Childbirth: An International Study of Maternal Care and Maternal Mortality, 1800–1950*. New York: Oxford University Press, 1993.

Manley, Kathleen. "The Woman in Process in Angela Carter's *The Bloody Chamber*." *Angela Carter and the Fairy Tale*. Eds. Danielle M. Roemer and Cristina Bacchilega. Detroit: Wayne State University Press, 2001.

Martin, Ann. "Generational Collaborations in Emma Donoghue's *Kissing the Witch*: Old Tales in New Skins." *Children's Literature Association Quarterly* 35.1 (2010): 4–25.

Mendlesohn, Farah. "Narrative." *An Unofficial Companion to the Novels of Terry Pratchett*. Ed. Andrew M. Butler. Westport, CT: Greenwood World Publishing, 2007.

Melchior-Bonnet, Sabine. *The Mirror: A History*. 1994. Trans. Katharine H. Jewett. New York: Routledge, 2001.

Miller, Nancy K. *Subject to Change: Reading Feminist Writing*. New York: Columbia University Press, 1988.

Morrison, Toni. Interviewed by Cecil Brown. "Interview with Toni Morrison." *Massachusetts Review* 36.3 (1995): 455–73.

Motte, Warren. "Reflections on Mirrors." *MLN* 120.4 (2005): 774–89.

Muller, John P., and William J. Richardson. *Lacan and Language: A Reader's Guide to* Écrits. New York: International Universities Press, 1982.

Murnaghan, Sheila, and Deborah H. Roberts. "Penelope's Song: The Lyric Odysseys of Linda Pastan and Louise Gluck." *Classical and Modern Literature* 22.1 (2002): 1, 1–33.

O'Reilly, Andrea. *Toni Morrison and Motherhood: A Politics of the Heart.* Albany: State University of New York Press, 2004.

Ostriker, Alicia Suskin. *Stealing the Language: The Emergence of Women's Poetry in America.* London: Women's Press, 1987.

———. *Feminist Revision and the Bible.* Oxford: Blackwell, 1993.

Pollitt, Katha. "Andrea Dworkin: 1946–2005." 2005. *Virginity or Death!: And Other Social and Political Issues of Our Time.* New York: Random House, 2006. 217–19.

Pollock, Linda A. "Embarking on a Rough Passage: The Experience of Pregnancy in Early Modern Society." *Women as Mothers in Pre-Industrial England.* Ed. Valerie Fildes. New York: Routledge, 1990.

Rank, Otto. "The Double." 1925. Trans. and Ed. Harry Tucker Jr. Chapel Hill: University of North Carolina Press, 1971.

Rich, Adrienne. "When We Dead Awaken: Women's Writing as Re-Vision." *Adrienne Rich's Poetry and Prose: Poems, Prose, Reviews, and Criticism.* Eds. Barbara Charlesworth Gelpi and Albert Gelpi. New York: W.W. Norton, 1993. 166–76.

Ryan-Sautour, Michelle. "Authorial Ghosts and Maternal Identity in Angela Carter's 'Ashputtle or the Mother's Ghost: Three Versions of One Story' (1987)." *Marvels and Tales* 25:1 (2011): 33–50.

Sceats, Sarah. "Flights of Fancy: Angela Carter's Transgressive Narratives." *A Companion to Magical Realism.* Eds. Stephen M. Hart and Wen-Chin Ouyang. Woodbridge, England: Tamesis, 2005. 142–50.

Smith, Kevin Paul. *The Postmodern Fairy Tale: Folkloric Intertexts in Contemporary Fiction.* New York: Palgrave MacMillan, 2007.

Tiffin, Jessica. *Marvelous Geometry: Narrative and Metafiction in Modern Fairy Tale.* Detroit: Wayne State University Press, 2009.

Tolkien, J.R.R. "On Fairy-Stories." 1947. *Tree and Leaf.* New York: HarperCollins, 2001. 1–81.

Troester, Rosalie Riegle. "Turbulence and Tenderness: Mothers, Daughters, and 'Othermothers' in Paula Marshall's *Brown Girl, Brownstones.*" *Double Stitch: Black Women Write About Mothers and Daughters.* Eds. Patricia Bell-Scott et al. 1991. New York: HarperCollins, 1993. 163–72.

Warner, Marina. *From the Beast to the Blonde.* London: Chatto and Windus, 1994.

White, Patricia. "Lesbian Minor Cinema." *Screen* 39.4 (2008): 410–25.

Wyatt, Jean. "Failed Messages, Maternal Loss, and Narrative Form in Toni Morrison's *A Mercy.*" *MFS: Modern Fiction Studies* 58.1 (2012): 128–51.

Zipes, Jack. *Fairy Tale as Myth/Myth as Fairy Tale.* Lexington: University of Kentucky Press, 1994.

———. *Relentless Progress: The Reconfiguration of Children's Literature, Fairy Tales, and Storytelling.* New York: Routledge, 2008.

Index